TRIUMPH
AND
TRAGEDY
IN MUDVILLE

TRIUMPH
AND
TRAGEDY
IN MUDVILLE

A Lifelong Passion for Baseball

STEPHEN JAY GOULD

Foreword by David Halberstam

JONATHAN CAPE

LONDON

Published by Jonathan Cape 2004

2 4 6 8 10 9 7 5 3 1

Excerpt from 'The Lesson for Today' from *The Poetry of Robert Frost*,
edited by Edward Conery Lathem. Copyright 1942 by Robert Frost,
© 1970 by Lesley Frost Ballantine, © 1969 by Henry Holt and Company.
Reprinted by permission of Henry Holt and Company, LLC. Interviews with
and letters by William Ellsworth 'Dummy' Hoy from Lawrence S. Ritter,
*The Glory of Their Times: The Story of the Early Days of Baseball
Told by the Men Who Played It* (New York: Macmillan, 1966).
Reprinted by permission of Lawrence S. Ritter

First published in the United States of America in 2003 by
W.W. Norton & Company, Inc.

First published in Great Britain in 2004 by
Jonathan Cape
Random House, 20 Vauxhall Bridge Road,
London SW1V 2SA

Random House Australia (Pty) Limited
20 Alfred Street, Milsons Point, Sydney,
New South Wales 2061, Australia

Random House New Zealand Limited
18 Poland Road, Glenfield,
Auckland 10, New Zealand

Random House South Africa (Pty) Limited
Endulini, 5A Jubilee Road, Parktown 2193, South Africa

The Random House Group Limited Reg. No. 954009
www.randomhouse.co.uk

A CIP catalogue record for this book
is available from the British Library

ISBN 0–224–05042–7

Papers used by The Random House Group Limited are natural,
recyclable products made from wood grown in sustainable forests;
the manufacturing processes conform to the environmental
regulations of the country of origin

Printed and bound in Great Britain by
Biddles Ltd, Guildford and King's Lynn

Frontispiece: Stephen Jay Gould at the ballpark of the
1993 Savannah Cardinals (now the Savannah Sand Gnats)
Credit: Yvonne Baron Estes

CONTENTS

Foreword
by David Halberstam

Stephen Jay Gould was one of the great public intellectuals of the second half of the twentieth century, a man of science who by dint of a formidable, relentless intellect, an insatiable curiosity, and an exquisite literary sensibility turned much of the nation (as well as millions of people in other nations) into students in what became a great extended classroom. Technically he was a paleontologist, which meant to most of his fellow citizens, that he was in the dinosaur business, but I thought of him operating under a broader mandate as a kind of all-purpose historian-detective, working on a span of time which covered a mere three and a half billion years, looking for a glitch here and a glitch there that would mark the extinction of one species and the perpetuation of another, intrigued always as to why one species of mammal—human beings—ended up on two legs and, in William Faulkner's well-chosen words, not merely endured but prevailed, when all around us, bigger, more powerful species disappeared. The race that we run, he seemed to be reminding us constantly, was neither to the swift nor the powerful.

I think of him as a man on the job all the time, not merely scouring the latest pile of dinosaur bones for newer, more

updated truths, but fascinated by the most trivial developments in
the world of snails, as well as changes and adaptations in the
world of baseball. To Steve Gould all of these areas had their
truths, and even more remarkably, their truths were often inter-
connected. He was the least narrow of intellectuals: what made
his intellect so admirable was his ability to connect seemingly
separate developments and truths in one field to developments in
another; he could connect dots where few of his colleagues could
even see the dots, let alone relate them. He was the most lumi-
nescent and valuable of citizens, able, as true intellectuals are
(one thinks of the towering sociologist David Riesman), to rise
above the boundaries of his own chosen profession and see things
that others could not. He was able to take what were seemingly
tiny bits of evidence, add historical and cultural dimension, thus
giving them larger meaning, and enhancing their value. He could
take big ideas and, through his skills as an analyst and writer,
make them small, thereby making their truths infinitely more
accessible. Equally important, he was capable of taking what were
seemingly small truths and, through the proper interpretation,
make them large, imbuing them with an importance and a dimension they otherwise lacked.

Nor was he simply some brilliant self-isolated figure, distanced
by the very nature of so superior an intellect from much of what
was around him; rather, he was in the best sense a major player
in the ongoing national arena of debate, the most engaged of public men, not just a witness to the human comedy around him but
a joyous appreciator of it. The descendant of an immigrant family
which had escaped from an infinitely crueler Europe, the compli-
cated, often painful lessons of assimilation were palpable in his
own childhood, as were the uses of adversity. The scions of his
generation of newly arrived, highly ambitious Jewish families
were involuntarily well schooled in the uses of adversity, in the
constant exhortations to work harder than those around them. He
had flowered in the new pluralistic, post–World War II American

democracy, and had great admiration for this society's possibilities, as well as a thoughtful wariness of its excesses. As his friend the distinguished First Amendment attorney Martin Garbus said of him—"his was the most imposing of intellects, one that seemed to have the widest possible uses, made all the more valuable to those of us around him because it was blended with a rich, enduring personal humanity—Steve was an almost perfect amalgam of great scientist and great humanist."

He was in all ways a valuable, pluralistic man, liberal in the best and broadest sense of the word; his liberalism was not merely an endorsement of a temporary fashionable political dogma, but liberalism in the better, classic sense: an abiding openness to new ideas and new forces. He understood earlier, and much more clearly than most of his peers, the public uses of science, and the ancillary lessons in history that science was capable of producing. He was a Darwinian, valuable in the ongoing debates with the creationists, in a debate he surely felt should have ended long ago. But he was a tempered Darwinian, he did not believe in a society where the powerful, armed with an arsenal of pseudoscientific data, could impose their will without restraints on those less blessed. He knew that was good for neither the weak nor the strong; even more, he knew that that those who appeared weak were not always weak, and those who appeared strong were rarely that strong.

That the creationists were still on the offensive late in the twentieth century, and that their newest proponents used the most modern means of communication to propagate what he considered myth-based views did not greatly surprise him. He was too wise and shrewd an intellectual to believe that good ideas which were science-based would, ipso facto, because of their elemental truths always triumph. He understood far better than most the power of passion bred by adversity. And he knew that the late-century backlash of the creationists in America was produced, if by no other force, by the most involuntary impulse to survive and live as in the past, on the part of people who thought the society as they knew it, and where they were most comfortable, was changing, driven by forces of modernity that they despised and felt were corrupting all that they treasured.

Stephen Gould was—perfectly in keeping with his own view of how immigrant families go through the process of Americanization—the most passionate of baseball fans; even his immigrant grandfather, born as he was in Hungary, liked going to games as a way of becoming that much more American, and it was through his own father, a court stenographer, that Steve eventually fell in love with the game, the Yankees, and Joe DiMaggio, in no particular order. That a bright, not particularly athletic child would love baseball was the most normal of possibilities in newly minted American homes at that time. There was less competition from other sports in what was essentially a pre-television, pre-entertainment–age childhood. Baseball was very accessible (all you had to do was turn the radio to 1010 and hear the honeyed voice of Mel Allen), and even if a child was not a gifted athlete, baseball offered early intellectual traction. It had all those wonderful numbers, batting and earned run averages that somehow seemed to unlock both past and present. Besides, the Yankees seemed to win all the time, which was comforting in a world where there were enough other defeats. In addition baseball is, as Bart Giamatti, the former president of Yale and later commissioner of baseball, once told me, the first thing a child can discuss with his or her parents—matters of sex and politics and religion are far beyond reach, but baseball offers a rare commonality and gives the very young an enviable social connection with their elders. Steve Gould's father took him regularly to Yankee games as a boy, offering him an almost textbook example of the role baseball played in the Americanization of its newest citizens, how it allowed them to feel more *American*. Equally important, he came of age in New York at a wonderful time, the late forties through the mid-fifties, a golden age of baseball in the city of his birth, when a subway series was virtually a given each year. Though born and raised in Queens and not the Bronx, he became the most dedicated of Yankee fans; in all other things, one friend noted, Steve always rooted for the underdog. But not in baseball; the Yankees were rarely the underdog.

And so we have in these pages the great distinguished scientist at both work and play, studying a world he loves, that of baseball, and producing some of his most lyrical writing. What better field for study could there be for someone who was fascinated by the mutations of societal change, the impact upon a given institution by forces produced by the society around it. After all, in his lifetime the changes in the game were quite profound and yet the game remained essentially the same. When he first became a fan in 1949, there were only sixteen big league teams, St. Louis was a western city and Washington a southern one. The teams played more often than not during the day, on grass, and traveled by train. The games were broadcast on radio. Owners had complete dictatorial power over players—they could offer a player a preselected salary of their choosing, and a player's only recourse, if he did not like the number, was to retire. Though Jackie Robinson had just integrated the National League and Larry Doby the American League, it was still a very white game. But it did reflect the changing demographics of America. On the Yankee team that faced the Dodgers in the second game of the 1949 World Series, there were four children of the new Italian immigration to America—DiMaggio, Rizzuto, Berra, and Raschi—in the starting lineup.

Fast-forward to today, thirty teams, eleven of them in the Sunbelt (if you count the Bay Area teams), the game always on television, teams traveling in chartered jets around the country, games played mostly at night, often on artificial surfaces in domed stadiums, with power having passed from owners to players, and some players making as much as $18–25 million a year. Ethnically, of course, it has changed as well. On occasion during the 2001 and 2002 seasons, his beloved Yankees fielded a lineup with seven black and Hispanic players. Thus baseball was a wonderful subject for him, something that essentially stayed the same (except for the designated hitter rule, which he quite predictably hated) and yet reflected the quite dramatic social and legal changes in the society around it.

His favorite ballplayer, as these pages will make abundantly clear, was Joe DiMaggio, the greatest player on the greatest team in baseball at the historic moment when Steve Gould first discovered the sport. When he was a boy, he and his father had once gone to a midweek game against the hapless St Louis Browns and his father had caught a foul ball off DiMaggio's bat. In time DiMaggio signed the ball for him. If he was idolatrous of few other things or people in his life, he idolized DiMaggio ("He was the glory of a time that we will not see again"). Late in his life he taught a class at Harvard jointly with Alan Dershowitz, the noted law school professor and a close friend, and they argued constantly over DiMaggio. Dershowitz, originally from Brooklyn, was a devoted Dodger fan, and thus a Yankee hater; he would readily admit to DiMaggio's greatness as a player but saw all kinds of flaws in him as a man, flaws that remained invisible to the worshipful Gould. In this case, at least, the adoration of the great scientist looking out at a chosen icon late in his life was no different from that of the little boy sitting in Yankee Stadium in the late forties, holding his father's hand and hearing how great a player DiMaggio was. Of the two great hitting achievements of 1941, the year he was born, he was vastly more impressed by DiMaggio's fifty-six-game streak than he was by Williams's .406 batting average. Was this, others might wonder, the purely scientific importance of the streak, or was it as well the enduring charisma of a childhood hero?

The collection of these pieces shows Steve Gould at his best, and readers will readily understand the richness and complexity of his mind. There is a lovely small piece composed on the death of Babe Pinelli, the umpire who had called Don Larsen's perfect game in October 1956. The final pitch to Dale Mitchell, a pinch hitter and twenty-seventh batter, with the count 1–2, was just a little high and outside. "Strike three!" said Pinelli. Naturally enough, Mitchell groused about the call. Gould, the historian-as-umpire, calls the play for Pinelli and against Mitchell—"A man may not take a close pitch with so much on the line. Context matters. . . . Babe Pinelli, umpiring his last game, ended with his finest, his most perceptive, his most truthful moment." Another wonderful piece is about Dummy Hoy, a deaf and dumb player, who played for fourteen years from 1888 to 1902. It is powered by Gould's rage against the cruelty of the era, the stupidity of the nickname, and the demeaning forces with which Hoy had to contend. In Gould's words Hoy emerges as one of the most gifted, intelligent players of his time, a man admirable in all ways. And there is his long essay on the disappearance of the .400 hitter, a rumination on why no one is likely to do it again, on how the forces both inside and outside of baseball have changed the context and made it so unlikely.

To place Steve Gould's baseball life in proper historical perspective, one should note that he was born in September 1941, a month before Mickey Owen dropped the third strike on Tommy Henrich in game four of the World Series, a mistake that cost the Dodgers not merely the contest but a 3–1 lead in games and greatly improved the Yankees chances of winning the Series. And he died some sixty years later in May 2002, just as Jason Giambi was making his debut as a free-agent Yankee first baseman, but perhaps even more important, as Alfonso Soriano, the young Dominican infielder, rose to superstar status. He and I never talked about Soriano, but I presume Steve would have been thrilled by Soriano's almost miraculous ascent to greatness, by the quickness of his bat, the amazing strength in his seemingly slim body, the explosiveness and elasticity in his muscles, and the fact that early in his major league career it was almost impossible to get him to lay off pitches and work his way on base by walking.

This, I think, is the part that Steve Gould would have loved, the deep sociocultural imprint of Soriano's native culture, and the fact that, as they say, you don't get off the island (the Dominican Republic) by taking pitches and walking.

In the second part of his life, positioned permanently in the Boston area by dint of tenure at Harvard, he became a season-ticket holder at Fenway Park and something of a naturalized Red Sox fan as well, and there is in some of his later writing a rare compassion and affection for the Red Sox. (Because I was born in the Bronx, about eight blocks from Yankee Stadium, but grew up partly in New England, and later ended up with a house on Nantucket, I have considerable sympathy for what are, if not divided loyalties, at least dual, or partially shared loyalties.) He loved Fenway Park, came to appreciate the complexity of being a Red Sox fan, and sired a son who was a Red Sox fan. That meant that he could still easily go to games and sustain his love of it; baseball, as readers of this book will soon understand, was not merely a source of pleasure, though certainly it was that, but it soon became one more field on which a great detective could test his intellect. Steve Gould believed in what might be called the contingency of history theory—that is, history is not a simple unbroken, almost predictable line of progress with certain almost guaranteed givens and thus assured outcomes. Rather, it is filled with pitfalls and ambushes and there are land mines everywhere; occasionally it is almost whimsical in the course it chooses. If you rewind certain sections of history and try to replay them, he believed, things might come out very differently: the Confederacy, say (these are my examples not his), might triumph at Gettysburg, Rommel might defeat Montgomery in North Africa, and Mickey Owen might hold on to the third strike from Hugh Casey. Interestingly enough, Dershowitz believes that Gould's view of baseball informed his larger view of history, rather than the other way around, because baseball is so accessible and it is so easy to see what might have happened in the outcome of a game with just the smallest of changes, say a different relief pitcher throwing to Bobby Thomson in 1951, or perhaps Casey Stengel in 1960 bringing in Whitey Ford for the final outs against the Pirates.

Baseball really begins for Steve Gould in the 1949 season, DiMaggio's last great year, when he missed the first two and a half months of the season with aching feet and then came back in late June to lead the Yankees to a three-game sweep in Boston, a series in which he hit four home runs and knocked in nine runs. If I have any regret, reading these pieces, it was that Gould did not seem to have made a comparable connection to Ted Williams, whom I think he would have adored. For someone who was fascinated by the complexity of human behavior and its effect on performance ("the human heart in conflict with itself," to use another phrase of Faulkner's), it has always struck me that Williams is a much more interesting, much richer subject than DiMaggio. I can just imagine Gould and Williams together—Gould with his wondrous, shrewd, and relentless curiosity, and Williams with his exuberant spirit, his ferocious and on occasion belligerent intelligence, delighted because he had finally found someone smart enough to understand him: "No goddamn it, Professor Gould, when I said pitchers are dumb by breed, I meant exactly that, *pitchers are dumb by breed. . . . Yes, of course pitchers are a breed—what else would they be? Why you ought to know that—I thought they told me you were a smart Harvard scientist!*"

I'd have loved to have been a fly on the wall for that one. After all, Williams's own philosophy (though he was technically a political conservative and Gould a liberal) paralleled Gould's with some surprising similarities, and Gould would have loved one of Williams's elemental truths of both baseball and life: "God gets you to the plate, but from then on, you're on your own." That is, natural talent has a lot of to do with the earlier rounds of selection in any enterprise, but what you put into it on your own, how hard you work and how much passion you bring to it, how much you study to improve yourself matters equally—it is our mark as individuals, our passions, our visions, our commitment on occasion to something larger than ourselves, which sets us apart. Fittingly, no baseball player ever studied the game more closely, worked harder to build himself up physically (especially in an age when players accepted their bodies and did not try to improve them) than Williams. He was, as much as any player I can think of, someone who reflected the qualities in a society that Steve Gould wrote about so well, the achievement of a seemingly ordinary man fighting not inconsiderable disadvantages, who raises himself to a position of excellence out of his own fierce will. For certainly there was a central theme which distinguished Gould's most important work: he was wary of classification of people by race and by ethnicity. Here he was well ahead of the curve; he understood that continuing breakthroughs in science—the coming of DNA with its awesome implications—would likely create an ever greater instinct to categorize people and to do it too quickly, based on what are presumed to be genetic characteristics, as if to rephrase Tolstoy, your genes are your fate. He was, in effect, the anti–bell curve man; other forces, he believed, determine our character and fate more than sheer DNA. He did not like people being pigeonholed based on presumptions about them, presumptions that had nothing to do with their character and their individuality. (As such, I believe he would have been fascinated by the revelations which came out about Williams, just about the time of both of their deaths in 2002—of the fact that May Williams, the ballplayer's mother, was half Mexican, and there was a virtually secret part of the Williams family, something which surely, given the prejudices of Southern California in that era, must have had something to do with Williams's exceptional rage to excel.)

Steve Gould, it should be said, was a devoted and somewhat ritualistic fan. One of the reasons he loved baseball so much was because the past casts so important a shadow on the present: players are measured not just against those whom they play today, but against those who have gone before them. Other sports did not catch his fancy. His friend Dershowitz was a serious basketball fan as well as baseball fan, but he could never get Steve to buy in on basketball, arguably our most balletic and athletically demanding sport. It simply did not move him, and he could not be reconnected with his boyhood as he was when he watched baseball. By contrast, when he watched baseball, the man could become a boy once again. He had learned to keep score as a boy, and as a man, ever meticulous, he still kept score. When he was a boy, he had always gone to games by public transportation, getting a feel for the excitement of the crowd even before it got to the stadium, and as a grown man he still demanded that he and his friends go to games by public transportation, never by car, in no small part because he still liked getting a feel for the mood of the crowd. In addition, though he liked eating well in good restaurants, no amount of pressure from his pals could convince him to go to a good restaurant and eat well before a night game. That was not the way it was done, because it was not the way it had been done when he was a boy. If he was going to a ballgame, he was going to eat at the game. Hot dogs it would be, not coq au vin.

At the game he was the most attentive of fans. Others might see a baseball game, with its languid rhythms, as a chance to get together and talk of other things, but not Steve Gould. He was not there to socialize. He was appalled once when Dershowitz brought a cell phone to a game and actually took incoming calls. Dershowitz might just as well have endorsed the DH rule. Gould protested vigorously and it did not happen again. He was there to see the game, to watch the field at all times, with one eye if need be on the scoreboard. He loved the subtle byplay of the game, certain pitchers against certain hitters in tight situations. Once he had gone to a game with his longtime editor, Ed Barber, and it was one of those nights when Roger Clemens was pitching and was absolutely on top of his game. About the eighth inning, Gould showed Barber his scorecard, and Clemens's line went something like this: eleven strikeouts and two hits, and one or two walks. Perhaps in all, a hundred or so pitches thrown. As he showed this statistical update to Barber, Steve turned as if to the crowd itself, and said, talking about the game Clemens was pitching, but perhaps more important, the whole scene, and the pleasure of being a part of it, his words as much as anything an epitaph for his own exceptional and occasionally magical life, "Isn't this wonderful!"

Editor's Note

In the months before his death on May 20, 2002, Steve Gould had been hard at work on this volume. The subject had come up between us in the seventies, when Steve began to write his vibrant essays about baseball for *Natural History* and elsewhere. Early on, he had displayed a unique skill in blending his science and his game in a way that humanized the former and deepened the latter. We agreed then that there would be a baseball book but that it must wait in line. He had in mind *The Mismeasure of Man*, *Wonderful Life*, and of course there followed hundreds of essays gathered into his wonderful collections as well as long work on his final scientific statement that became *The Structure of Evolutionary Theory*.

So, time passed. Steve lived a busy life, constantly balancing teaching, research, writing, speaking, travel, and a personal life that prominently featured baseball, as well as, tragically, the first onset of his cancer, over fifteen years ago. But by late 2001 he was ready to go out to the literary ballpark. In 1992, his friend Stephen King had written him a letter suggesting that Steve "devote a small but not inconsequential block of time" to writing a novella-sized memoir about baseball, a pivotal exhortation. In the introductory piece that follows, Gould says that this book "exists to fulfill a promise" made to King, meaning the memoir to come.

Steve went to work, first gathering all of his writings on baseball, choosing and revising the pieces to accompany the memoir and lining up an order of presentation. He'd always been good at titles, and the title here is his. This was the same procedure Steve had always used in turning his various essays into book form. At last he turned to the long, personal work which was to have been the book's cornerstone, only to be overcome by the cancer that would take him from us. Game and enthusiastic to the end, Steve called in the early spring of 2002 to assure me that he would deliver the book, and he has. He had left it, neatly organized and in good hands, in his office at Harvard. With the revised earlier essays, designed to accompany the memoir, were two new pieces: the warm introduction to this volume and his fond—and analytical—story of a boyhood spent playing stickball on the neighborhood streets of Queens, as far as he could go with the longer work.

We at Norton are proud to present this book, and we are grateful to Patricia Chui for her invaluable work and to Kay McCauley who so professionally smoothed the way.

Steve Gould loved baseball; and he loved the New York Yankees, loved them not so much because they were champions, but because they were *his* champions—he'd grown up with them. Millions of readers have, in a way, grown up in science with Steve Gould. With this last legacy, he offers to us a celebration of both as only he could, with depth, grace, wit, and passion.

Edwin Barber

W. W. Norton & Company

September 2002

TRIUMPH
AND
TRAGEDY
IN MUDVILLE

Seventh Inning Stretch:
Baseball, Father, and Me
Introduction and Rationale

This introductory and longest piece of the book exists to fulfill a promise made to one of my best baseball friends, author Steve King, who wrote to me in late October 1992: "I think you should set aside a small but not inconsequential block of time—three weeks, maybe a month—to write a long (20,000 to 30,000 words) 'linchpin essay' that would place your love and knowledge of baseball among the other landmarks of your rather remarkable life."

Obviously, I appreciated the implied compliments in Steve's remarks. But I quickly resolved to follow his suggestion for a set of more literary and personal reasons. I have published eleven volumes of essays, ten from my monthly series in *Natural History* magazine that ran to three hundred successive pieces, without a break, from January 1974 until January 2001, and an eleventh (*Urchin in the Storm*) based primarily on essays originally published in the *New York Review of Books*. I have been writing about my serious dedication to baseball (in a wide variety of formats, from short op-ed statements to fairly lengthy articles) since the early 1980s; and I suppose that, for at least fifteen years, I have been intending to collect these baseball scribblings into a volume once enough material had accumulated. Steve King's suggestion

of a decade ago (I began this "novella" in mid April 2002) made
my resolve firm, but the press of other commitments and the need
to accumulate more material made this palindromic year of the
new millennium an appropriate time to begin in earnest.

As much as I have loved and followed baseball all my conscious
life, I never thought, before deciding to "cash out" Steve's suggestion in an opening novella, that I would ever try to discourse
(at any length or seriousness) about why the game continues to
hold me so tight after more than half a century of serious and continuous rooting. After all, one loves what one loves, and unless
the activity causes clear and intrinsic harm to others, no explicit
defense need be provided for following one's bliss.

Yet I have developed personal answers to the two major questions so often thrown at academics and other professional intellectuals as challenges to their baseball commitments, and my
responses might be worth sharing, especially since discussion on
these issues never seems to abate. First, why are so many American intellectuals so serious about their baseball commitments? Or
(to put the matter more specifically, as this form of inquiry so
often does), why has baseball alone among major American
sports, with boxing as the only other possible contender, generated so much writing of not insubstantial literary quality? Second,
does this favoritism toward baseball arise in any way from the
plethora of common claims about baseball's imitation of the central rhythms and patterns of our lives? Does life imitate the World
Series in any way that might transcend lame and meaningless
metaphor? Does time begin on opening day in any sense that
might help us, at least by analogy, to accept the loud evenings of
July 4 or the silly costumes of neighborhood kids on October 31?

I have devised, over the years, a definite way of treating general
questions of this sort, including these two particular inquiries—
and though my resolutions satisfy me both rationally and emo-
tionally, I cannot claim for them any abiding status as provable or
general truths. These resolutions do, however, set a groundwork

for permitting me to begin this baseball book with an autobio-graphical rationale.

I have written two general books (*Wonderful Life*, 1989, and *Full House*, 1996) dedicated to viewing the history of life as a sensible and interpretable unfolding of one actual pattern among the countless alternative (and equally sensible) scenarios that just didn't happen to attain the privilege of empirical realization. We live in a basically unpredictable world, featuring histories domi-nated by contingency—that is, actual patterns that make good sense and become subject to interesting and sensible explanation once they unfold as they did, but that could have proceeded along innumerable alternative routes that would have yielded just as sensible a history, but that did not gain the good fortune of actual occurrence.

Thus, if it be true that intellectually inclined American sports fans tend to enjoy and follow baseball at a higher frequency than other popular national sports, I don't for a moment attribute such favoritism to any inherent property of the game itself. Baseball became America's pastime for a complex set of reasons, explored throughout this book, but the game is not intrinsically more dif-ficult or inherently harder to fathom than any other major sport—and I therefore reject the common assumption that strong rootership among intellectuals can be related in any important way to the nature of the activity itself.

Rather, I would argue that sports plays an important role in the lives of many people (either by direct participation or by follow-ing it as a fan), and that intellectuals roughly match the norms of any other group in their predisposition to such avocational inter-ests. Thus, if baseball has captured the serious attention of many scholarly fans, I would seek no special cause beyond the general appeal of the game among all aficionados of sport. By this argu-ment, baseball holds its favored place as a general phenomenon in the history of American sport, and not because the game holds any special or intrinsic appeal to the intellectually minded fans.

As I argue within this volume, modern baseball coagulated from a variety of stick-and-ball games, played in England and perhaps in other European nations and imported to this country by early settlers. In essentials, the modern form of the game coalesced by the mid-nineteenth century, having evolved as a truly popular sport, played by farm boys and city slickers alike. By contrast, other currently popular team sports, football and basketball in particular, arose primarily as university activities at a time when only a small percentage of Americans achieved any tertiary education. During my childhood in the late 1940s and early 1950s, for example, professional football and basketball played short seasons and commanded only quite restricted popular attention. Hockey was, and to a large extent remains, an import from a great land just to our north. (I remember going to a hockey game at Madison Square Garden in the late 1940s and reading in the program that almost every starting player for the New York Rangers was Canadian by nationality.)

And so, I would argue (at least for myself and, I suspect, for most baseball fans of scholarly bent as well) that a serious personal affection for the sport does not follow, either logically or intrinsically, from any particular inherent property of the game's uniqueness, but rather needs to be explained in the same basic mode as most autobiographical phenomena—that is, as a contingent circumstance that did not have to unfold as it did, but that makes perfectly good sense as a reasonable outcome among a set of possibilities. In this general sense, and for a large array of excellent reasons, baseball became America's "signature sport." I can think of no reason why its appeal should be any less or greater among intellectuals than among any other segment of our population. So I would suspect that the appeal of baseball should, at least as an initial hypothesis, be equally strong among intellectually minded fans as among any other group of Americans.

I am not, however, either in this introductory piece or in the book in general, trying to advance general explanations of the appeal or success of our national pastime. Thus, I can only speak for myself and from my own life. If any of my personal reasons apply more generally, then we will need the confirming testimony of others. I view the major features of my own odyssey as a set of mostly fortunate contingencies. I was not destined by inherited mentality or family tradition to become a paleontologist. I can locate no tradition for scientific or intellectual careers anywhere on either side of my eastern European Jewish background. I myself am the oldest member of the third cohort, the offspring of immigrant grandparents who passed through Ellis Island—that is, the generation destined for university education and professional careers outside the garment district and the world of small shopkeepers.

I accepted this circumstance gladly (not that we have much choice in such matters). And I view my serious and lifelong commitment to baseball in entirely the same manner: purely as a contingent circumstance of numerous, albeit not entirely capricious, accidents. In other words, my affection for baseball does not predictably follow from any generality of my being (in a "laws of nature" type of explanation preferred by scientists like myself), but rather from a set of "accidents" arising from the particulars of my personal life.

Among these particulars, I would single out two for special emphasis. In fact, I rather suspect that versions of these two factors tend to rank high on the list of contingencies for explaining the inclinations and commitments of many serious fans.

1. Issues of how, or whether, to assimilate to the language and customs of an adopted land stood in the forefront of consciousness for the millions of immigrants (including all members of both sides of my family) who arrived in America during the great wave of the late nineteenth and early twentieth centuries. Some chose to retain native languages and customs so far as they could, and to assimilate only to the minimal degree required for basic success and solvency. Others consciously abjured their natal

tongues and traditions and struggled to speak only English and to learn and practice the history and customs of their adopted land. This second assimilationist group tended to dismiss the traditionalists and newcomers who had not yet made up their minds as "green horns" or "greenies." My maternal Hungarian grandparents (the relatives I know best and who served as my surrogate parents during World War II, when my father fought in Europe and Northern Africa) were devoted assimilationists who spoke Hungarian only when they didn't want me to understand, and who took great pride in their accommodation to America. I doubt that they ever understood the limits to their success, particularly as expressed in strong accents that they actively denied, but never lost nonetheless.

Immigrants who opted for assimilation tended to choose particular American institutions or customs as public foci for their commitments. Some veered toward politics of democratic systems that they and their families could enjoy for the first time— as in, for example, the domination of local governments in several major cities by new Irish and Italian citizens. (The WASPs of old Brahmin Boston feared the death of their beloved city when poor Irish immigrants took local political power away from traditional sources, but the Hub persevered and prospered.)

Particularly for men, and especially commonly for Jewish men, a dedication to a distinctively American sport provides the major tactic for assimilation. The three Bs in particular (boxing, basketball, and especially baseball) assumed great importance in the lives of many Jewish and other immigrants. Few Jews grow very tall, so we were probably not destined for basketball triumph as players (although Abe Saperstein put together and coached the Harlem Globetrotters, and many important teams in the early history of basketball—notably the SPHAs, for South Philadelphia Hebrew Association—were formed and staffed by Jewish players).

Boxing and baseball offered stronger possibilities, where champions like Benny Leonard, Max Baer, Moe Berg (a mediocre player,

but absolutely outstanding character) and especially Hank Greenberg and, later, Sandy Koufax could become heroes and role models for entire generations, and where even your average city street
kid (like me) could play with reasonable success. As a happenstance of personal contingencies, the men of my strongly assimilationist maternal side took up baseball as their major sign and
symbol of "Americanization," and became serious and knowledgeable fans, eager to pass this new tradition to subsequent generations.

Thus, baseball became a centerpiece of family life in my house-
hold—and, as several essays in this book acknowledge and discuss, I take pride in being enmeshed within an unbroken string of
four generations of serious baseball rooting. The sequence began
with my maternal grandfather, Papa Joe, a dedicated Yankee fan
from, by his testimony, 1904, when he thrilled to Jack Chesbro's
forty-one victories in a single season—a pitching record that will
stand unless the game undergoes radical changes in scheduling
and counting—until his death in 1953. All three of his sons followed in serious fandom, although his only daughter, my mother,
never really caught the bug despite a personal crush on Mel Ott.
("She thinks a foul ball is a chicken dance," if I may quote a
misogynist line from my father.)

Moving to the other side, my father passed his boyhood rooting for the great Yankee team of Ruth and Gehrig—and his dramatic and detailed memories provided me, a lifelong skeptic in
religion, with my closest insight into the potential nature of a
deity. In this familial context, my own adoption of serious interest can scarcely be deemed surprising! I must also confess to a
feeling of personal pride that my youngest son, Ethan, has now
continued a family tradition into a fourth generation—although
he grew up in Boston, and three generations of Yankee fandom
have now been eclipsed, understandably of course, by his exquisite pain of rooting for the Red Sox, and hoping to live long
enough to win another World Series—last achieved in 1918!

2. If we honor the entertainment and real estate industries'
cliché that the three most important factors for success are "location, location, location," then we must aver, I think, that my being
a baseball fan requires no special explanation and should evoke no
surprise, whereas we might become puzzled and feel the need for
some resolution if I were indifferent to the game. As a pure contingency of my own life, I happened to come of baseball fandom's
age in the greatest conjunction of time and place that the game
has ever known: in New York City during the late 1940s and early
1950s. (I was born on September 10, 1941.)

The situation was entirely unfair to the rest of the country,
but—hey—you can't possibly cast any blame on me, so I owe no
one any apology. From 1947 to 1957, New York City had the three
greatest teams in major league baseball. (Many fans do not understand why a county or borough, rather than a full city, had its own
team as the Brooklyn Dodgers. But New York City did not incor-
porate its outer boroughs into a single city until 1897, so the
Dodgers represented an independent city when the team first
formed and played major league ball.)

During these eleven years, one of the three New York teams
(the Yankees of the American League and the New York Giants
and Brooklyn Dodgers of the National League) won the World
Series in all but two years, when the Cleveland Indians prevailed
in 1948 and Milwaukee in 1957. Only in 1948—Cleveland vs. the
Boston Braves—did a New York team not play in the Series at all.
In seven of these years ('47, '49, '51, '52, '53, '55, and '56) two
New York teams played each other in the World Series—all won
by my beloved Yankees except for the ultimate tragedy of '55,
when the Dodgers won their single victory over the Yanks as a
Brooklyn team. We got them back the next year, though, in '56!

My earliest vague memories of baseball date to the 1946 or
1947 season. I remember the great 1948 season in substantial
detail—the year that should have been the Boston subway series,
but the Indians tied the Red Sox and then won the single game

playoff for the right to play the Boston Braves in the World Series. Starting in 1949, I suspect that I could narrate at least the major events of all World Series games through the Yankees' revenge on Milwaukee in the 1958 contest.

But my point is simply this—and plausible though the claim may be as an abstraction, one really had to "live it" to know the full extent of the pull and the virtual inevitability—during these years, nearly all boys in New York City and quite a few girls, as well, became passionate baseball fans, spending a good bit of each day, from April to early October, tracing the developing fate of one's favorites.

Patterns of rooting were neither entirely capricious nor entirely predictable. Nearly all of Brooklyn's two million citizens rooted passionately for the Dodgers. I'm still mad at my cousin Steve Sosland for failing to protect me, as he promised he would, when I admitted to being a Yankee fan while playing stickball with his Brooklyn neighborhood friends—the worst street beating I ever received, but a rite of passage in the coming of age for any New York street kid.

The still solid Jewish and Italian ethnic communities of the Bronx lived and died with the Yankees (a.k.a. The Bronx Bombers), of course. The Polo Grounds, home of the New York Giants, located in northeastern Manhattan and literally within sight of Yankee Stadium across the Harlem River, did not command so clear a geographic region of nearly exclusive rooting—and Giants fans tended to be scattered throughout the city. Many kids, myself included, rooted for two New York teams, one from each league. Affection for the Yankees and Dodgers proved difficult, for they played each other too often in the World Series ('41, '47, '49, '52, '53, '55, and '56, all won by the Yanks except 1955). By contrast, the Yankees and Giants only met in 1951—on my watch at least, for several Yankee-Giant Series had been played before my birth in the 1920s and 1930s.

I grew up in Queens, the most "neutral" borough, with no team of its own (the expansion Mets did not begin until the early 1960s, and I have never been able truly to view them as a "home team," despite substantial affection based on pure accidents of birth and upbringing—and some wonderful memories of going to Shea Stadium whenever Sandy Koufax of the Los Angeles Dodgers pitched against the Mets, and invariably won).

Memory, of course, is the ultimate trickster, but I do have a very clear impression that at least 50 percent of boy-talk between April and October in Queens focused on the fates of our three teams, with constant bets, threats, and bickerings about pennant races and World Series outcomes. I rooted for the Yanks and Giants. But I even managed to tolerate the Dodger fanaticism of some of my best friends.

The final point is simply this: All New York City boys of the late 1940s and early 1950s were baseball nuts, barring mental deficiency or incomprehensible idiosyncrasy. How could one not be? This decade was the greatest conjunction of quality and place that the game has ever known. Grossly unfair to the rest of the country, of course, but a fabulous piece of luck that made the "coming of age" for me and a million other New York kids ever so much easier—and what purely contingent blessing of ontogeny could be more precious?

REFLECTIONS AND EXPERIENCE

Streetball from a
New York City Boyhood

I do understand the practical and sensible reasons behind such a profound change. But when I grew up on the streets of Queens in New York City, school ended at 3 P.M., and then, weather permitting, we went outdoors to play with our friends until our parents called us in for dinner at about 6 P.M. And, yes, most families did then eat dinner together, every single day—no TV allowed (we didn't yet own one), no newspapers; just conversation.

My mother still lives in the same neighborhood, and nowadays no kid would venture outdoors alone. Children make "play dates" with their friends, and parental tracking has become ubiquitous. By contrast, and throughout the 1950s until we left for college in 1958, Roger Keen (still my best friend) and I played stickball or some other variety of baseball together practically every afternoon of our lives.

A lot of different games "erupted" each day in Fresh Meadows, our neighborhood of three-story garden apartments with adequate greenery separating the buildings, and with space aplenty on the streets (and few cars to hog all the potential parking spaces). We boys—and I must speak of "boy culture," for very few girls ever ventured to inquire about joining us—played so many different games, many just one kid against another, others by teams always "democratically" selected by sequential choices of two designated captains. One did not want to be chosen last—and I still say thank God for Ira, wherever he may be now, the shortest kid in the neighborhood, and almost invariably the final selection; I usually got my assignment in the lower half, but not embarrassingly far down.

The point has been made many times, in this book and elsewhere, but the phenomenon really did define New York at the time. Throughout the 1940s, and until 1958 when New York City began a serious decline with the migration of the Brooklyn Dodgers and New York Giants to California, baseball virtually defined the joys of city life.

Almost all the neighborhood boychicks (about half Jewish and half Catholic in our vicinity of rising working-class families, "ruled" by fathers still recently returned from service in World War II) lived and breathed baseball all the time, for our city then boasted three truly great teams. Nearly all our street games—the main point of this chapter—applied baseball rules to the object of the contest. To this day, my memory remains tickled by the diversity that I can remember, and frustrated by the several versions beyond my recall.

I don't mean to claim that we did nothing else but adapt our activities to the rules of baseball. For example, I was also an avid philatelist (particularly on rainy days), but I never really warmed up to the Lionel electric train set that my Uncle Milton insisted on giving me. A few outdoor games did not follow baseball conventions. I did enjoy my roller skates, and we did play touch football, but only in season. The big kids hogged the few basketball courts in the schoolyard, while adults took constant possession of the four handball courts. Indeed, in the weirdest "time warp" I have ever experienced, the same men have never yielded their ground. When my mother moved back to the old neighborhood about twenty years ago, I walked over to the schoolyard and found the very same men—not their sons and not their cousins—still presiding over the handball courts!

I remember only three street games not played by baseball rules, and only one of these held any interest for me. Some kids played marbles (I didn't), or one of the various versions using bottle caps and known as skelley. Others played mumbledepeg (called "land" or "territory" in my neighborhood), but you needed a switchblade, or at least a pen knife. I owned neither and couldn't have brought such an implement to school in any case.

Chinese handball enjoyed substantial vogue and was the single exception that captured my participation. As a key to spontaneous street games in major cities, one must acknowledge the two controlling variables: the nature of the projectile (the ball), and the geometry and distribution of sidewalk boxes. To play Chinese handball, you first need to put together a substantial and uninterrupted row of chalked boxes, all abutting a wall. Each player gets a box and the game proceeds as follows: using the canonical pink rubber ball (not always called a "spaldeen," but more about this in a moment), a player hits the ball with his palm against the wall on a bounce. The ball must bounce into the chalked box of another player, who must then bounce it against the wall and into someone else's box. Whenever a player fails to execute this maneuver properly, and his ball does not bounce clearly into another player's box, then he has "lost" the round and must move down to possess the box at the end of the line, while all players below him move up a box. And so the game proceeds, until Mom calls you in for dinner. Really good players—not including yours truly, who never really got the hang of this particular activity—could hold onto their top boxes nearly forever.

Let's get to those spaldeens. Yes indeed, those smooth, hollow, pink rubber balls made by the A. G. Spalding company were the sine qua non of boy play. Prices varied, but I remember ten or fifteen cents as the usual cost. And you never abandoned a ball until all potential utility had been extracted. Each was made as a two-piece mold with a full center seam. Eventually, the ball would split in half, and Roger and I played many a full stickball game with half a ball—either because the drug store was closed on weekends or because neither of us could get our allowances for another day or two.

Quite a bit has been written about New York streetball over the past two decades or so, and I have tried to follow the claims carefully. As usual in such circumstances, a few prominent errors emerge and then become entrenched by constant and mindless repetition. Let me then dispel the most prominent of these mistakes, citing as evidence no more than my own absolutely firm memories of Queens in the late 1940s and early 1950s.

To be sure, very few kids owned a real bat (although we did play softball occasionally and some neighborhood kid would then turn up with a proper bat). Mom's broom or mop handle served our daily needs, and stickball became the standard everyday game. Yes again, we always played stickball with that ubiquitous pink rubber projectile. But now consider the two errors. Most sources insist that the ball bore only one name—a "spaldeen." Well, my Brooklyn friends did so designate the ball, but in my neighborhood we called it a "spalding," with strong accent on the final syllable. (These variations, of course, record the same theme, for the balls, made by the A. G. Spalding company, carried the name embossed in black letters.)

Second, the impression has grown that New York stickball followed one set of rules—played in the street, with sewers used as standards of distance (two for a double, four for a homer, for example). Well, I knew the sewer version, and my Brooklyn friends did play by these standards, but on my turf in Fresh Meadows we almost always played stickball by chalking a box (the strike zone) against a wall (usually of a store or an apartment building), and then pitching toward the batter and into the box, with prearranged distances counting for hits of various merit.

New York City stickball, circa 1940s. *Credit: Bettmann/Corbis*

Broken windows—not so rare, by the way—were automatic outs and usually the game's end as well.

While I cannot provide an exhaustive description of even the major forms of New York City street games played by baseball rules, let me at least briefly describe five major forms. Each occupied a distinctive role in our overall play.

Punchball: the canonical "recess" game. In that blessed half hour or so of midmorning schoolyard recess, when the girls jumped rope and the teachers sat and smoked, the boys invariably gathered at the concretized baseball diamond to play the unvarnished "standard" form of baseball with a Spalding—punchball by our name. No pitching. The fielders of the opposing team took their positions and the "batters" of the other team then proceeded by throwing up the Spalding and punching it with their fist. Some kids threw the ball high and punched it overhand; most (including me) tossed it up a foot or two and punched it underhand. Pure baseball rules applied. No exceptions. (And you could often get in a three- to five-inning game during a full half hour of recess time.)

Punchball truly held status (in my neighborhood at least, but not in other, even adjacent, turfs). It was the game we would play unless kids specifically called for another form. If we played by teams rather than twosomes after school, we "automatically" went to punchball, which required no equipment beyond the ball and a spontaneously laid-out field with bases.

Just one (true) story illustrates the kid–grown-up issues that arose on a daily basis. Boys on first and second; no one out. The batter pops one high in the infield. I, playing third base, shout out "infield fly rule" and insist that the batter is automatically out. Most players have never heard of this "arcane" rule and dispute my claim (it didn't really matter because I caught the pop-up in any case). We agreed, by standard custom, to ask the first adult man who passed by, and to abide by his judgment. Thank goodness. The gent turned out to be a knowledgeable fan who not only affirmed the existence of such a rule but even gave a well-wrought explanation for its necessity.

By utter contrast, one summer at camp I got into an argument with a bunkmate about whether humans and dinosaurs had coexisted: me, already a budding paleontologist, in the correct negative; he, citing Alley-Oop, in the wrongly positive. We bet a candy bar and agreed to abide by parental opinion at the forthcoming weekend visitation. My parents were unable to come. His father affirmed that, of course, humans and dinosaurs had coexisted— just look at Alley-Oop—and I had to pay, Hershey's chocolate with almonds. What can be more galling than absolutely to *know* you're right but to have to submit anyway! I don't remember the guy's name, but I'll murder him (something slow and painful like drawing and quartering comes to mind) if I ever find him.

Stickball, the second "standard" form, either by pairs or by teams. Much is known about New York City stickball. The rookie Willie Mays worked on his game by playing stickball with neighborhood kids in Harlem, for example. I have little to add to the consensus, except to note the enormous variety of norms and styles. Each neighborhood, each tiny subdivision of each neighborhood, developed its own local customs.

Stickball could be played by twos or by teams. Twosomes predominated on my turf, and I suspect that Roger and I logged more stickball hours during the 1950s than I spent in any other activity.

As mentioned above, we pitched toward a chalked box on a wall and the batter flailed away. Distance determined the status of a hit. Caught pops and flies were outs, and cleanly fielded ground balls were also outs (probably the most common mode, along with strikeouts). We tried to play seven innings, but didn't always have enough time for a full game. Roger, by the way, is a lefty—a great advantage in this forum (and I think he won about two-thirds of our games over the years). And, yes, it isn't easy to hit a Spalding with a broomstick, but when you swing hard and catch the "sweet spot," the ball really sails—up and away, often far enough to count as a home run.

Stoopball, much of a muchness, but each a bit different. Baltimore may be the greatest American city for stoops, but New York owes no apologies to anyone. The garden apartment buildings of Fresh Meadows each have three entryways, each up a stoop of several concrete steps. Each stoop leads to nine apartments, three to a floor.

Stoopball, usually played one to a side, works basically like stickball, with the Spalding as projectile, the status of a hit determined by distance, and the steps of the stoop as the analog for a bat. The "batter" throws the Spalding against a step and the fielder tries to catch the rebounding ball on the fly or ground.

As almost every player knows, each step has a pronounced

A boy playing stickball catches a ball thrown to home plate, represented here by the manhole cover. *Credit: Ralph Morse/TIMEPIX*

"sweet spot" located at the perpendicular intersection of the hor-
izontal and vertical portions of the step. If a batter manages to hit
this spot with his Spalding (called a "pointee" or a "pointer" on
my turf), then the ball really flies—usually over the head of the
fielder and often into home run territory. An extensive mythology
surrounded the issue of whether anyone could figure out a way to
hit the point of a step in some systematic way and at high probability. We all tried, but so far as I know, nobody ever succeeded.

As any kid will affirm, the chief fascination of stoopball lies in
the fact that no two stoops are exactly alike, and that, consequently, each stoop generates its own unique and idiosyncratic set
of rules. A little story in conclusion: I once dislocated my arm during a stoopball game as I crashed into the side rail of the stoop
when I ran in to catch a pop-up. So, one day, I'm sitting on the
stoop, arm in a sling, when the local beat cop—as big, tough, and
Irish as any stereotype of the profession could possibly suggest—
sidles up to me and simply says, thus suffusing me with immense
pride: "How's the other kid?"

Boxball-baseball and using the sidewalk. We played a wide variety
of games by hitting a Spalding between two or three sidewalk
chalk boxes. One could, for example, put a penny on the crack, to
be awarded to the first contestant who hits it with a Spalding.

We called our local favorite "boxball-baseball" and played the
game across three boxes, one belonging to each contestant, with
the middle box neutral. The "pitcher" had to toss the Spalding
into the neutral box, and the "batter" then had to slap the ball
with the palm of his open hand into the pitcher's box and hope-
fully far beyond on the subsequent bounce, with (just as in stickball and stoopball) the value of the hit determined by distance of
the first bounce.

Baseball cards before the full hegemony of capitalism. We had baseball cards in the late 1940s and throughout the 1950s. I even kept,
while discarding all others, my favorite set of 1948 Bowman
cards—black and white photos of players rather than Topps's car-

icatures. My set is now worth several thousand dollars, but I'm not selling.

Nothing amuses (or puzzles) a fan of my generation more than the current treatment of baseball cards as commodities of distinctive monetary value. I confess that I laugh every time I see a kid these days acquire a new card and immediately transfer it to a plastic binder, lest, God forbid, an edge should become frayed, thus destroying the pristine value.

We collected cards, but never with a thought of money. We *used* them in a variety of games. You could stick them in the spokes of your bicycle wheel, where they made a pleasant whirring sound as you rode. But two utilities in real games predominated. First, we played flipping or matching. One contestant took a card and, from belt height, flipped it toward the ground, making sure that it turned several times on the way down. The other contestant then flipped his card—taking both if his matched the other in "heads" or "tails" of the final position, but losing both if his fell in the opposite orientation. Unlike the inability to hit pointers systematically in stoopball, a few neighborhood kids did learn—don't ask me how, for I could never master the method—how to throw a heads or a tails almost every time.

Second, we scaled them against a wall. In this paper version of "pitch pennies," each contestant scales a card, and the card closest to the wall wins them all. I once had sixteen identical cards of Ewell Blackwell—a fine pitcher, but not the greatest—and lost every one of them in a scaling game!

I could go on, but enough's enough. We derived a great deal of enjoyment from these games. They also kept us out of trouble and away from girls. And what more could a boy have desired in preadolescence?

The Babe's Final Strike

Tiny and insignificant reminders often provoke floods of memory. I have just read a little notice, tucked away on the sports pages: "Babe Pinelli, long-time major league umpire, died Monday at age 89 at a convalescent home near San Francisco."

What could be more elusive than perfection? And what would you rather be—the agent or the judge? Babe Pinelli played the role of chief umpire in baseball's unique episode of perfection—a perfect game in the World Series. It was also his last official game as arbiter—October 8, 1956. Twenty-seven Dodgers up; twenty-seven Bums down. The catalyst was a competent but otherwise undistinguished Yankee pitcher, Don Larsen.

The dramatic end was all Pinelli's, and controversial ever since. Dale Mitchell, pinch hitting for Sal Maglie, was the twenty-seventh batter. With a count of one ball and two strikes, Larsen delivered a pitch low and outside—close, but surely not, by any technical definition, a strike.[1] Mitchell let the pitch go by, but

First published as "The Strike That Was Low and Outside" in the *New York Times*, November 10, 1984. Reprinted with permission of the *New York Times*.
[1] Gould would later realize that he had slightly misremembered the moment— Larsen's pitch had actually been *high* and outside. See page 315. [Ed.]

Don Larsen pitches the only perfect game in World Series history, leading the New York Yankees to victory over the Brooklyn Dodgers in game five on October 8, 1956. The Yankees ended up winning the Series in seven games. *Credit: Bettmann/Corbis*

Pinelli didn't hesitate. Up went the right arm for a called strike three. Out went Yogi Berra from behind the plate, nearly tackling Larsen in a frontal jump of joy.

"Outside by a foot," groused Mitchell later. He exaggerated, for it was outside by only a few inches, but he was right. Babe Pinelli, however, was even more right. A man may not take a close pitch with so much on the line. Context matters. Truth is a circumstance, not a spot.

I was a junior at Jamaica High School. On that day, every teacher let us listen, even Mrs. B., our crusty old solid geometry teacher (and, I guess, a secret baseball fan). We reached Mrs. G., our even crustier French teacher, in the bottom of the seventh, and I was appointed to plead. "You gotta let us listen," I said. "It's never happened before." "Young man," she replied, "this class is a French class."

Luckily, I sat in the back just in front of Bob Hacker (remember alphabetical seating?), a rabid Dodger fan with earphone and portable radio. Halfway through the period, following Pinelli's last strike, I felt a sepulchral tap and looked around. Hacker's face was ashen. "He did it—that bastard did it." I cheered loudly and threw my jacket high in the air. "Young man," said Mrs. G. from the side board, "I'm sure the verb *écrire* can't be that exciting." It cost me ten points on my final grade, maybe admission to Harvard as well. I never experienced a moment of regret.

Truth is inflexible. Truth is inviolable. By long and recognized custom, by any concept of justice, Dale Mitchell had to swing at anything close. It was a strike—a strike low and outside. Babe Pinelli, umpiring his last game, ended with his finest, his most perceptive, his most truthful moment. Babe Pinelli, arbiter of history, walked into the locker room and cried.

The Best of Times, Almost

L ook, I'm a Yankee fan—have been since long before most of you were born. I have benefited from Boston's suffering (most, after all, for Yankee gain) all my life. I reacted with boyish glee when, in 1949, Boston faced the Yanks one game up with two to go—and my guys won both for the pennant. And, although (honest to God) I didn't want Yaz to make the last out by popping to third, I decided that Bucky Dent was the greatest living American one afternoon in early October 1978. The Red Sox, in other words, began as my mortal enemies.

That is, until 1967, the year of the Impossible Dream, and my rookie season in the Harvard professoriat. I loved that pennant race and cheered Boston on (why not, the Yanks were out of it, and one of my New York heroes, Elston Howard, was catching for the Sox). For the first time in my life, I suffered with you through the seventh Series game—though the final result was inevitable (I mean nobody but nobody could beat Bob Gibson, not even Lonborg, especially on two days' rest).

My affection for Boston crept slowly apace until it blossomed in 1975, and I began to understand Boston pain. I watched the

First published in the *Harvard Crimson*, November 5, 1986.

sixth game of the Series from a hotel room in Salt Lake City (no beer, not even before the seventh inning), and exulted in Carlton Fisk's homer with a glee unmatched since Bobby Thomson's for the Giants in 1951. I also watched, from the same room, the next day as the Sox, in the finale, took a 3–0 lead into the sixth, and then blew it.

This cocky Yankee fan, accustomed to victory as a rite of fall, began to understand the uniqueness—also depth—of Boston's special pain. Not like Cubs pain (never to get there at all), or Phillies pain (lousy teams, but they did take it all)—but the deepest possible anguish of running a long and hard course, again and again, to the very end, and then self-destructing one inch from the finish line.

Well folks, guess what? Call it shallow, fickle, or anything else you want. But this year I was with you all the way. The Yanks never had a real shot (and Steinbrenner does wear on you after a bit). Maybe you thought I would switch caps for the Series and start chanting "Let's Go, Mets." Not on your life. I'm a loyal New Yorker, to be sure, but the Mets are nothing to me. They didn't exist when I was a kid, and loyalties are shaped by those early years of splendor in the grass and glory in the flower.

I rooted for the Sox all the way, as hard and as diligently as I ever rooted in all my life (and spurred by my son Ethan, a Sox zealot too young to remember any previous postseason play).

What can possibly be said? It's a week later, and I'm still numb. To hell with the French Revolution; to hell with Dickens. This, not that, was the very best, and then the absolute worst, of times.

When, a millimeter from final defeat (with the champagne already uncorked in the Angels' dressing room), Dave Henderson hit that fifth-game homer, I reacted as I never had before. I didn't cheer or jump; I wept—not a few tears stifled by the customs of manhood, but copiously. Then, alone again in a hotel room (this time in D.C.), I had to watch when Henderson, reaching for immortality, apparently won the Series with another homer in the tenth inning of game six, and, with two outs and nobody on, the Sox came—not once but four times—within a micron of taking it all, only to blow it once again.

The Mets' scoreboard had already flashed "Congratulations Red Sox." NBC had already named Marty Barrett player of the game, and Bruce Hurst the Series MVP. But the Sox knew better. They had peeled the aluminum off the champagne bottles, but they hadn't popped the corks. You all know what the great Yogi Berra says about when it's over—and when it ain't.

Yes, I do understand finally. I came to it late, but I do understand now. This was worse, more bitter than ever. A total self-immolation, by guys we love and admire—by Calvin Schiraldi, who got us there; Rich Gedman, who performed with such quiet efficiency; Bill Buckner, who, though hobbled, had fielded flawlessly. I even grieved for Bob Stanley (nine times out of ten, Gedman stops that ball, even though it must technically be ruled a wild pitch; and Stanley did what he was brought in to do—he got Mookie Wilson to hit an easily playable ground ball). Yes, this was much worse—worse than selling that great lefty pitcher named Ruth, worse than Pesky holding the ball in 1946, worse than facing the Gibson machine in 1967, worse than Joe Morgan in 1975, worse even than Bucky Dent and Yaz's pop to third in 1978.

What does it all mean? (We academics do have to ask that question after all.) I held and abandoned my hypotheses in this vein during postseason play. After Henderson's resurrection in playoff game five, I actually dared to suggest that God was a Red Sox fan. After the most providential rain delay in recent sports history, between games six and seven of the Series, I decided that God cannot influence human actions, but still controls the weather. After the last game, I realized that He must hate the DH rule so much that He only favors the Sox within the American League. (I must, of course, now also entertain the possibility that

either he doesn't exist at all or doesn't give a damn about baseball.) We are left alone with our pain.

The finale was too typical—an early Sox lead, eroded near the
end; a late Sox surge, almost but not quite enough. Ethan cried
when it was all over—and this was only his first time. I tried to
console him, but ended up joining him. It's a puzzle, isn't it? I
don't know why grown men care so deeply about something that
neither kills, nor starves, nor maims, nor even scratches in our
world of woe. I don't know why we care so much, but I'm mighty
glad that we do.

Innings

Time flows in many ways, but two modes stand out for their prominence in nature and their symbolic role in making our lives intelligible.

Time includes *arrows* of direction that tell stories in distinct stages, causally linked—birth to death, rags to riches.

Time also flows in *cycles* of repetition that locate a necessary stability amid the confusion of life—days, years, generations.

Cycles of repetition, based in nature, once surrounded us and shaped our daily lives. We sowed in the spring, reaped in the fall, froze in the winter, and frequented the ol' swimmin' hole in the summer.

Urban life has vitiated these rhythms. We become insensible to seasons in a world of air-conditioning and nectarines available throughout the year at Korean all-night fruit stores.

We must therefore create cycles from the flow of culture—for our need has not abated. Thus, we celebrate holidays and other largely artificial rituals, set at appointed times. The seasons may be utterly lost in Southern California, but San Diegans still eat

First published in the *New York Times*, April 4, 1988. Reprinted with permission of the *New York Times*.

turkey in November, spend money in December, and watch fire-
works in July.

Spring marks the true beginning of the year. Spring signifies
renewal, rebirth. Spring (up here in New England, where season-
ality still pokes through the asphalt jungle) is the yearly sequence
of crocus to forsythia to tulip to rose. The Romans understood
and began their year at this right time—so that September, October, November, and December (as their etymology still proclaims)
were once the seventh, eighth, ninth, and tenth months of a year
that started in March.

But spring, to all thinking, feeling, caring, red-blooded Americans, can only mean one thing—if you will accept my premise that
culture must now substitute for nature in symbols of cyclic repetition.

Spring marks the return of baseball—opening day, the true
inception of another year. Forget the inebriation of a cold January
morning. Time, as Tom Boswell so aptly remarked, begins on
opening day.

Baseball fulfills both our needs for arrows (to forge time into
stories) and cycles (to grant stability, predictability and place).

Opening day marks our annual renewal after a winter of discontent. But opening day also records the arrow of time in two
distinct ways.

It evokes the bittersweet passage of our own lives—as I take my
son to the game, and remember when I held my father's hand and
wondered if DiMag would hit .350 that year.

And opening day promises another fine season of drama—an
arrow that will run through October, telling its stories of triumph
and tragedy as the world turns and yet another summer cycles
past.

More Power to Him

I n 1927, when my father turned twelve, Al Jolson inaugurated the era of sound movies with *The Jazz Singer*, Jerome Kern and Oscar Hammerstein's *Show Boat* opened on Broadway, Charles Lindbergh flew the *Spirit of St. Louis* across the Atlantic nonstop to Paris, the state of Massachusetts executed Sacco and Vanzetti, and Babe Ruth hit 60 home runs in a single season.

Roger Maris bested the Babe with 61 in 1961, the summer of my nineteenth birthday, with teammate Mickey Mantle batting just afterward and reaching 54 in one of the two greatest home run derbies in baseball history. This summer, Mark McGwire has already broken 61, and may even reach 70—with Sammy Sosa of the Chicago Cubs just behind, or perhaps in front, in the other greatest derby ever. My two sons, both fans in their different ways, will turn twenty-nine and twenty-five.

This magic number, this greatest record in American sports, obsesses us for at least three good reasons. First, baseball has changed no major rule in a century, and we can therefore look and compare, in genuine continuity, across the generations. The sea-

First published as "How the New Sultan of Swat Measures Up" in the *Wall Street Journal*, September 10, 1998.

sons of our lives move inexorably forward. As my father saw Ruth, I followed Maris, and my sons watch McGwire. But the game also cycles in glorious sameness, as each winter of our discontent yields to another spring of opening day.

Second, baseball records are unmistakably personal accomplishments, while marks in most other team sports can only be judged as peculiar amalgams. Wilt Chamberlain once scored 100 points in a single basketball game, but only because his teammates elected the odd strategy of feeding him on essentially every play. Home runs emerge from a two-man duel, *mano a mano*, batter against pitcher.

Third, and how else can I say this, baseball is just one helluva terrific game, long paramount in American sporting myths and athletic traditions. Babe Ruth put it best when he said, in his famous and moving speech at Yankee Stadium in 1947, that "the only real game in the world, I think, is baseball . . . You've got to start from way down . . . when you're six or seven. . . . You've got to let it grow up with you."

As a veteran and close student of the 1961 Mantle-Maris derby, I thrill to the detailed similarity of McGwire vs. Sosa. The two Yankees of 1961 embodied different primal myths about great accomplishments: Mantle, the deserving hero, working all his life toward his year of destiny; Maris, the talented journeyman, enjoying that one sweet interval in each man's life when everything comes together in some oddly miraculous way. (Maris never hit more than 39 home runs in any other season.) That year, the miracle man won—and more power to him (and shame on his detractors). Fluke or destiny doesn't matter; Roger Maris did the deed.

Sammy Sosa is this year's Maris, rising from who-knows-where to challenge the man of destiny. Mark McGwire is this year's Mantle. Few other players have been so destined, and no one has ever worked harder and more single-mindedly, to harness and fulfill his gifts of brawn. He is the real item, and this is his year. No one, even Ruth, ever hit more than 50 homers in three successive sea-

The Cardinals' Mark McGwire rounds the bases after hitting his 70th home run, the last of his record-breaking season, in a game against the Montreal Expos in St. Louis on September 27, 1998. Sammy Sosa ended the season with 66 home runs for the Chicago Cubs. *Credit: AP/Wide World Photos*

sons as McGwire has now done. (But will anyone ever break Ruth's feat of hitting more than 40 in all but two years between 1920 and 1932? Hank Aaron was a marvel of consistency over twenty-three seasons, but he never hit more than 47 in a single year, and only once did he hit more than 40 in two successive seasons.)

Though we cheer both Sosa and McGwire—may they each hit at least 70—we nonetheless rightly focus on McGwire for the eerie and awesome quality of his particular excellence. Most great records descend in small and even increments from the leader, and no single figure stands leagues ahead of all the other mere mortals. The home run record used to follow this conventional pattern: Maris with 61; Ruth with 60 and again with 59; Jimmy Foxx, Hank Greenberg, and McGwire (last season) with 58; Hack Wilson and Ken Griffey Jr. (also last season) with 56.

However, a few champions stand so far above the second-place finisher that they seem to belong to another category altogether. Consider DiMaggio's fifty-six-game hitting streak in 1941 (regarded by most sports statisticians, myself included, as the most improbable figure in the history of American athletics), compared with second place Willie Keeler and Pete Rose, both far away at forty-four. Or Jim Thorpe's lopsided victories in both the pentathlon and decathlon of the 1912 Olympics. Or, marking a single man's invention of the art of home run hitting, Babe Ruth's first high figure of 54 in 1920, a number exceeding the sum total for any other entire team in the American League!

McGwire belongs to this most select company of superhuman achievers. He may well hit 70, thus creating the same sweep of empty space that separates DiMaggio and Thorpe from their closest competitors. Moreover, the character of his blasts almost defies belief. Four hundred feet is a long home run; the vast majority of major league dingers fall between 300 and 400. Well, only 19 of McGwire's first 62 failed to reach 400 feet (including number 62, which was a mere 341 feet), and several have exceeded 500, a figure previously achieved only once every few years.

When faced with such an exceptional accomplishment, we long to discover particular reasons. But no special cause need be sought beyond the good fortune of many effectively random moments grafted upon the guaranteed achievements of the greatest home run hitter in the history of baseball.

I don't care if the thin air of Colorado encourages home runs. I don't care if expansion has diluted pitching. I don't care if the ball is livelier and the strike zone smaller. And I especially don't care if McGwire helps himself train by taking an over-the-counter substance regarded as legal by major league baseball. (What cruel nonsense to hold McGwire in any way accountable, simply because we fear that kids may ape him as a role model for an issue entirely outside his call, and within the province of baseball's rule makers.)

Mark McGwire has prevailed by creating, in his own person, an ultimate combination of the two great natural forces of luck and effort: the gift of an extraordinary body, with the steadfast dedication to training and study that can only inspire wonderment in us all.

Rough Injustice

I have spent a paleontological career studying the fickleness of fate and the myriad might-have-beens of evolution.

The Earth would feature no life at all if any of several past ice ages had ever been intense enough to freeze the entire planetary surface, and no humans would grace this world if an extraterrestrial impact had not driven dinosaurs to extinction 65 million years ago and given mammals a lucky opportunity.

This ultimate chanciness, this power of unpredictable events to alter global histories, applies at all scales, from each person's daily dreams to the destiny of our planet. Only an iota of pure circumstance—an inch up or down, a microsecond sooner or later—separates the permanent genius from the eternal goat, the victorious hero engraved in eternal memory from the answer to a future trivia question.

In the most famous successful hunch of postseason baseball history, Philadelphia Athletics manager Connie Mack started the 1929 World Series (against the Chicago Cubs, believe it or not) with Howard Ehmke, an aged and forgotten hurler who had not

First published as "Fickle Fate Rules Sox Destiny" in the *Boston Herald*, October 8, 1998. Reprinted with permission of the *Boston Herald*.

pitched for a month—and not with his stars Lefty Grove (who ended his stellar career with the Sox) or George Earnshaw. Ehmke won the game, giving up just three hits and whiffing a record-breaking (for them) thirteen Cubbies. The Athletics won the Series, Mack became a genius, and everyone forgot Ehmke's terrible final-game outing, saved by good relief pitching and timely hitting.

Last Saturday, in a comparable situation (with Pete Schourek playing Ehmke and Pedro Martinez as Lefty Grove on the bench), Sox skipper Jimy Williams missed Mack's immortality by a whisker of chance. With the Sox down two games to one in a must-win fourth contest against Cleveland, Schourek surrendered only two hits and no runs in a gut-wrenching, not particularly pretty, but completely effective five and one-third innings. In the eighth, with the Sox leading 1–0, our masterful closer Tom Gordon on the mound, and Boston just five outs away from a decisive game five (and an almost guaranteed victory by Martinez), three quick hits, starting with a lucky broken-bat single and ending with a double dose of rough (David) Justice, scored two runs for the Indians and spelled oblivion once again for the Sox.

And so, for no particular reason, by fate's fickle finger (the true and only source for the Bambino's nonexistent curse), Schourek, who did more than anyone had a right to ask, becomes a poignant moment of transient memory, rather than a permanent New England hero.

The fans in Fenway's brimming bandbox rocked with hope until the very end, saluted their brave team with a final cheer, and then filed out once again into an early night (literally and figuratively). I hugged my seatmates Jenny, Ruth, and Jeff, partners in expectation and agony for so many seasons. We will return, by habit and with hope, in 1999. The forces of fate are indifferent to human feeling, and some year our time must come.

But for now, there will be no first-time-ever, most-wonderful-of-all-to-contemplate, full postseason series between the Yanks and the Sox. As a Yankee fan, new to Boston, I saw the only previous postseason encounter of these two archrivals—the Bucky Dent fiasco (and my joy) of 1978. My son Ethan, then four years old, watched with me, and now knows the bliss of being too young to remember.

Last Saturday, Ethan sat beside me, a young man bearing a lifetime of Red Sox pain and devotion. I too have learned to love this crazy, maddening team. How I would have relished the chance to step once again into the breach of my ambivalent rooting in next week's might-have-been! Instead, Ethan and I walked out of Fenway Park and down Yawkey Way in the full understanding of complete silence.

Tripping the Light Fantastic

My grandmother, a proud immigrant with a heavy accent, taught me to sing "The Sidewalks of New York." But my four-year-old mind could not comprehend the description of what folks do on those sidewalks: "we'll trip the light fantastic."

I should have asked (not that she would have known), but my nascent stubborn self decided to go it alone. I concluded that the line must refer to changing traffic signals. (At that age, I was not troubled about the difference between adjectives and adverbs.)

I grew up in far distant Queens and attended only one ticker-tape parade in my youth: the welcome for Gen. Douglas MacArthur after President Harry Truman dismissed him for his refusal to wage a limited war in Korea. School wasn't officially canceled, but teachers hinted in no uncertain terms that they'd look the other way if we traded grammar for grandeur that day—when Mrs. Ponti undoubtedly taught the class about adjectives and adverbs.

In any case, I loved the crowds and confetti, but my pleasure

First published as "At Last, I Love a Parade" in the *New York Times*, October 24, 1998. Reprinted with permission of the *New York Times*.

was seriously tainted, and I've felt just a tad guilty ever since, for my entire family stood with Truman against any extension of war into China.

Sometimes, most of life passes by before childhood confusions get resolved. The New York Yankees have brought me enormous pleasure in exactly fifty seasons of rooting. My first baseball memories extend to the 1949 pennant, when the Yanks faced the Red Sox, one game behind Boston with two games to go in the season—and, obviously, had to win both. And did.

In another misapprehension, my father called these two final games "the crucial series." Only as a young adult did I discover that "crucial" was an ordinary English word and not a proper noun for those two particular contests. But I must also thank the Yankees for two little alleviations of childhood misconceptions.

I now live downtown (after a thirty-year Boston hiatus, with unswerving Yankee devotion, even in Fenway Park). I have just returned from my second ticker-tape parade, this time to honor our transcendent team of 1998. And I finally understand the meaning of such wonderfully traditional celebrations as Mac-Arthur received in 1951, when I was too young and too ambivalent to understand. Long, crowded subway rides from Queens to honor a man you regard as wrong (if not dangerous) cannot convey the meaning or the emotion.

This time, on a crisp and sunny day, I walked to the parade— and immediately recognized why these celebrations must be held at the very southern end of Broadway, on an ordinary working day when kids can miss school (and not on the more convenient weekend for televisors and traffic controllers).

This rule of time and place must be observed because ticker-tape parades stand out (and move along) as one of the few unaltered joys of our past, still vibrant enough to face the present and future in uncompromised form. "See, the conquering hero comes"—and the entire city may watch and celebrate as the procession moves up the full length of main street, and everyone

New York Yankees World Series victory parade, October 23, 1998. *Credit:*
AP/Wide World Photos

walks to the event from home. The surrounding buildings must
be alive with workaday activity, so that shredded computer paper
(substituting for the genuine ticker tape of yore) can cascade from
all the windows, propelled by real human hands.

I was still in Boston during the 1996 victory and celebration. I
even missed the final game of the World Series because, during
those very hours, I was singing in a performance of Handel's
oratorio on Milton's text "L'Allegro ed il Penseroso." At one point
in the performance, no doubt as the Yankees scored the winning
run, the tenor soloist intoned Milton's lines about vibrant and visceral joy:

Come and trip it as you go
On the light fantastic toe.

Another childhood misconception, finally resolved: "light" and "fantastic" are both adjectives!

Yes, Joe, Scott, David, Derek, Mariano, Paul, Tino, Andy, Chuck, Bernie (please stay, you'll never find a better team), El Duque, and all you others down to the very last and entirely essential man. Yes, especially, Darryl. And yes, even George. We'll trip the light fantastic on the sidewalks of New York.

Fenway Crowns
the Millennium

As performers in daily life, each of us can honor the best in our common human nature when we do justly, love mercy, and walk humbly. But as spectators of great accomplishments, we thrill to the transcendent moment of peak achievement in any honorable skill.

These rare and wondrous incidents—for we can only hope to witness a precious few in a full lifetime—unfold in two distinctly different modes. One is essentially democratic. Any good player—although odds favor the best, of course—can propagate a glorious moment of victory if circumstances conspire and skills permit: Carlton Fisk's great home run in the 1975 World Series, or Ted Williams's last hurrah, when he hit a dinger in his final at bat, to cite two local examples.

But the second mode is elite. We may, on the rarest of occasions, enjoy the privilege of watching a person who can do something so much better than anyone else on the planet that we have to wonder if he really belongs to our universal tribe of *Homo sapiens*. I can cite only two such experiences in my previous fifty-seven years of life, both musical: when, in the late 1960s, I heard Diet-

First published as "Greatness at Fenway" in the *Boston Globe*, July 16, 1999.

rich Fischer-Dieskau sing Schubert's *Die Schöne Müllerin*, and even his triple pianissimos penetrated like pinpricks of utter beauty to my seat in the last row of the last balcony of Symphony Hall; and when, two years ago at the Metropolitan Opera, I saw the world's greatest performers in each part boost their combined talents far above the sum of their individual strengths when they sang the first act of Wagner's *Die Walküre*: Placido Domingo as Siegmund, Deborah Voigt as Sieglinde, and Matti Salminen as Hunding, with James Levine conducting the finest orchestra ever assembled in operatic history.

In Boston, we have just been treated to a fabulous double-header of similar import as the millennium closes on our shrine of Fenway Park—and I shall never forget the thrill and privilege of simply being there.

The All-Star Game itself is a spectacle, not a sporting contest (for no manager out to win a meaningful game would remove his best players early and use his final substitutes for a last comeback attempt). But spectacles serve the different function of show-casing excellence and affirming traditions worth preserving in a volatile and increasingly commercialized world, where material quantity becomes confused with ultimate worth, and where we seem unable to recognize and honor our older standards of human quality.

Mark McGwire's baker's dozen dingers in Monday night's home run derby scarcely belong in a human league. His shortest shot over the Green Monster almost exceeded the longest single ball hit by any of the other nine contestants. (In the most awe-some Fenway homer I had ever seen in thirty years of attendance, Jack Clark once hit the second row of lights in the left field tower that soars above the Green Monster; one of McGwire's shots hit the very top of the same tower, while several others went higher and farther.)

Then, to begin the game itself on Tuesday night, our own Pedro Martinez struck out five of the six batters he faced, includ-

American League starting pitcher Pedro Martinez pitches in the first inning of the All-Star Game at Fenway Park on July 13, 1999. *Credit: AP/Wide World Photos*

ing, in order, Larry Walker, Sammy Sosa, and the same Mark McGwire.

Above it all (spiritually, as he linked my middle age to my childhood passion for baseball; materially, as he firmly threw out the first ball with the one side of his body that the ravages of stroke have spared; and literally, as he then watched the game from his left-field sky box), Ted Williams presided as the closest surrogate for God that such activities can muster.

Ted may not have been a "nice man" during his tumultuous playing days in Boston; and, although he didn't starve, he never amassed a monetary fortune from baseball either. But Ted Williams directed all his maniacal dedication, and his gifts of body and mind, to pursuing—and achieving—his own dream of transcendence. He did not submit to the rules of corporate blandness or false modesty (now so essential for a lucrative life of commercial endorsements) in stating the driving goal of his choice in life.

As he has said so often, he "simply" wanted to become so good that when people saw him on the street they would turn their heads and say: There goes the greatest hitter who ever lived. And so he is. And so is Mark McGwire in the different art of power hitting, and Pedro Martinez in pitching finesse. And this—may we never forget, and never cease to practice—is the true significance and essence of enthusiasm, which literally means "the intake of God."

Times to Try a Fan's Soul

In 1949, when Joe DiMaggio became my hero and the Yankees my passion, the Boston Red Sox led the Yanks by one game as the teams met in a final confrontation at the season's very end. The Yanks won both and then took the World Series against their second-greatest rivals, the Brooklyn Dodgers.

A generation later, in 1978, my son (matching my own age in 1949) and I watched in delight as Bucky Dent's flyball over the Green Monster (an out almost anywhere else, but a dinger in Fenway Park) beat the Red Sox in the only postseason episode—a one-game playoff to resolve a regular-season tie—of the greatest rivalry in the history of baseball.

The classicist Emily Vermeule, a colleague of mine at Harvard and an ardent Sox fan, wrote that destiny had deep-sixed the Sox because their drama with the Yanks had to unfold within the rigid norms of Greek tragedy. Roger Angell replied, in the greatest one-liner ever written about sports, that the pathways of history cannot be so foreordained. Mr. Angell offered the alternative view that—just as Yaz, representing the potential winning run, popped to third to end the game—God (who must support the Sox if the

First published in the *Wall Street Journal*, October 15, 1999.

poor shall inherit the earth) became distracted, and chose this worst possible moment to shell a peanut.

And now these greatest rivals meet for the first time in a full postseason series (impossible previously, because two teams in the same division could not face each other in full postseason play before the recent introduction of the otherwise abominable "wild card"). Pedro Martinez vs. Roger Clemens on Saturday marks a promotion to reality of such fictional dreams as a poetry slam between Shakespeare and Marlowe, or a composition derby between Bach and Handel—as good as it gets in our imperfect world.

The first-round victories that have brought these teams together followed the scripted route for this quintessential drama. The Yankees, with the ruthless efficiency of baseball's greatest and most frequent champions, dispatched Texas in a minimal three games, allowing the Rangers one paltry run in twenty-seven innings. (This year's team features a wonderfully likable group of players—not always a hallmark of Yankee history, to say the least—but their personal amiability does not reduce the deadly force of the team's juggernaut.)

I grew up in New York, now live here again, and have loved and followed the Yankees all my life. I would, moreover, never break a fealty of three generations extending from my immigrant grand-father who learned to love America by watching Jack Chesbro win a record forty-one games for the Yanks (then called the High-landers) in 1904, to my father who worshiped Ruth and Gehrig, and who cried when Alexander struck out Lazzeri in the 1926 World Series. But after living in Boston for thirty years and hold-ing season tickets in Fenway Park, the most captivating of all inti-mate bandboxes, how can I not love the Sox as well?

In maximal contrast to the Yankees' smooth sail, the Sox lost the first two games in their best-of-five first round to the Indians in Cleveland, as their only two genuine stars, pitcher Pedro Mar-tinez and shortstop Nomar Garciaparra, both went down with injuries. At Fenway for the third game, I sat with my seatmates of so many fruitless years, Jeff, Jay, Rob, Leo, and Jenny, all anticipating a wake but acknowledging the duty of our presence. The Sox won, 9–3. On Sunday, we enjoyed an even more improbable party as the Sox fractured the postseason record for runs, winning by a football score of 23–7. On Monday, back in Cleveland, Pedro Martinez, still hurting and unable to throw his best fastball, pitched six hitless innings, while Troy O'Leary's two homers powered Boston to the most improbable comeback of recent memory.

Logic and reason dictate a swift Yankee victory in this second round, but such noble principles cannot buy a ticket to Fenway Park, where God may again shell peanuts at the crucial moment, or may not care enough even to attend, or may not give a damn about baseball, or may not even exist. This spectacle—the first postseason series ever played between baseball's two oldest and greatest rivals—lies well beyond rationality. As Red Smith wrote, in the second greatest one-liner of sports literature, following Bobby Thomson's series-ending home run in the 1951 playoff between the Brooklyn Dodgers and the victorious New York Giants: "The art of fiction is dead. Reality has strangled invention."

Nothing can explain the meaning and excitement of all this to nonfans. No sensible person would even try. This is church—and nonbelievers cannot know the spirit. One can only recall Louis Armstrong's famous statement about the nature of jazz: "Man, if you gotta ask, you'll never know."

I can only experience this Yankee vs. Red Sox series as eerie, for a rooterless benignity has descended upon me within an activity that demands partisan passion. I cannot abandon my lifelong fealty to the Yankees, but how can one live with Sox pain for thirty years and be unmoved or unattracted by the hope of redemption?

Just consider the possible scenarios. Yes, the first subway series since 1956 if the Yanks win and, however improbably, the Mets manage to vanquish the Braves. But suppose that the Sox win and

the Mets also triumph. Then, in the last chance of the millennium, Boston gets an utterly unexpected opportunity to undo a
century of humiliation from New York. This second round against
the Yanks would redeem 1949 and 1978. A subsequent World
Series victory over the Mets would then cancel the greatest pain
of 1986 and restore the earth's moral balance just before our great
calendrical transition.

Boston could then exorcise the curse of the Bambino—the
well-known hex put on the Sox when Boston owner Harry Frazee
sold Babe Ruth to the Yanks in 1920 to raise enough cash to take
a flutter on a Broadway show. (Boston last won the World Series
in 1918.) The dreaded date of 1986 could be uttered again in
Boston, and Bill Buckner, a fine player and gentleman who
deserves a far better fate, can live the rest of his life in peace.

And Boston would stage its biggest and most memorable party
since a group of hotheaded patriots dumped some tea into the
harbor, an act that has reverberated for more than two hundred
years—with the invention and spread of baseball, rather than
cricket, as a primary ramification. These are indeed, as Thomas
Paine said in an early reverberation, the times that try men's
souls.

Freud at the Ballpark

A highly inconvenient law of physics states that two objects cannot occupy the same space at the same time. Consequently, as New York rejoices in the first "subway series" since my high school days of 1956, we also lament that two of the three sacred places of past contests—Brooklyn's Ebbets Field and the Giants' Polo Grounds in upper Manhattan—now exist only as memories beneath housing projects, and not as material realities.

But I suggest a look on the bright side, spurred by a metaphor that Freud devised to begin his book with a quintessential New York title: *Civilization and Its Discontents*. Freud acknowledged the physical reality cited above, but he celebrated, in happy contrast, the mind's power to overlay current impressions directly upon past memories. The mind, he argued, might be compared with a mythical Rome that could raise a modern civic building upon a medieval cathedral built over a classical temple, while preserving all three structures intact in the same spot: "Where the Coliseum now stands we could at the same time admire Nero's vanished

First published in the *New York Times*, October 19, 2000. Reprinted with permission of the *New York Times*.

Golden House. . . . The same piece of ground would be supporting the church of Santa Maria sopra Minerva and the ancient temple over which it was built." The physical fable fails, but we can,
as Freud notes, make such an "impossible" superposition in our
mental representations, for our memories survive, long after fate
has imposed a sentence of death or the wrecking ball upon their
sources: "Only in the mind," Freud adds, "is such a preservation
of all the earlier stages alongside of the final form possible."

Thus, I can watch Roger Clemens striking out fifteen Mariners
in a brilliant one-hitter and place his frame right on top of Don
Larsen pitching his perfect game in 1956. And I can admire the
grace of Bernie Williams in center field, while my teenage memories see Mantle's intensity, and my first impressions of childhood
recall DiMaggio's elegance, in exactly the same spot. I can then
place all three images upon the foundation of my father's stories
of DiMaggio as a rookie in the 1936 Series, and my grandfather
Papa Joe's tales of Babe Ruth in the first three New York series of
1921–1923.

The count of the last millennium stopped at unlucky thirteen
in 1956. The reality of a subway series grew from more modest
roots and routes. The first two New York series of 1921 and 1922
never left the Polo Grounds (for both the Yanks and Giants then
played in the same park). Yankee Stadium opened in time for the
1923 three-peat of Yanks vs. Giants (and the first Yankee victory),
but a short walk across the Harlem River sufficed, as the two ballparks stood in literal shouting distance, one from the other. Yankee victories over the Giants in 1936 and 1937 also required no
more than a stroll. The first true subway series occurred a month
after my birth in 1941, as distant Brooklyn finally prevailed. Six
more subway contests between the Yanks and Dodgers followed
('47, '49, '52, '53, '55, and '56), all won by Yanks, with a tragic
exception in 1955. One strolling series between the Yanks and
Giants intervened in 1951, as I struggled to restore my Yankee
loyalty after rooting so hard for the Giants against the hated

Home-plate umpire Charlie Reliford separates Yankees pitcher Roger Clemens from Mike Piazza in the second game of the 2000 subway series. Clemens had fielded a fragment of Piazza's bat and thrown it in the Mets catcher's direction as Piazza ran to first base on a foul ball. *Credit: AP/Wide World Photos*

Dodgers—and being so gloriously rewarded by Bobby Thomson's immortal homer in the last inning of the last playoff game.

Geography then expanded even more dramatically from immobility in 1921, to a short stroll in 1923, to a subway ride in 1941, to a transcontinental flight, as several subsequent series pitted the Yanks against the transplanted Dodgers and Giants of California. But, to any real New Yorker, these contests simply don't count. They left in 1958, broke our hearts, and then ceased to exist in that wondrous domain of Freudian superposition. The Mets, to me, are still an expansion team, but who's complaining after a forty-four year drought, as subway series number fourteen initiates the new millennium?

What can I say? The subway series of my youth shaped my life and my dreams, and established the milestones of timing and memory for all later accomplishments. In the peace of midlife, just a few years shy of those senior discounts, I can even place the

Freudian calm of experience upon the passions of unforgiving boyhood—and finally come to terms with the Dodgers' victory, and the spoilage of Yankee perfection, in 1955. I met Roy Campanella at a university cocktail party several years ago. Incredibly, for this wonderful man exceeded all others present by an order of magnitude in interest and achievement, he sat alone, talking with no one. So I walked over, still in the awe of remembered youth, and knelt by his wheelchair for the most memorable half hour of conversation in all my life. He wore a World Series ring on each finger of his left hand, but one exceeded all the others in size and brilliance. So I said to him: "I know the year of that biggest ring. That must be for 1955, when you finally beat us." And this great man simply replied with such heartfelt candor and pleasure: "Yes, I am so proud." And, at that moment, and forever, a little, but persistent, wound of my youth healed, and all shone bright and good.

A Time to Laugh

O n October 6, 2001, for the first time in nearly a month of tragedy, the *New York Post* ran a headline on a different and happy subject. This screamer, despite its telegraphic mode and our preoccupation with other matters, conveyed a clear message in its numerical minimalism (to honor maximal achievement). The headline simply stated: "72." Barry Bonds had fractured Mark McGwire's "unbeatable" record for home runs in a single season, set at 70 just three years ago. (Two games later, he added another and finished the season with 73.) We are not callous. The thousands dead on September 11 shall remain in our lacerated hearts so long as we live. We now honor them by moving on in full memory, for "there is," the Preacher tells us (Ecclesiastes 3:4), "a time to weep, and a time to laugh."

As we cherish a happy note in the diapason of our emotional lives, we also wonder why this good news must dismember a comforting plateau of relative stability. Ruth's 60 and Maris's 61 set enduring standards, each lasting more than thirty years. We expected the same extended glory for McGwire's 70, now fallen

First published as "A Happy Mystery to Ponder: Why So Many Homers?" in the *Wall Street Journal*, October 10, 2001.

San Francisco Giant Barry Bonds hugs his son Nikolai after hitting his 70th home run against the Houston Astros on October 4, 2001. The next day, against the Los Angeles Dodgers, Bonds would hit his 71st and 72nd home runs to break Mark McGwire's three-year-old record. *Credit: AP/Wide World Photos*

before we could even explore the appearance and meaning of this new Everest.

We may, I think, best grasp Bonds's achievement by struggling to understand two numerical aspects of his remarkable deed—one conventional among sporting records, the other surprising. First, Bonds's 73 dingers follow the usual pattern of incremental improvement, rather than shattering breakthrough. When Ruth hit 60 in 1927, he broke his own record of 59 from 1921. Maris's 61 in 1961 also added a minimal increment. These heights, then, slide evenly down to Greenberg and Foxx at 58, Wilson at 56, Mantle at 54, etc. McGwire's 70 seemed to fracture the scale, but the disturbing gap quickly filled, restoring a comforting incrementalism with McGwire at 70, Sosa at 66 in the same 1998 season, McGwire at 65 in 1999, Sosa with 64 this year, and Sosa again with 63 in 1999.

But in a second and disconcerting feature, this Giant has broken all decorum by so accelerating the pace of fracture that we can hardly stabilize our admiration before transcendence forces a reorientation. Sure, "records are made to be broken," as the cliché proclaims. But truly great records should endure for a *little* while, at least long enough to potentiate the stuff of legend across a single generation: "Son, I remember when . . . Oh yeah, Dad, you were there? Really, honest!"

Our discombobulated lives need to sink some anchors in numerical stability. (I still have not recovered from the rise of a pound of hamburger at the supermarket to more than a buck.) Ripken waited a long time to break Gehrig's feat of endurance. DiMaggio's fifty-six-game hitting streak remains unchallenged (with a distant forty-four for second place), but may one day fall. Cy Young's 511 career victories will never be exceeded unless surgeons invent an iron arm, or pitchers return to the old practice of working every fourth day and finishing what they start.

This acceleration therefore raises a question that I, as a statistician of the game, generally regard as inappropriate. Broken records usually demand no special explanation, despite our inclination to view any increment as a uniquely heroic feat accomplished for a particular reason of valor. In this case, however, we do need to understand our current epidemic of homers, permitting three great players to exceed, and several others to challenge, all within the past four seasons, a plateau of 60 reached only twice before in 120 years of major league baseball. No random "blip" can encompass so much done so quickly by so many.

I tend to dismiss the three most common conjectures, but wish to defend a fourth notion rarely aired in this growing debate. First, we cannot ascribe this outburst to the sociology of changing fan preferences for displays of raw power. The great sluggers of the past—from the versatile Ruths to the single-minded Kiners or Killebrews—played "long ball" just as assiduously, and the domination of hitting over pitching peaked during the 1920s and 1930s, not in modern baseball.

Second, despite all conspiratorial suspicions and reasoned

arguments, numerous tests of old vs. new balls find no "juicing up" of the projectile, either consciously ordered or accidentally achieved. Third, and finally, knee-jerk arguments about the general decline of pitching won't wash. I suspect that Ruth enjoyed better prospects in his time, before the "invention" of relief pitching in several varieties of subspecialization. (At the very least, he never had to hit against himself, for Ruth was also baseball's best left-handed pitcher.) I wonder how many dingers the Babe hit off tired starters in the late innings?

Only one explanation makes any sense to me as an innovation that might sufficiently boost the output of the best sluggers. Several years ago, *American Heritage* asked me to write an article on the greatest athlete of the twentieth century. I considered the inestimable Jordan and Ali, but finally decided upon the consensus favored at midcentury (when, as a sports-addicted kid, I read everything on this subject): Jim Thorpe, who put miles of space between himself and the clumped second- to fifth-place finishers in both the pentathlon and decathlon of the 1912 Olympics, who reigned as the best player in American football, and who also performed adequately in major league baseball (whereas Jordan really couldn't hit a curve and barely broke .200 in a full minor league season). Contemporaries invariably described Thorpe as an Adonis, whose gorgeous body bristled with strength and muscles. But if you judge a photo of Thorpe by contemporary standards of bodily perfection, you will probably recall the ninety-eight-pound weakling of those old Charles Atlas ads. Thorpe now looks scrawny and ill-developed, no match for half the guys at the local gym.

I therefore suspect that one consistent and important thing separates then from now: scientific weight training for highly specific changes in particular muscles and groups—a regimen now rigidly followed by all serious athletes, yet completely unknown in Ruth's time. Scientific training, by itself, does nothing, and cannot convert even a very good hitter into a home run champion.

But such assiduous, specialized work, rigorously followed by those few surpassingly gifted athletes who combine the three essential attributes of bodily prowess, personal dedication, and high intelligence, can probably raise Greenberg's 58 to McGwire's 70.

To Mark McGwire, a truly splendid man who deserved to savor a longer reign, we can only say that "there is . . . a time to get, and a time to lose: a time to keep, and a time to cast away." You were the firstest with the mostest. We will always love you, and revere your amazing grace in that wonderful season. You and Sammy (and the ghosts of Roger and Mickey) will always be the boys of our most exquisite summers. And to Barry Bonds, who by quirks of temperament has never matched McGwire in public appeal, but who did his deed with honor, consistency, and fortitude at the most tragic of all times, may you enjoy every moment as you remember another verse in the third chapter of Ecclesiastes: "There is nothing better than that a man should rejoice in his own works; for this is his portion." Barry, that was one helluva portion! God bless you, and God bless us every one. You gave us some lightness of being to face an unbearable time.

HEROES LARGE, SMALL, AND FALLEN

Mickey Mantle:
The Man versus the Myth

I was nine years old when the Yanks brought up Mickey Mantle in 1951. I hated him. DiMaggio was my hero, but even I could tell his skills were eroding. I longed for that center-field job, and I knew that it would be mine if only DiMag could hang in there long enough for me to finish high school. But now, at the brink of realizing this beautiful fantasy, I faced a usurper from Commerce, Oklahoma.

In 1952 I began to change my mind, for even a child can empathize with the victims of cruel treatment and ill fortune. One day, as the senseless booing continued to envelop Mantle (he hit .311 with twenty-three homers in his sophomore year), Yankee emcee Mel Allen broke the cardinal rule of dramatic performance by forsaking his appointed role and conversing directly with his audience. As I listened on the radio, Allen leaned out of his press box and accosted a fan in the midst of a raucous Bronx cheer: "Why are you booing him?" The fan replied, "Because he ain't as good as DiMaggio"—and Allen, rendered momentarily speechless (for once) by simple fury, busted a gut.

"Mickey Mantle" first appeared in *Sport* magazine, December 1986.

Suddenly I realized something in a cold sweat. Mickey was actually closer to me in age (ten years older) than he was to DiMaggio (nearly seventeen years younger). Before then I had simply lumped all full-sized people into the single, undifferentiated category "adult." But Mickey was more like me, and I would have been scared shitless out there in center field. My heart went out to him—as it had, for the first time, when he caught his spikes on a drainage spout during the 1951 World Series and almost ended his career with the first and most serious of many leg injuries.

In 1956, his magical year of the triple crown, I came to love Mickey Mantle. I suspect you had to be a kid growing up on the streets of New York to appreciate the context in all its glory. The fifties—before the great betrayal and flight to California by Stoneham and O'Malley—were the greatest baseball years that any single city ever experienced. I was lucky to be the right age in the right place. We had three great teams (and seven subway World Series in the ten years between 1947 and 1956). All Yankee fans hated either the Giants or Dodgers with blazing passion (we loved individual players, but the corporate entity was Satan incarnate). Affiliation was no laughing matter or passing fancy. I received my worst street beating—and deserved it—when I had the temerity to admit, while playing with a cousin and his friends in Brooklyn, that I was a Yankee fan.

Success had smiled on my side. The Yanks had beaten the Dodgers in all five of their subway series between 1941 and 1953. But then, in 1955, it happened—the impossible, the soul searching, the unimaginably painful, the always feared but never really anticipated. The Dodgers won in seven and the *Brooklyn Eagle* featured on its front (not its sports) page a smiling derelict under a banner headline "Who's a Bum?"

We waited all year for revenge, through a winter of discontent and into a summer of Mantle's blooming greatness. We recovered our pride in 1956 (the last subway series), a victory sweetened to true perfection by Don Larsen's twenty-seven bums up and twenty-seven bums down. Mantle both won and saved that game for Larsen, first with a home run off Sal Maglie, and then with a dandy catch on Hodges's 430-foot drive to left-center.

His next year, 1957, was even better, probably the greatest single season by any player in baseball's modern era. Mantle's achievements in 1957 have been masked by a conspiracy of circumstances, including comparison with his showier stats of the year before and the fact that his career-best batting average of .365 came in second to Ted Williams's .388. In 1957 Mantle had a career high of 146 walks, with only 75 strikeouts. (In no other year did he come even close to this nearly two-to-one ratio of walks to strikeouts; in ten of eighteen seasons with the Yanks, he struck out more often than he walked.) This cornucopia of walks limited his official at-bats to 474 and didn't provide enough opportunity for accumulating those (largely misleading) stats that count absolute numbers rather than percentages—RBIs and home runs for example. Superficial glances have led to an undervaluing of Mantle's greatest season.

Sabermetrics (or baseball number crunching) has its limits and cannot substitute for the day-to-day knowledge of professionals who shared the playing field with Mantle, yet numerical arguments command our respect when so many different methods lead to the same conclusion. As Bill James points out in his *Historical Baseball Abstract*, all proposed measures of offensive performance—from his own runs created for outs consumed, to Thomas Boswell's total average, Barry Codell's base-out percentage, Thomas Cover's offensive earned run average, and Pete Palmer's overall rating in *The Hidden Game*—judge Mantle's 1957 season as unsurpassed during the modern era. Consider just one daunting statistic, Mantle's on-base percentage of .512. Imagine getting on base more often than making an out—especially given the old saw that, in baseball, even the greatest fail about twice as often as they succeed. No player since Mantle in 1957 has come close to an on-base percentage of .500. Willie Mays reached .425 in his best year.

In 1958 the Yankees' general manager, George Weiss, a tough old bastard, had the audacity to offer Mantle a contract with a $5,000 pay cut, reasoning that 1957 had not matched his triple crown performance of the year before!

In a nation too young to generate truly mythical figures, Americans have been forced to press actual, rounded people into service, and to grant these special folks a dual status as human and legend. When, as with Mickey Mantle, sports heroes exemplify the cardinal myths of our culture, their conversion to parable and folklore is all the more rapid and intense.

Mantle's legend is the most powerful and enduring since Babe Ruth's because he mixed into the circumstances of life and career three of the most potent folk images of American mythology. First, Mantle was young, handsome, and bristling with talent. His skills satisfied both sides of the great nature-nurture debate, for he combined the struggle of Horatio Alger with the muscles of John Henry. He was big and strong and could hit a ball 565 feet. His father, an impoverished miner, lived and breathed for baseball. He named his son after his favorite catcher, Mickey Cochrane, and made a playing area (usually against a barn) wherever they lived. Mutt Mantle converted his son, a natural righty, into a switch-hitter by delaying dinner each night until Mickey had taken enough successful swings from the left side.

Second, Mantle was the gullible and naive farmboy who prevailed by good will and bodily strength in a tough world. Commerce, Oklahoma, as Mantle describes it, is a movie theater, a cafe, four churches, a motel, and a lot of grassroots (or rather slag heaps, in this bleak mining region) baseball. Mantle's father labored in the mines all his brief life, except for a failed stint at farming. Mantle grew up as an Okie in the depths of the Depression—a family that stayed while Tom Joad and his compatriots moved westward.

Third, his country innocence met the Big Apple. Mickey hit New York, symbol of immensity, rapacity, and sophistication, at age nineteen. He was soon bilked by a sleazy agent and victimized in a phony insurance scheme. His dad was so awed and disoriented on his first visit to Manhattan that he mistook the monument of Atlas at Rockefeller Center for the Statue of Liberty.

Yet even this conjunction of unparalleled talent and naivete alone in the big city cannot in itself set an enduring legend. Mythological heroes need flaws and tragedies, the Achilles' heel that defines an accessible humanity. Mantle's innocence was tainted by tragedy and dogged by disappointment. He did it all for (and because of) his father, but Mutt Mantle lived to see only the dicey beginnings of Mickey's then uncertain career. After Mickey's injury in the 1951 World Series, Mutt took his son to Lenox Hill Hospital. As they got out of the cab, a hobbled Mickey put his weight against his father, and Mutt collapsed on the sidewalk. They ended up together in a double room—Mickey to recover from torn ligaments, his father to begin the slow process of dying from Hodgkin's Disease, a form of cancer now usually curable.

Serious injuries continued to plague Mantle. He never could put together a long string of healthy seasons, and he often played in pain, wrapped in more bandages than Boris Karloff as Im-Ho-Tep the Mummy. He had four glorious seasons (1956–1957 and 1961–1962) but also several distinctly subpar years. Playing hurt in his last season (1968), his skills prematurely eroded, Mantle batted .237 and watched in frustration as his lifetime batting average slipped below the magic line to .298.

Moreover, Mantle put his heart and life into baseball before the era of great material reward. His top salary never reached even

Mickey Mantle in 1955. Mantle died on August 13, 1995. *Credit: Bettmann/Corbis*

half of what any utility infielder might command today. Year after year he was forced into humiliating negotiation with Weiss, the archetypal skinflint and belittler of men. He worried continually about finances, and diverted much energy to schemes that no one in his position would dream of needing today. He moved from Oklahoma to Dallas in order to run a bowling alley that he hoped would secure his financial future (though it eventually failed). He established a chain of country-cooking outlets, also unsuccessful in the long run. The sport that had been his lifelong obsession did not repay his investment, and he joined Willie Mays in heartless and senseless exile after commissioner Bowie Kuhn ruled that no employee of an Atlantic City casino could also represent major league baseball (a galling judgment since widely revoked by Peter Ueberroth).

I do not wish to debunk this legend. It contains enough truth to pass muster, and, as argued above, Mickey the myth has a different (and legitimate) status from Mickey the man. Still, the rounded man is so much more interesting than the cardboard legend. The myth really fails only in one crucial way. Achilles' heels are blemishes beyond the control of heroes. It was not Achilles' fault that his mother had to grasp some part of his anatomy when dunking him in the river Styx. But Mantle's disappointments were not, as the legend holds, solely the result of congenitally weak legs and an unlucky series of freak accidents.

Though no one ever matched Mantle's fierce commitment and competitive desire, he did not train properly and actively disregarded almost all medical advice for rehabilitation from his injuries. As for the injuries themselves, several were just bad luck, but others (covered up at the time) were the consequences of foolishness and excessive drinking. Mantle teetered for years on the edge of a serious problem with alcohol, and his legendary late nights cannot be called a mere innocent exuberance of youth, but a pattern that hurt and haunted his career.

Mantle's autobiography, *The Mick*, presents an honest account of this tension between high jinks and harm. Mantle told me that, if his book contains any lesson, he hopes that kids with great talent will understand why they must take better care of their bodies. As we sat in the press box three hours before a night game with Baltimore, Mantle looked down on the field and said to me witsfully, "Look, there's Mattingly, my favorite player. I love the man. He's out there for extra batting practice with the rookies. He doesn't need to be there; I never was."

Mantle's failure to sustain his full potential is all the more poignant because he harbors deep regret, and for reasons that transcend mere ambition and desire for personal fame. He writes in his autobiography: "When somebody once asked me what I'd want written on my gravestone, I answered, 'He was a great team player.' "

Now I'm not from Commerce, Oklahoma. I'm a prototypical cynical, streetwise, New York kid. When I read such statements, upholding values we all mouth but seldom follow, I get suspicious and assume a bit of dissembling. But I accept Mantle's judgment absolutely. Everything fits too well. Mantle struggling for his team and not for personal stats is the man himself, not the myth.

I remember so clearly, because I watched the scene often, how Mantle would circle the bases after a home run—head down and as fast as he could, as if to shut out the personal adulation and limit its duration.

I asked him about his proudest achievements and deeper disappointments. He takes greatest pride, he said, not in his triple crown or his home runs, but in playing more games as a Yankee (2,401) than any other man. As his worst moments he cited his return to the minors during his first season in 1951 (not sufficient help to the team) and Bill Mazeroski's home run that won the 1960 World Series for the weaker Pittsburgh club ("I cried all the way home in the plane after that")—though Mantle had played his heart out and harbored no feelings of personal failure. Above all, he told me, he regretted his "stupidity" (his own word, and the only one uttered with real vehemence during our interview) in allowing his prodigious skills to erode more quickly than nature required, forcing his retirement just before his thirty-seventh birthday, while those who share Mantle's fire for the game but take better care of themselves, the Yazes and the Roses, play with grace well into their forties.

During my youth nothing so obsessed the minds of New York fans as the great Mantle-Mays-Snider center-field debate. We all love the Duke, but men of good conscience must see the real contest as between Mickey and Willie. Hindsight has usually given the nod to Mays. Mays was a better fielder (Mantle was also damned good), and Mays sustained his greatness longer and more consistently. But Mantle at peak value in his four great seasons,

was—by any measure, sabermetric, conventional, or simple subjective memory—clearly superior to Mays or any player since.

The Yanks of the fifties and sixties were probably the greatest
team of all time. Mantle dominated this superlative bunch. He led
the team for nine years in a row in runs scored, five in total hits,
seven in homers, three in RBIs, nine in walks, six in stolen bases,
and six more in a row in slugging average. In 1961 Mantle hit a
career-high fifty-four home runs and might have fractured Ruth's
record along with Roger Maris if he hadn't visited a quack medico
to cure a cold and ended up flat on his back during the end of this
greatest baseball derby. Mantle won the MVP award for three of
his four great seasons (finishing second to Maris in the year of the
asterisk).

Mantle played at the acme of the most one-dimensional style
the game has ever known—put men on base and wait around for
someone to hit a long ball. We sometimes forget that Mantle, for
all his size and power, was also the fastest man in baseball, and a
great drag bunter (practically unbeatable when bunting for a hit
from the left side). He maintained a career success rate of 80 percent for stolen bases (compared with 77 for Mays), but only once
was he allowed to swipe more than twenty in a season. Imagine
what Mantle's speed and bunting ability might produce in our
present game, especially with the return of scrappy, one-run baseball.

But enough already. You can carry abstract analysis so far—and
although I may be an academic by trade, I write primarily as a fan,
as a man who loved Mickey Mantle and whose childhood was
brightened by his glory. To hell with what might have been. No
one can reach personal perfection in a complex world filled with
distraction. Williams had his best years cut short by World War II
and Korea; DiMaggio played in the wrong park; Shoeless Joe Jackson, acquitted by the courts, was executed by major league baseball. What happened is all we have. By this absolute and

irrefragable standard, Mantle was the greatest ballplayer of his time.

Mantle also taught me something very special: the universality of excellence. We intellectuals, in our crass parochialism, often imagine that scholars succeed only by a struggle of long years devoted to study but that athletes triumph by untutored skill—the pain of brain versus the gift of brawn. But if I have learned anything from studying the lives of great ballplayers, Mantle's in particular, I have come to understand the common denominator of human excellence. The potential must be present (and we do not all possess it), but the universal agents of realization are passion to the point of obsession combined with hard, unrelenting work. All achievers are kinsmen in a tough and crowded world.

I do not seek moral lessons from my sports heroes. The thrill of witnessing rare excellence will suffice. My relationship with Mickey Mantle was forged by a single image. Probably a quarter of a million people will swear they saw it in the flesh (though Yankee Stadium then held but a quarter that many), but I was really there.

I took a trip to New York a month before my graduation from college in 1963. On May 22, Mantle, batting lefty, hit a line drive off Kansas City pitcher Bill Fischer. It rose and rose until it struck the facade above the third deck in right field—the closest that anyone has ever come to hitting a fair ball out of Yankee Stadium ("the hardest ball I ever hit," Mantle told me). It was still rising when it struck the parapet. I remember particularly the stunned silence before the roar of the crowd. Six more feet up, and Mantle would have fused himself to my profession of scientific exploration in more than the abstract character of excellence. Six more feet up, and that ball would have become a moon of Uranus.

Dusty's Moment

C ircumstance is the greatest leveler. In a world of too much predictability, where records by season and career belong only to the greatest players, any competent person in uniform may produce one unforgettable feat. A journeyman pitcher, Don Larsen, hurled a perfect game in the World Series of 1956. Does Bill Wambsganss, with his unusual name and strictly average play as an infielder, ever evoke any memory beyond the unassisted triple play that fortuitously fell his way in the fifth inning of the fifth game of the 1920 World Series?

All ship's carpenters are named "Chips," all radio engineers "Sparks." By a similar custom, anyone named Rhodes will end up with the nickname "Dusty." James Lamar "Dusty" Rhodes, an alcoholic utility outfielder from Mathews, Alabama, made me the happiest boy in New York when he won the 1954 World Series for the New York Giants, all by himself. (I will admit that a few other events of note occurred during these four short days—Mays's legendary catch off Vic Wertz among others—but no man, and cer-

First published as "Dusty Rhodes" in *Cult Baseball Players: The Greats, the Flakes, the Weird, and the Wonderful*, ed. Danny Peary (New York: Simon & Schuster, 1990).

tainly not a perpetually inebriated pinch hitter, has ever so dominated our favorite days of October.)

The 1954 Cleveland Indians were probably the greatest team of modern baseball (although we might also argue for the 1998 Yankees and a few others). They compiled the best record of the modern era, 111–43 for an incredible winning percentage of .721. People forget the ironic fact that the Yankees, who won the American League pennant in every other year from 1949 to 1958, actually compiled their best record of the decade by coming in second to the Indians at 103–51 in 1954. With a pitching staff of Bob Lemon, Early Wynn, and Mike Garcia (not to mention an aging, but still able, Bob Feller), Cleveland was an overwhelming favorite to slaughter my beloved Giants with dispatch.

The Giants won that World Series in the greatest surprise of modern history, matched only, perhaps, by the 1969 Mets, whose victory, or so George Burns tells us, was the only undeniable miracle since the parting of the Red Sea. Those two Series, 1954 and 1969, share two other interesting elements, but in each case the 1954 Giants provide the cleaner and more memorable case. First, both the Giants and the Mets were overwhelming underdogs, yet both won commandingly with four straight victories. But the 1969 Series lasted five games, because Baltimore beat Tom Seaver in the first contest; the Giants put the Indians away in four—clean, simple, and minimal. Second, both victories were sparked by the most unlikely utility ballplayer. Al Weis (remember Big Al?) won the Mets' first game with a two-out single in the ninth, then tied the last game with an improbable homer. Dusty Rhodes fared even better. He won, tied, or assured victory in each of the first three games. By then, the Indians were so discouraged that they pretty much lay down and died for the finale.

If Leo Durocher, the Giants' manager, had been able to call the shots, Rhodes wouldn't have been on the team at all. In fact, Durocher told Giants' boss Horace Stoneham that he would quit as manager unless Rhodes were traded. Durocher had two objec-

The New York Giants greet Dusty Rhodes after his pinch-hit, tenth-inning home run wins the first game of the 1954 World Series. *Credit: AP/Wide World Photos*

tions to Rhodes: he couldn't field, and he couldn't stay sober. Stoneham agreed and put Rhodes on the block, but no other team even nibbled. As Durocher said, "Everybody else had heard about Mr. Rhodes, too. Any club could have claimed him for a dollar bill. Thank the Lord none did." Durocher was appeased by Stoneham's honest effort, and even more by Rhodes's stellar performance as a pinch hitter in 1954, when he batted .333 in that role at 15 for 45.

Rhodes won the first game of the 1954 Series with a three-run homer in the tenth after Willie Mays had saved the game with his legendary catch off Vic Wertz. Rhodes's dinger wasn't the most commanding home run in the history of baseball, but they all have the same effect, whether Carlton Fisk grazes the left-field foul pole in Fenway Park or Mantle hits one nearly into orbit. I loved the old Polo Grounds, but the ballpark had a bizarre shape, with a cavernous center field and short fences down the lines to compensate. The right-field corner sat at a major league minimal distance of 258 feet from home plate. Dusty just managed to nudge one over the right fielder's outstretched glove—an out anywhere else.

In game two, Durocher called upon Rhodes earlier. Wynn held a 1–0 lead in the fifth, but the Giants had two on and nobody out. Rhodes, pinch-hitting for Monte Irvin, dumped a single to center, tying the score. In the seventh, he added an insurance run and silenced the grousing about his "cheapie" of the day before by blasting a massive homer that was still rising when it hit the Polo Grounds' upper facade, 350 feet from home.

Durocher, on a roll, inserted Rhodes as an even-earlier pinch hitter in game three. He came in with the bases loaded in the third inning and knocked in two more runs, including the ultimate game-winner, with a single.

All this happened long ago, but my memories of joy and vindication could not be more clear or immediate. I had taken all manner of abuse, mostly from Dodger fans, for my optimism about the Giants. I had also bet every cent I owned (about four bucks) at very favorable odds. I ended up with about fifteen dollars and felt like the richest kid in New York. I'd have bought Dusty a double bourbon, but we never met, and I was underage.

Dusty Rhodes, a great and colorful character, was a strictly average ballplayer who had a moment of glory. You will find him in record books for a few other items—he once hit three homers in a single game, two pinch-hit homers in a single inning, and has the most extra-base hits in a doubleheader. But he was no star during his seven-year career, all with the Giants. People tend to focus on great moments and forget averages. They then falsely extrapolate the moment to the totality. Thus, many fans think that Dusty was a great pinch hitter throughout his career. Not so. As Bill James points out, Dusty's career pinch-hitting average is

.186. He could do no wrong in 1954, but his pinch-hitting averages in his other six years were .111, .172, .250, .179, .152, and .188.

Who cares? Our joys and our heroes come in many modes and on many time scales. We treasure the consistency of a Ted Williams, the resiliency of a Cal Ripken, but we hold special affection for the journeymen fortunate enough to taste greatness in an indelible moment of legitimate glory. We love DiMaggio because he was a paragon. We love Dusty Rhodes because he was a man like us. And his few days of majesty nurture a special hope that no ordinary person can deny. Any of us might get one chance for an act of transcendence—an opportunity to bake the greatest cake ever, to offer just the right advice or support, even to save a life. And when that opportunity comes, we do not want to succeed because we bought the lucky ticket in a lottery. Whatever the humdrum quality of our daily life, we yearn to know that, at some crucial moment, our special skills may render our presence exactly right and specially suited for the task required. Dusty Rhodes stands as a symbol of that hope, that ever-present possibility.

This Was a Man

When Mel Allen, the Voice of the Yankees, died last week at eighty-three, I lost the man who ranked second only to my father for sheer volume of attention paid during my childhood. (My dad, by the way, was a Dodger fan and Red Barber devotee.)

As I considered the surprising depth of my sadness, I realized I was mourning the extinction of a philosophy as much as the loss of a dear man. And I felt that most of the warm press commentary had missed the essence of Allen's strength. The eulogies focused on his signature phrases: his invariable opening line, "Hello there, everybody"; his perennial exclamation of astonishment, "How about that!"; and his home run mantra, "It's going . . . going . . . gone!"

But I would characterize his immense appeal by two statements I heard him make during a distant childhood. They have stayed with me, one for its integrity, the other for its antic humor. One exemplifies the high road, the other an abyss, however charming.

The comments could not be more different, but they embody,

First published as "A Voice With Heart" in the *New York Times*, June 26, 1996. Reprinted with permission of the *New York Times*.

when taken together, something precious, something fragile and invariably lost when institutions become so large that the generic blandness of commercial immensity chokes off spontaneity and originality.

The phenomenon is not confined to broadcasting. In my academic world, textbooks have become longer, duller, and entirely interchangeable for the same reason. Idiosyncratic works cannot sell sufficiently, for curricula have been standardized (partly by conventional textbooks), and originality guarantees oblivion. The great texts of the past defined fields for generations because they promulgated the views of brilliant authors—Charles Lyell's geology, Alfred Marshall's economics—but modern writers are faceless servants of a commercial machine that shuns anything unique.

One day in 1952, as Mickey Mantle struggled in center field the year after Joe DiMaggio's retirement, fans started booing after Mickey struck out for the second time in a row. In the midst of his play-by-play, an infuriated Allen shouted at a particularly raucous fan, "Why are you booing him?" When the fan shot back that Mickey wasn't as good as DiMaggio, Allen gave him a ferocious dressing-down for his indecency in razzing an enormously talented but unformed twenty-year-old just because he couldn't replace the greatest player of the age.

The Yankees were sponsored by Ballantine beer and White Owl cigars. Mel never lost an opportunity for supplementary endorsements. Home runs became "Ballantine Blasts" or "White Owl Wallops" depending on the sponsor of the inning. When a potential home run passed just to the wrong side of the foul pole, Allen would exclaim, "Why, that ball was just foul by a bottle of Ballantine beer."

One day, Mickey hit one that seemed destined for success, and Allen began his mantra, "It's going . . . going . . ." He stopped as the ball went foul by no more than an inch or two. "Folks, that ball was foul by no more than a bottle of Bal—" Then he stopped,

Mel Allen in 1951. Allen died on June 16, 1996. *Credit: AP/Wide World Photos*

thought for a fraction of a moment and exclaimed, "No, I've never seen one so close. That ball was foul by no more than the ash on a White Owl cigar!"

A man of grace and integrity, a shameless huckster of charming originality. But above all a man who could only be his wonderful cornball self—Mel Allen, the inimitable human Voice of the Yankees. So join my two stories, and let us share Shakespeare's judgment in *Julius Caesar*: "The elements so mixed in him that Nature might stand up and say to the world, 'This was a man!' "

The Greatest Athlete
of the Century

T he fin de siècle, an arbitrary phenomenon created by cal-
endars of our own construction, elicits some mighty peculiar behavior in that biological oddball known as *Homo
sapiens*—from mass suicides designed to free souls for union with
spaceships behind cometary tails to trips to Fiji for a first view of
the new millennium. Among the more benign manifestations, we
might list our own propensity for making lists of the best and the
worst where calendrical cycles end by our own fiat.

Among the various impediments to fair and honorable listing,
no factor could be more distorting—or of more immediate concern to devotees of this magazine—than the virtual erasure of historical knowledge among so many people who grew up with a
television in each room, not a book in the house, and a convction
that last year's models must be antiquated, and last decade's versions both extinct and erased from memory. In this context the
greatest American athlete of the century must stand directly
before us, either in the full flower of current performance or in
constantly reiterated images of various media. Therefore the title

First published as "The Athlete of the Century" in *American Heritage*, October 1998.

could go only to Michael Jordan or Muhammad Ali, and why should anyone want to look elsewhere when directly confronted with such magnificence? (I make this last statement in full belief and without a trace of sarcasm, for these two men continue to awe and thrill me.)

Any great cycle also deserves recognition at the halfway point. In 1950 the Associated Press conducted an extensive poll of American sportswriters and broadcasters to determine the best football player of the half-century. Jim Thorpe beat Red Grange by 170 votes to 138, with Bronko Nagurski a distant third at 38. Three weeks later the same professional group voted for the greatest male athlete of the preceding fifty years, with the same winner, but by a larger margin: Jim Thorpe received 252 of 393 first-place votes, with Babe Ruth second at 86, Jack Dempsey third at 19, Ty Cobb fourth at 11, and at a distance surely recording the realities of racism, Joe Louis sixth at 5.

I was then, at age eight, a nascent sports nut and statistics maven. I well remember both these polls and the consensus among sports fans of all generations that Jim Thorpe was the world's greatest living athlete—an impression heightened in 1951, when the popular film *Jim Thorpe—All American*, starring Burt Lancaster, told his story in the conventional hagiographic mode for youngsters like me who had never seen Thorpe in action.

This consensus has since evaporated. In fact I wonder if most younger fans have even heard of Jim Thorpe, a situation that can only be chalked up to the status of history (defined as anything unexperienced) as a tabula rasa for the "now" generation. Yet as I contemplated this assignment to write about the greatest American athlete of the twentieth century and thought about my own heroes, from Louis and DiMaggio in childhood to Jordan and Ali today, I could only conclude that the old consensus cannot be seriously challenged (except, just perhaps, by Man o' War—and he couldn't hit a curve, among other disqualifying factors of a more directly zoological nature).

For the bare bones, Jim Thorpe (1888–1953), of predominantly Sauk and Fox descent, grew up in a region now called Oklahoma but formerly designated as Indian Territory. He attended the Carlisle Indian Industrial School in Pennsylvania, where he starred on football teams drawn from small numbers of impoverished students playing with poor equipment under terrible conditions—but coached by the legendary "Pop" Warner. The Carlisle team regularly defeated the best Ivy League, Big Ten, and military squads. Thorpe, who excelled in almost every sport he ever attempted, won both the pentathlon and decathlon at the 1912 Olympic Games in Stockholm. He played professional baseball, mostly with the New York Giants, for several years (1913–1919), and then became the greatest star in the early days of American professional football (1915–1929).

Despite my affection for statistics, I do not think that such assessments can be made "by the numbers." Thorpe's incomparable greatness must be viewed as a singular tapestry, woven from several disparate threads into a unity for one distinct time and one unrepeatable set of circumstances: the off-the-scale numbers, the intense dedication and unbounded enthusiasm, the crushing obstacles posed by racism and a sanctimonious sports establishment.

In a run for the title of greatest athlete—not best boxer (Ali, Louis, Dempsey, Robinson, or Marciano), basketball player (Jordan hands down, as much as I loved Bird), or home run hitter (Ruth, Maris, Aaron, McGwire, now don't get me started on this one!)—Thorpe wins by several laps for two key reasons.

1. Versatility. Superlative athletes often perform well in several sports. No one but Thorpe has ever been the best of all in so many. He was America's number one football player and general track-and-field man at the same time. He also played major league baseball for several seasons and excelled in lacrosse and swimming (while dabbling with success in boxing, basketball, and hockey). He won *both* of the most diverse and grueling Olympic competitions in 1912—the pentathlon (running broad jump, javelin throw, two-hundred-meter dash, discus throw, and fifteen-hundred-meter race) and the ten-event decathlon (these multiple events had been introduced into the 1912 Olympics at the behest of European athletes, who complained that American styles of training, based on intense specialization, failed to showcase European strength in general fitness). John McGraw, the feisty New York Giants manager, did not like Thorpe and branded him with an unfair epithet that stuck: the old charge that he couldn't hit a curve ball. In fact, Thorpe performed competently (though not brilliantly) in professional baseball, compiling a lifetime batting average of .252 in six seasons as an outfielder.

2. *Extent of excelling.* In the same sense that Maris's home run record is vulnerable (and will probably fall this season), while DiMaggio's hitting streak may stand for generations, Thorpe not only won all these events but usually relegated the opposition to embarrassing relative incompetence, putting more distance between himself and the second-place finisher than the full range from the penultimate score to the very bottom.

The narratives of Thorpe's collegiate football career frequently descend to near comedy (for the relative ineptitude of others), as Thorpe wins game after game, virtually all by himself (often scoring all the points by kicking field goals every time his team penetrates the opponent's territory). Thorpe won the pentathlon with 7 points (on the basis of a scoring system of 1 for a first-place finish, 2 for second place, and so on). The next six competitors scored 21, 29, 29, 30, 31, and 32. He then won the decathlon with 8,413 out of 10,000 possible points. The runner-up scored 7,724, with five others above 7,000.

A heroic tale in a decent nation would end here, but if you know anything about Jim Thorpe, you recognize that I must now

Jim Thorpe in 1925. *Credit: Bettmann/Corbis*

add the sad and final chapter. Like so many athletes, Thorpe knew
no other life and could never adjust to other professions and realities once his bodily strengths faded. He tried the usual range of
activities, from inspirational speeches before civic groups to bit
parts in movies. But nothing worked for him, and Thorpe died in
poverty, wrecked by alcohol and the early deaths of close family
members.

To this sad generality, we must add Thorpe's additional burden
of an Indian heritage in a largely racist nation, a burden that
destroyed him in both a general and a specific way. I cannot begin
to measure, or even understand, the generality, but a man of
Thorpe's intense pride must have railed inwardly—with a galling
bitterness that may have propelled him to self-destruction—
against the stereotype of his people (gross enough as an abstraction) constantly applied to his own being. I read several
biographies of Thorpe to prepare this piece, and nothing struck

me more profoundly than the constant drumbeat of this deprecation, from the paternalism of Pop Warner, speaking of his good-hearted but naive braves (led by a great chief who would always need his white handler) to the caricatures of even the best-intentioned reporters, as in this characteristic newspaper account of a Carlisle victory over Georgetown in 1911: "Not since Custer made his last stand against Sitting Bull at the Little Big Horn had a battle between redskins and palefaces been so ferociously fought as that which was waged on Georgetown field yesterday afternoon, when the husky tribe of chiefs from Carlisle savagely forced Georgetown's weak, though gallant, cohorts to bite the dust 28 to 5."

The specific story must rank among the saddest incidents in American history—for all its implications about ideals versus actualities and for all the personal pain thus inflicted upon the greatest athlete this country has ever produced. As an impoverished Indian college student, Thorpe received a few dollars for playing semiprofessional baseball in the summers of 1909 and 1910. He was following a common practice among athletes—just a more pleasant way than farm work to make some necessary and minimal cash during the summer break—but he didn't know the accepted ruse of not using one's real name and therefore not jeopardizing one's amateur status. His "handlers," including Pop Warner, must have known (for Thorpe hadn't hidden his activities and didn't recognize their consequences for amateur athletes), but these coaches couldn't forgo such a grand opportunity as the Olympics, and they let Thorpe compete.

When the Amateur Athletic Union (AAU) discovered this "transgression" of their sacred rules, Thorpe lost his medals, and the distant second-place finishers received both the titles and the objects. (To complete the humiliation, Thorpe not only lost his records but was also browbeaten into returning the medals themselves, even after humbling himself and begging forgiveness for his supposed sins, and despite support from most major sportsmen and the American public.)

The resulting humiliation marked and destroyed this wonderfully proud man. Thorpe's name became inextricably linked with the incubus of this supposed misdeed. (I purposely left this topic for the end, and I'll wager that most readers have been wondering throughout the piece, "Well, when is he going to discuss those Olympic medals?") Chief Meyers, Thorpe's roommate and a great catcher for the New York Giants, recalled (note also the paternalism reflected in the almost automatic decision to pair Indian players as roommates, and in the epithet "Chief" applied to nearly all Indian ballplayers at the time): "Jim was very proud of the great things he'd done. A very proud man. . . . Very late one night Jim came in and woke me up. . . . He was crying, and tears were rolling down his cheeks. 'You know, Chief,' he said, 'the King of Sweden gave me those trophies, he gave them to me. But they took them away from me. They're mine, Chief, I won them fair and square.' It broke his heart and he never really recovered."

Far too late to appease Thorpe's wounds, and despite arguments and pleas that never abated, the U.S. Olympic Committee finally restored Thorpe's amateur status in 1973, twenty years after his death. The Olympic medals were returned to his family in 1982. (Avery Brundage, a "gentleman" of wealth and breeding, had competed against Thorpe, and lost, in both the pentathlon and decathlon in 1912. He later became the aristocratic and sanctimonious head of the International Olympic Committee and never wavered on this issue, while hypocritically proclaiming his personal sympathy with Thorpe.)

Any further moralizing could only be tendentious. As Ethel Barrymore famously said, "That's all there is, there isn't any more." I would only close with this footnote: According to legend, the King of Sweden, in presenting the Olympic medals to Jim Thorpe, said, "Sir, you are the greatest athlete in the world." To this basic factual judgment, Thorpe replied, in his own elegantly simple way, "Thanks, King." And what can we say but "Thanks, Jim."

The Amazing Dummy

The society of males, especially when bonded by a shared physical activity, often promotes a distinctive and curious form of camaraderie, neatly balanced on a fulcrum between near cruelty and ferocious loyalty. The nicknames given to professional athletes stand as telling testimony to this important social phenomenon. The press, particularly in earlier times of more leisurely and flavorful prose, may have christened Joltin' Joe Dimaggio, The Yankee Clipper; or Babe Ruth, the Sultan of Swat. But ballplayers themselves usually favored the pungent and the derogatory. Ruth, to his peers, was usually called "Niggerlips."

We should interpret this apparent harshness as a badge of acceptance into a special sort of guild, with membership strictly limited both by the skills needed to play, and the toughness required to brave the daily struggle. If you can't take a nasty name without an eyeblink ("like a man," as folks of my gender tend to say), how will you survive the fastball thrown at your head next time you crowd the plate, or the spikes aimed at your calf the next time you cover second base on a force play?

These derogatory names were often fixed upon the particular mishaps or weaknesses of individuals. Thus, Fred Merkle, the first baseman of the New York Giants during the early years of the century, remained "Bonehead" throughout his distinguished career, for a stupid mistake in a crucial contest of his sophomore season (1908), when he forgot to touch second base on his teammate's supposedly game-winning single. But my greatest sympathy goes to H. S. Cuyler, Hall of Fame outfielder of the 1920s and 1930s— but known only as "Kiki" because he stuttered badly and frequently tripped over his own last name (pronounced Ki-ler).

Another and more common class of nicknames uses the tactic of the ethnic slur by labeling individuals with a pejorative name for their group—as in numerous short players called "Stump," or "Specs" for players with eyeglasses. In the early days of baseball, all Indian players were "Chief" (with Philadelphia pitcher Chief Bender and New York catcher Chief Meyers as the leading stars), while naïfs from the farm became "Rube" (with Hall of Fame pitchers Rube Marquard and Rube Waddell as most notable bearers of the label).

Early baseball did dispense an odd form of rough justice based on the elite but democratic premise that all men who could stand the heat and hazing would be named for their weakness but judged only by their play. (Lest we descend into maudlin romantic reverie about these times, let us remember the restrictive covenant applied to such "democracy": black men could not play, whatever their talent.) Several deaf men also played major league baseball during the game's early years—and every last one of them bore the name "Dummy." As another linguistic cruelty by extension, the etymology of "dumb" refers only to muteness, not stupidity—as in the old phrase "deaf and dumb" for people who could neither hear nor speak. These men played at a time when few deaf people learned to vocalize, and when signing was not yet regarded as true language. To the hearing world, therefore, they did not speak, and were consequently regarded as mute or dumb—hence "Dummy" in a world of derogatory nicknames.

Two deaf players of baseball's early years stand out for excellence of performance—Luther Haden "Dummy" Taylor, a fine pitcher who won 112 games for the New York Giants between 1900 and 1908; and the subject of this essay, William Ellsworth "Dummy" Hoy, a superb center fielder with a lifetime .288 batting average for six teams in four major leagues between 1888 and 1902. The career of Dummy Hoy—Mr. Hoy bore that nickname with pride and dignity during his career and later life—also offers us great insight into the history of American sports by virtue of Hoy's keen intelligence through such a long life, for he died in December 1961 at age ninety-nine, just five months shy of his one-hundredth birthday. He was, at the time, the longest lived of all major league players. Since then, one man has slipped past the century boundary by a mere eight days—an unknown pitcher named Ralph Miller, who compiled an undistinguished record of five wins and seventeen losses in a two-year career from 1898 to 1899. So Dummy Hoy remains the most longevitous major leaguer of note.

Note a central paradox and irony in the career of Dummy Hoy, a peculiarity that would have appealed to his wry sense of humor. We are drawn to this man because his disability, as recorded in a nickname now regarded as cruel, attracts our attention in an age of greater sensitivity toward human diversity. But when we study his career, we discover that he stands out not for his unusual deafness (which he regarded as largely irrelevant to his profession and, at most, a nuisance), but rather because he was such an exemplary performer and human being.

Dummy Hoy's biography typifies baseball's early history, when the game reigned supreme as a national pastime, but drew professional players almost entirely from the proletarian population of agricultural and industrial workers. Knowledge of this background remains essential for understanding many key features of baseball's social and organizational ways. Consider the paternalism of wealthy owners and their horror and confusion at the successful unionization of players during our generation, or the structure of advance that leads from minor to major leagues, rather than from college teams to professional leagues, as in sports that rose later, including basketball and especially football (which began as an elite college sport).

Dummy Hoy was a farmboy from the tiny rural hamlet of Houckstown, Ohio. He was born on May 23, 1862, and became deaf at age three following an attack of meningitis. He did not attend school until his parents learned about the Ohio School for the Deaf in Columbus. Beginning at age ten, but advancing rapidly, he finished both primary and high school, learned the trade of a cobbler, and graduated as valedictorian of his class at age eighteen. Hoy recalled that his father gave his sister a cow and a piano for a legacy when she turned eighteen, and then provided a suit of clothes, buggy, harness, and saddle to each of his brothers at age twenty-one. When Dummy Hoy reached majority, however, his father give him just the suit, and free board until age twenty-four, for the family had decided that, due to his deafness, Hoy should remain at home and become a cobbler.

He began as an assistant to the local Houckstown shoemaker, but eventually saved enough money to buy his boss out. Hoy recalled: "I got the good will for nothing, but the leather, lasts, tools, and sewing machine cost me about $100." The rest of the recorded story smacks a bit of bucolic mythology and was, no doubt, more complicated; but as Hoy told the tale: Rural people went barefoot in the summer and business became slow. Hoy therefore encouraged the local kids to gather around his shop and play ball. Hoy recalled in a 1947 interview:

> This went on for years until one day a citizen from Findlay, Ohio, nine miles away passed through the town. He

paused to watch the fungo hitting for a while, then accosted me. Disappointed at finding I was a deafmute he continued on his way. The next day he passed through the town and again stopped to watch players, me in particular. Taking out a pad and pencil he wrote me asking me if I would accompany him to Kenton, Ohio, a town some twelve miles further on and play for its team against its bitter rival from Urban. . . . I hit so well against them that it gave me an idea. The following spring I set out for the great Northwest and caught on with Oshkosh, Wis. That was in 1886. I stuck to baseball for 18 years, retiring at the end of 1903.

Hoy signed his first contract (with Oshkosh of the minor Northwest League) for $75 a month, with a stipulation that he could leave at the beginning of August because work was piling up at his cobbler's shop. But Oshkosh offered him $300 to finish the remaining two months of the season, and Hoy never looked back again. He starred in his sophomore season at Oshkosh (following an indifferent rookie year), hitting .367, stealing sixty-seven bases, and leading his team to a pennant. He was then promoted to Washington in the major National League, where he enjoyed a fine rookie season in 1888, batting .274 and stealing a league leading eighty-two bases. (Steals were defined differently and more generously in baseball's early years, so we cannot compare this figure with modern records. For example, a player was awarded a stolen base when he reached third from first on a single that, in the scorer's judgment, would usually advance a man only one base).

Dummy Hoy followed a peripatetic career thereafter, although his play remained consistently excellent. After two seasons with Washington, he cast his lot with baseball's first prominent revolt and joined the Players' League, organized by New York Giants' captain John Montgomery Ward in hopes of winning fairer pay and working conditions, especially freedom from the peonage of the reserve clause that bound players to their owning teams and did not fall until the legal battles of our current generation. But Hoy landed with the particularly inept Buffalo team in 1890, and the league failed in any case. In a letter written at age ninety-three, Hoy recalled this season in writing to thank a journalist for sending him a photograph of the 1890 Buffalo Club:

> I recall those three clubowners. I thought they were good people to have behind the club, but that they were unlucky. . . . It was the poor playing of the team that caused them to lose money. One day the leading members . . . called a meeting of the team. It was suggested that, as the club was in financial difficulties, each player should be assessed a certain sum and share in the profits, if any. The majority, including myself, after due deliberation, decided to let the ship "sink" and go home, rather than throw good money after the bad.

In 1891, Hoy therefore moved to St. Louis in the American Association (then a major league), and thence back to the National League, where he played for Washington (1892), Cincinnati (1894), and Louisville (1898). But he bolted again to join the fledgling (but this time successful) American League in 1901. After the 1902 season, he could have continued in the majors, but decided to see another part of the country, and played all 211 games for Los Angeles in the minor Pacific Coast League in his last season of 1903.

Dummy Hoy may not have stood in the very first rank of players, but he certainly played as a star of the game's early history. He played 1798 games, nearly all as center fielder, in fourteen seasons, and compiled an excellent lifetime batting average of .288. But his greatest skills lay in three other areas: his speed and superior baserunning abilities (with 597 lifetime steals); his acknowl-

edged intelligence and savvy understanding of the game's subtleties; and his excellent fielding, particularly his rifle arm. In his
most famous single achievement, Hoy once threw three players
out at home plate—from the outfield, of course—in a single game
in 1888.

Dummy Hoy accomplished all these feats under an additional
disadvantage potentially more serious than his deafness; he was
one of the smallest men in the major leagues, even in these early
days of lower average height for the general population. Hoy
stood between 5' 4" and 5' 5" (sources differ) and weighed about
145 pounds.

On the more universally human side of our admiration, Hoy's
later life remained a rare model of prosperity and apparent con-

William "Dummy" Hoy, at the age of ninety-eight, throws out the first pitch
at a Cincinnati Reds game on April 11, 1961. *Credit: AP/Wide World Photos*

tentment. Hoy saved his money and bought a dairy farm in his native Ohio upon retirement. He married Anna Lowery, a teacher of the deaf (and a deaf woman herself) late in his career, and had three surviving children, two daughters (both of whom taught in schools for the deaf), and a son (who became a distinguished judge in Ohio). Hoy also left seven grandchildren and eight great-grandchildren when he died in 1962.

After selling his farm in 1924, Hoy worked as a personnel director for deaf employees at the Goodyear Rubber Company in Akron, and then for the Methodist Book Concern in Cincinnati until his retirement. He maintained a home, and continued to walk at least five miles a day, until his wife died during his early 90s. He then lived with his son until his death, just a few months shy of his one hundredth birthday. As a wonderful last baseball hurrah, Dummy Hoy, at age ninety-eight, threw out the first ball both on opening day and (having turned ninety-nine in May) at one of the World Series games, for the 1961 Cincinnati Reds, the principal team of his own career (1894–1897, and again in his last major league season of 1902). Dummy Hoy had a truly wonderful life.

In addition to what one might call his more generic excellence, Dummy Hoy commands our attention (and commends our study) for at least three particular reasons that illuminate the history of American sports and our social history in general.

His deafness. One cannot (and should not) fail to recognize the defining feature that gave Dummy Hoy his baseball name. First, as all aficionados of the game will instantly recognize, Dummy Hoy played center field—and center fielders must serve as generals of the outfield by calling which balls they will catch, and which should be handled by the right or left fielder. How could a mute player express such leadership? That he played center serves as testimony to the acceptance and respect that Hoy commanded among his fellow players. Wahoo Sam Crawford (from Wahoo, Nebraska), one of the game's early stars, played with Hoy in the outfield, and provided personal testimony in his interview for Lawrence S. Ritter's wonderful 1966 book, *The Glory of Their Times*, an oral history told by the few survivors of baseball's early years:

> We played alongside each other in the outfield with the Cincinnati club in 1902. He had started in the Big Leagues way back in the 1880's, you know, so he was on his way out then. But even that late in his career he was a fine out-fielder, a great one. I'd be in right field and he'd be in cen-ter, and I'd have to listen real careful to know whether or not he'd take a fly ball. He couldn't hear, you know, so there wasn't any sense in me yelling for it. He couldn't talk either, of course, but he'd make a kind of throaty noise, kind of a little squawk, and when a fly ball came out and I heard this little noise I knew he was going to take it. We never had any trouble about who was to take the ball.

But you did have to be tough to survive in these rough-and-tumble days. Tommy Leach, another early player, told this anec-dote to Ritter about his first day with Louisville in 1898:

> My own bat hadn't arrived yet, so I just went over and picked one out I liked and went up to hit. After I was through, I hardly had time to lay the bat down before somebody grabbed me and I heard this strange voice say something like, "What are you doing with my bat?" Scared the dickens out of me. I looked up, and it was a deaf mute. We had a deaf mute playing center field, Dummy Hoy. . . . I roomed with Dummy in 1899, and we got to be good friends. He was real fine ballplayer.

Leach later became friendly with Hoy's wife as well, and he recalled their styles of communication (Hoy, evidently, was not entirely mute, though he usually communicated by sign, or by writing—and he read lips superbly):

They could read lips so well they never had any trouble understanding anything I said. They could answer you back, too, in a little squeaky voice that usually you could understand once you got used to it. We hardly ever had to use our fingers to talk, although most of the fellows did learn the sign language, so that when we got confused or something we could straighten it out with our hands.

Hoy also won the appreciation of fans as well as players. Sportswriter Vincent X. Flaherty heard about Hoy's play as a child, and wrote an appreciation for Hoy's ninetieth birthday:

But perhaps none of these gilded facets of his all-around ability impressed me nearly as much as the fact that he was a deaf-mute. In a kid's mind, that made him unique. It set him apart from all others, and made him something special.

Several witnesses remembered Hoy's popularity among fans. When Hoy made a good hit or fielding play, the fans would stand up and wave their arms, hats, and handkerchiefs in easily visible appreciation. They called him "The Amazing Dummy."

But it would be dishonest and unfair to gild a reality with the claim that deafness didn't matter, or even proved more of an advantage for the appreciation thus engendered than a detriment for jeers received or possibilities foreclosed. One has only to read standard press accounts of the time to get a flavor of old-style political incorrectness. Consider the following 1892 report on a salary dispute under the headline, " 'I Won't Sign,' Says Hoy.": "Wagner [the club owner] offered to split the difference and raised his figure to $3250, but the dummy wouldn't sign and the matter was dropped."

The practices of journalism usually worked to Hoy's great disadvantage by the opposite route of silence. Press coverage didn't

matter as much then as now, but players' popularity and reputa-
tions still correlated strongly with journalistic attention. Few
reporters ever bothered to interview Hoy at all, even though he
was probably the smartest player in baseball at the time. They
were discomfited, didn't know how, or just didn't want to bother
with the extra time needed to read and write answers. Disability
then carried no cachet, and not a single reporter ever followed
Hoy or interviewed him extensively. In the revealing letter quoted
earlier, and written when he was ninety-three, Hoy recalled the
origin of official confusion about his age—and with a most
poignant final line:

> I was 28 with that club [Buffalo in 1890] and 93 on my
> last birthday—May 23, 1955. Why do not the records tally
> with those figures? I will tell you and go bail on the cor-
> rectness of my figures—they were copied from the family
> Bible: One rainy day in the Spring of 1886, the Oshkosh
> (Wis.) players were assembled in the club house getting
> ready for the opening day. A newspaper man, representing
> the local press, entered to take down the age, height, and
> weight of each player. When it came to my turn to be
> interviewed he omitted me because I was a deaf mute.
> Also because he had not the time to bother with the nec-
> essary use of pad and pencil. When I read the write-up the
> next day I saw where he had me down as 20 years old. He
> had made what he considered a good guess. Now, during
> my school days I had been taught to refrain from correct-
> ing my elders. Then, too, he had *whiskers*. After thinking
> the matter over I decided to let his figures stand. Later, the
> Associated Press copied them. In this way, I became
> known as the twenty-year-old Oshkosh deaf-mute player.
> Thus, I got along fine by telling all inquirers that I had my
> birthday last May 23 and that I was past the age in ques-
> tion. My looks satisfied them, too, as I was always looking

younger than my real age. What would you have done if you had been in my place?

Journalist Robert F. Panera cites the following anecdote in an article for the *Rochester* (New York) *Democrat and Chronicle*:

> The first few months were difficult for Hoy, being unable to hear or speak. Often he was the butt of ridicule by his fellow players. But Hoy persisted and let his play speak for itself. . . . He soon showed that he was not only literate but also had a keen sense of humor. Using pad and pencil to communicate with a reporter during an interview, he wrote, "What is your name?" The reporter, taken aback, voiced to those standing nearby, "Oh, I didn't know he could write!" Proving he could lipread too, Hoy snatched back the pad and wrote, "Yes, but I can't read."

Finally, we must acknowledge the contingent good fortune that gave Hoy a chance to develop his playing skills at all. Luckily, Hoy attended the Ohio School for the Deaf; and, luckily, his school became the first of its kind to institute baseball, sometime around 1870. In 1879, several players of the Ohio School organized the first semiprofessional deaf club, the Ohio Independent Baseball Team. They barnstormed through several eastern states, playing town clubs, and even some National League teams. Major league baseball's other deaf star, pitcher Dummy Taylor, also graduated from the Ohio School for the Deaf.

His intelligence, independence, and education. Hoy played at a time when most players were semiliterate and lacked much formal education. Very few had ever attended college. (The great pitcher Christy Mathewson spent a few terms at Bucknell, but never graduated. Still, and to this day, neither standard baseball prose nor Bucknell's promotional office will ever let you forget this tidbit.) Hoy never progressed beyond high school either, but his unusual literacy shines forth in the few letters, most written during his nineties, that the Hall of Fame Library in Cooperstown supplied to me from their files. (One has to be familiar with the awkward and utterly ungrammatical prose of most early players to appreciate what a rare jewel these letters—and Hoy's equally articulate spontaneous testimonies—represent.)

But we needn't rely only on these documents. Contemporary accolades from Hoy's teammates and fans tell the same story. Thomas Lonegran, a St. Louis baseball historian, watched Hoy play throughout the 1891 season and remarked:

> Hoy is one of the brainiest ballplayers I ever saw. . . . Hoy was as swift as a panther in the field. . . . I have seen balls hit for singles that would have been doubles or triples with other players fielding them. With men on bases, Hoy never threw to the wrong spot. No player ever returned a ball faster from the outfield. . . . Hoy was a "Cobb" on the bases. I never saw him picked off base. . . . Hoy, a deaf mute, didn't bother about coaches. He did his baserunning on his own. There'll never be another like him.

In an interview for his ninetieth birthday, Hoy recalled how he had used his own intelligence to make up for clues usually supplied by others:

> As to the yelling of my own coaches, that meant nothing to me. They meant well but I could not take my eyes off the ball in play to watch them. So I had to go solo. I was always mentally figuring in advance all possible plays on the bases and in the field.

I also wonder if Hoy's intelligence and pride (as well as his understanding of loneliness and the unfairness of labeling) can help to explain his restlessness in frequent moves between clubs, particularly his willingness, twice in his career, to jump from the established National League to "outlaw" (the Players' League, as defined by owners!) or "upstart" (the American League at its inception in 1901) organizations. We do know that Hoy was one of the few early players willing to contest his tendered salary in public, and to withhold signing in hopes for negotiation of a higher wage. In his age of limited options, the reserve clause forced a player to sign with his own club or not to play at all.

The success and prosperity of Hoy's later life also reflects his unusual intelligence and integrity. I was particularly touched by a small story told by Wahoo Sam Crawford about their post-baseball friendship:

> Another interesting thing about Dummy Hoy was the unique doorbell arrangement he had in his house. He had a wife who was a deaf mute too, and they lived in Cincinnati. Instead of a bell on the door, they had a little knob. When you pulled this knob it released a lead ball which rolled down a wooden chute and then fell off onto the floor with a thud. When it hit the floor they felt vibrations through their feet, and they knew somebody was at the door. I thought that was quite odd and interesting, don't you?

Above all, and in conclusion, I love the wit and clarity of Hoy's letters over so many years. To cite just two examples from mid- and late life, Hoy wrote to the owner of the Cincinnati Reds in 1925, responding to an invitation sent to former players to join a celebration for the club's fiftieth anniversary: "Your invitation . . . is accepted with pleasure. Like all young players on the eve of a spring training trip, I am 'raring to go.' " After the event, Hoy wrote (and I quote his witty, if formal, note in full):

> I wish to express to you and the Red directors my thanks and appreciation for the handsome manner in which you entertained us "oldtimers" yesterday.
>
> The chance which the occasion afforded in the renewing of old acquaintances and the forming of new ones did us all much good, I assure you.
>
> It was a good game we saw. It resulted in a win because we brought you good luck—probably.
>
> We sure were surprised at the fine dining room you have up in the grand stand. Most of us did not know it existed. And the eats and drinks, and the smokes! As a host you have the job down fine and we take our hats off to you.
>
> If the Reds would only play as well on the diamond as you entertain in the dining room, the pennant would be Cincinnati's easily.

On the day of his ninety-eighth birthday, May 23, 1960, Dummy Hoy wrote to his journalist friend J. M. Overfield:

> Only a few days ago I decided to carry a walking stick, a stick I have been treasuring for 74 years, which I never used except the year it was presented to me by a bunch of Oshkosh baseball fans. Just why a walking stick was selected for a present is understandable because in the year 1886 the craze in the U.S. was the carrying by young people of slender bamboo sticks, priced at ten cents and up. They were put in cylinder containers, placed on the sidewalk in front of shops for the passerby to stop, select one, go inside and pay for his choice. Mine was and is a gold square-handled ebony cane, suitably engraved. The presentation ceremony was published in the Oshkosh

newspapers of the period. I imagine the sporting editor of whatever paper it was would be surprised to learn that the centerfielder of the 1886 Oshkosh baseball club began his 99th year by carrying that same treasured stick for real aid in his walking.

His legends and their history. Standing in the way of history, but reflecting something precious about human foibles, legends inevitably arise about old-timers from supposedly golden ages, particularly players remembered for their excellences or eccentricities. Two particular legends both dog and surround Dummy Hoy—and I end this essay with a short recitation in order to make an explicit point.

First, he did throw three runners out at the plate from the outfield in a single game in 1888—and only a handful of players have ever accomplished this feat. We should, of course, mention and even highlight this peculiarity of genuinely superior fielding skills combined with the luck of odd circumstances in a single game. (Outfielders, no matter how good, rarely get three opportunities even to try for such long-distance assists in a single game). But we make a terrible mistake—though the stuff of legends directs our focus to such oddly heroic events—when we write endlessly about single grand moments (partly fueled by luck) and neglect the daily grind of consummate play over many years.

Second, nearly all popular sources hold that Hoy initiated a ubiquitous, if minor, tradition of baseball practiced ever since—the hand signals used by umpires to call balls and strikes. I suppose that the pathways of legend must conjure up stories to render the oddly contingent both purposeful and anecdotally touching—in short to vest the origin of a general practice in a sensible and particular source. We should therefore always be wary of tales that sound "so right." Perhaps the story is true, but best evidence indicates that the first umpire to use such signals did not enter baseball until 1905, two years after Hoy's retirement (although Hoy's teammates probably did signal him from the dugout, and perhaps with the same signs eventually adopted by umpires).

I stress these legends, and urge a proper placement in one case and a refutation in the other in order to make a plea. The Hall of Fame Library, in sending me their files on Hoy, included an extensive set of testimonials surrounding a campaign, still continuing, to persuade the Veterans' Committee to vote Dummy Hoy into the Hall of Fame. Most of these testimonials come from organizations of and for the deaf (Gallaudet College, among others) and—to put the matter diplomatically, but honestly—were obviously not written by people steeped in baseball history or current knowledge of the game. These letters continually emphasize only two aspects of Hoy's career—his three putouts in one game, and his role in inspiring the use of umpire's hand signals. One letter even states that Hoy belongs in the Hall solely because he initiated, however unwittingly, this custom that now occupies a space in the cultural knowledge of millions of Americans.

May I object strenuously to rationales that make such an unfortunate use of legend, while legend itself veils so much of our important history?

A real baseball fan, told that Hoy should be in the Hall of Fame for one great day or for possibly instigating one item of cultural history, will rightly laugh and dismiss your argument. Athletes belong in the Hall for sustained excellence in play—for career performance, not momentary happenstance. Citing a legend only obscures the real point—or even suggests (to folks who do not consult the actual records) that the proper criterion may not truly apply in this case. But the real point could not be simpler: Dummy Hoy belongs in the Hall of Fame by sole virtue of his excellent, sustained play over a long career. His case seems undeniable to me. A dozen players from Hoy's time have been elected with records no better than the exemplary statistics—particularly the great fielding and savvy baserunning, not to mention the more than adequate hitting—of Dummy Hoy.

I have tried not to stress Hoy's deafness in citing his virtues throughout this article. But I suspect that Hoy's deafness did deprive him of a necessary tool for the later renown that gets men into the Hall by sustained reputation. As mentioned earlier, Hoy never received much press coverage. Journalists refrained from interviewing him, even though he was the smartest and most articulate player in baseball. So Hoy was forgotten after he left the field—and his fierce pride prevented any effort at self-promotion. His inbuilt silence abetted the unjust silence of others.

I therefore end with one last example of Hoy's wit—again from the letter written on his ninety-eighth birthday:

> I am finding it harder and harder to write, to think, to decide on anything, or to act properly. In short, I am rapidly slowing up.

Let us therefore enshrine Dummy Hoy for whatever eternity means in baseball. Only then will we break the circle of silence that still surrounds this intelligent, savvy, wonderfully skilled, and exemplary man who also happened to be deaf, while giving his life to a sport never well played by ear.

The Glory of His Time, and Ours

I n our sagas, mourning may include celebration when the hero dies, not young and unfulfilled on the battlefield but rich in years and replete with honor. And yet, the passing of Joe DiMaggio has evoked, in me, a primary feeling of sadness for something precious that cannot be restored—a loss not only of the man, but also of the splendid image he represented.

I first saw DiMaggio play near the end of his career in 1950, when I was eight and Joe was having his last great season, batting .301 with 32 homers and 122 RBIs. He became my hero, my model, and my mentor, all rolled up into one remarkable man. (I longed to be his replacement in center field, but a guy named Mickey Mantle came along and beat me out for the job.) DiMaggio remained my primary hero to the day of his death, and through all the vicissitudes of Ms. Monroe, Mr. Coffee, and Mrs. Robinson.

Even with my untutored child's eyes, I could sense something supremely special about DiMaggio's play. I didn't even know the

First published as "Harvard Prof. Pays Homage to Joe D." for the Associated Press on the day of DiMaggio's death, March 8, 1999. Reprinted with permission of the Associated Press.

words or their meanings, but I grasped, in some visceral way, his gracefulness, and I knew that an aura of majesty surrounded all his actions. He played every aspect of baseball with a fluid beauty in minimal motion, a spare elegance that made even his rare swinging strikeouts looks beautiful.

His stance, his home run trot, those long flyouts to the cavernous left-center space in Yankee Stadium, his apparently effortless loping run—no hot dog he—all were perfect. If the cliché of "poetry in motion" ever held real meaning, DiMaggio must have been the intended prototype.

One cannot extract the essense of DiMaggio's special excellence from the heartless figures of his statistical accomplishments. He did not play long enough to amass leading numbers in any category—only thirteen full seasons from 1936 to 1951, with prime years lost to war, and a fierce pride that led him to retire the moment his skills began to erode.

DiMaggio also sacrificed records to the customs of his time. He hit a career high .381 in 1939, but would probably have finished well over .400 if manager Joe McCarthy hadn't insisted that he play every day in a meaningless last few weeks, long after the Yanks had clinched the pennant. DiMaggio, who was batting .408 on September 8, had developed such serious sinus problems that he lost sight in one eye, could not visualize in three dimensions, and consequently slipped nearly thirty points in his average. In those different days, if you could walk, you played.

DiMaggio's one transcendent numerical record—his fifty-six-game hitting streak in 1941—deserves the usual accolade of most remarkable sporting episode of the century, Mark McGwire notwithstanding.

Several years ago, I performed a fancy statistical analysis on the data of slumps and streaks, and found that only DiMaggio's shouldn't have happened. All other streaks fall within the expectations for great events that should occur once as a consequence of probabilities, just as an honest coin will come up heads ten

Joe DiMaggio in 1949. *Credit: Bettmann/Corbis*

times in a row once in a very rare while. But no one should ever have hit in fifty-six straight games. Second place stands at a distant forty-four, a figure reached by Pete Rose and Wee Willie Keeler.

DiMaggio's greatest record therefore ranks as pure heart, not the rare expectation of luck. We must also remember that third baseman Ken Keltner robbed DiMaggio of two hits in the fifty-seventh game, and that he then went on to hit safely in sixteen straight games thereafter. DiMaggio also compiled a sixty-one-game hit streak when he played for the San Francisco Seals in the minor Pacific Coast League.

DiMaggio was a man of few words, and by no means a "nice guy" in his personal and private life. But he was possessed of consummate style and integrity on the field. One afternoon in 1950, I sat next to my father near the third baseline in Yankee Stadium.

DiMaggio fouled a ball in our direction and my father caught it. We mailed the precious relic to the great man and, sure enough, he sent it back with his signature. That ball remains my proudest possession to this day.

Forty years later, during my successful treatment for a supposedly incurable cancer, I received a small square box in the mail from a friend and book publisher in San Francisco, and a golfing partner of DiMaggio. I opened the box and found another ball, signed to me by DiMaggio (at my friend's instigation) and wishing me well in my recovery. What a thrill and privilege—to tie my beginning and middle life together through the good wishes of this great man.

Ted Williams is, quite appropriately, neither a modest nor succinct man. When asked recently to compare himself with his rival and contemporary DiMaggio, the greatest batter in history simply replied, "I was a better hitter; he was a better player."

Paul Simon captured the essence of this great man in his famous lyric about the meaning and loss of true stature: "Where have you gone, Joe DiMaggio? A nation turns its lonely eyes to you."

He was the glory of a time that we will not see again.

Eight More Out

In *The Godfather, Part II*, gambler Hyman Roth laments that the real movers and shakers of society—kings and princes of the underworld—do not receive their proper public acclaim. He suggests that, above all, a statue should be erected to Arnold Rothstein for his brilliant and audacious job of fixing the 1919 World Series. In the lyrical novel *Shoeless Joe*, W. P. Kinsella tells the story of Ray, an Iowa farmer who, seated one spring evening on his porch, hears a voice stating, "If you build it, he will come." Ray somehow knows that the unnamed man could only be Shoeless Joe Jackson, and that if Ray builds a ballpark in his cornfield, Jackson will come to play.

These tales, from such disparate men and sources, illustrate the continuing hold that the Black Sox scandal had upon the hearts and minds of baseball fans and, more widely, upon anyone fascinated with American history or human drama at its best. The "eight men out" of Eliot Asinof's wonderful book—eight players of the Chicago White Sox, banned for life from baseball for their roles in dumping the 1919 World Series to the Cincinnati Reds—

First published as the introduction to *Eight Men Out: The Black Sox and the 1919 World Series*, by Eliot Asinof, paperback edition (New York: Holt, 2000).

do not represent an isolated incident in an otherwise unblemished history of baseball. Links between players and gamblers, and the subsequent fixing of games, had become a scarcely concealed sore that threatened to wreck professional baseball in its youth during a difficult period of declining attendance and waning public confidence. Bill James pays homage to this book (in his *Historical Baseball Abstract*) by titling his discussion of game fixing during the teens and twenties "22 men out"—to show how many more beyond the Black Sox were accused. The others included such greats as Ty Cobb, Tris Speaker, and Smokey Joe Wood, but no plot was so sensational, no resolution so fierce as the Black Sox scandal. The "eight men out" of the Black Sox embody what can only be called baseball's most important and gripping incident.

If we ask why this story so interests us more than a half century later, I would venture three basic sets of reasons:

First, so many aspects of the scandal are intimately bound—in interestingly ambiguous rather than cut-and-dry ways—with our most basic feelings about fairness and unfairness. We bleed for these men, banned forever from a game that provided both material and personal sustenance for their lives. They were not naive kids, tricked by some slick-talking mobsters, but seasoned veterans, embittered and disillusioned by a sport that had promised much, but had sucked them dry. We feel that, whatever they did, they were treated unfairly both before and after. Sox owner Charles Comiskey was not only the meanest skinflint in baseball, but a man who could cruelly flaunt his wealth, while treating those who brought it to him as peons. Later, when the Black Sox had been acquitted in court, the brass of baseball, behind their first commissioner, Kenesaw Mountain Landis, continued the ban nonetheless. On the other side, whatever the justice of their bitterness, the Black Sox did throw the Series, thereby betraying both their uninvolved (and mystified) teammates and a nation of fans. The oldest of all Black Sox legends, the story of the boy who tugged at Jackson's sleeve as he left the courtroom and begged, "Say it ain't so, Joe," still has poignancy.

Second, history's appeal for us lies largely in the fuel thus provided for the ever-fascinating game of "what if?" How would the subsequent history of baseball have differed if the 1919 World Series had been honest, or if other men and teams had been involved? We can focus on many themes, from the persistence of the reserve clause and the failure of players' organizations (until recently) to the continuing power of the commissioner of baseball, an office set up in direct response to the Black Sox scandal. But consider only one personal item, perhaps the saddest result of all. Most of the Black Sox were fine players; pitcher Eddie Cicotte (29–7 with an ERA of 1.82 in 1919) might have made the Hall of Fame. But one man, Shoeless Joe Jackson, stands among the greatest players the game has ever known—and his involvement in the scandal wiped out an unparalleled career. His lifetime batting average of .356 ranks third (behind Cobb and Hornsby) in modern baseball, and the few who remember say that they did not see such a hitting machine again until Ted Williams arrived. Jackson turned thirty-three in 1920 (while batting .382), his last year of play. If age had begun to creep upon him, the records give no indication. Moreover, batting averages increased dramatically in 1920 and stayed high for twenty years, so Jackson's unplayed 5–10 seasons might not have decreased this career record. Not that I can vote, and not that it matters, and not that this old issue will ever be settled—but Joseph Jefferson Jackson is the first man out whom I would put in the Hall of Fame. His sin is so old, the beauty of his play so enduring.

Third, putting emotion and speculation aside, the Black Sox scandal had an enormous and enduring impact on the nature of baseball, as much as any event since Cartwright or Doubleday or Ms. Rounders, or whomever you choose, first laid out the base paths.

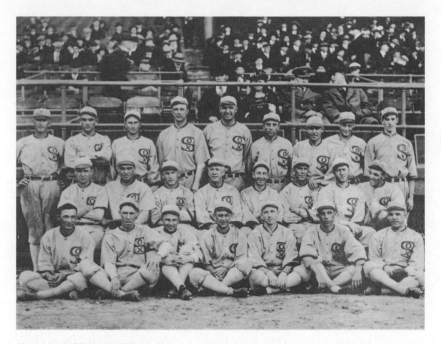

The 1919 Chicago White Sox. *Credit: Bettmann/Corbis*

A few years ago, I began to study the statistics of batting averages through time. Ever since the professional game began in 1876, league averages for regular players have hovered at about .260. This equilibrium has been broken several times, but always quickly readjusted by judicious changes in rules. (For example, averages soared in 1894 when the pitcher's mound was moved back to its current sixty feet, six inches, but they equilibrated within two years thereafter. Falling averages in the 1960s, culminating in Yaz's league-leading .301 in 1968, led to a lower pitcher's mound and a smaller strike zone—and averages quickly rose to their conventional .260 level.)

But one exception to this equilibrium stands out for impact and endurance. Starting in 1920, league averages rose into the .270s and .280s and remained high for twenty years (the *average* hitter in the National League exceeded .300 in 1930). The rise signaled the most profound change that baseball has ever undergone. Scrappy, one-run, slap-hit, grab-a-base-at-a-time play retreated and home run power became the name of the game.

Babe Ruth became the primary agent of this transformation. His twenty-nine homers in 1919 served as a harbinger of things to come, but his fifty-four in 1920—more by himself than almost any entire team had ever hit before in a season—sparked a revolution. Fans have long assumed that this mayhem was potentiated by the introduction of a "lively ball" in 1920, but Bill James has summarized the persuasive evidence against any substantial change in the design of baseballs (see his *Historical Baseball Abstract*). Rather, the banning of the spitball along with other trick pitches and, particularly, the introduction of firm and shiny new balls whenever old ones got scuffed or scratched were the primary agents—and based on equipment rather than people. (Before 1920, foul balls were thrown back by fans, and fielders would help their pitchers by scratching and darkening the ball whenever possible.)

If Ruth so destabilized the game, why didn't the brass change the rules to reequilibrate play as they always had done before (and have since)? Why, in fact, did they even encourage this new trend with a changed attitude toward putting new balls into play and removing other advantages traditionally enjoyed by pitchers? The answer to this question lies squarely with the Black Sox and their aftermath.

The game had been in trouble for several years already. Attendance had declined, and rumors of fixing had caused injury before. The Black Sox scandal seemed destined to ruin baseball as a professional sport entirely. Thus, when Ruth's style emerged and won the heart (and pocketbooks) of the public, the moguls of the game chose to view his style of play as salvation; and they permitted him to instigate the greatest and most long-lasting change in the history of baseball. Bill James puts the issue well in writing: "Under those unique circumstances [the Black Sox scandal and its sequelae], the owners did not do what they quite certainly would have done at almost any other time, which would have been to take some action to control this obscene burst of offensive productivity, and keep Ruth from making a mockery of the game. Instead they gave Ruth his rein and allowed him to pull the game wherever it wanted to go."

Educator and historian Jacques Barzun wrote, in a statement often quoted, that "whoever wants to know the heart and mind of America had better learn baseball." If baseball's appeal, beyond the immediacy of the game itself, lies in its history and its mythology, then the Black Sox scandal represents a pivotal moment. For this incident sparked changes in all these areas: in the character of the game itself, in the history of baseball's links to American society at large, and in mythology, by dispelling forever the cardinal legend of innocence. Innocence may be precious, but truth is better. Babe Ruth visited sick kids in hospitals, but he also did more than his share of drinking and whoring—and his play didn't seem to suffer. Do we not all prefer *Ball Four* to the cardboard biographies of baseball heroes that were de rigueur before Bouton published his exposé? We must also understand the Black Sox if we ever hope to comprehend baseball. With sympathy, and with a tear.

NATURE,
HISTORY,
AND STATISTICS
AS MEANING

Left Holding the Bat

A dvertising, as its primary goal, must create a desire for objects not really needed. Fads and fashions, advertising's analogue in the realm of ideas, can be recognized in the same way: they substitute strained and far-fetched explanations for simple common sense or honest and appropriate ignorance. Since the separation of insight from fashion ranks high on any list of worthy intellectual pursuits, this criterion for identifying fads may be worth exploring.

Of all current psychological fads, none has transgressed the border between fact and overextended fantasy so far as the supposed distinction between right and left brains. This fashion, like so many, has a root in firm and fascinating fact. The two halves of our brain are not mirror images, and the asymmetry of form underlies important distinctions of function. Language and most sequential, logical operations are generally localized in the left brain. Spatial and other styles of perception often labeled as gestalt or analog are monitored by the right brain. In one study, for example, people were asked to think about a piece of music. Those who tried to remember the melody activited their right

First published in *Vanity Fair*, August 1983.

brains, while those who visualized the notes on a staff of music activated their left brains. Cerebral asymmetry also runs beyond our own species; songs of most male birds are more profoundly altered by experimentally induced lesions of the left brain than of the right.

Overextended, even silly, speculation has issued from this interesting foundation—speculation fostered, I suspect, by the apparent resonance of left and right brains with several facile dichotomies of our popular press. The left brain is rational, the right intuitive; the left reflects linear and logical Western culture, the right, contemplative and integrative Eastern thought. The left, Harvard pretension; the right, California psychobabble. This invalid extension often overwhelms common sense, thus meeting our criterion for identifying fads.

For example, neurologists have long known that a curious crossover occurs between brain and body, so that the left brain regulates the right side of the body, while the right brain controls the left side. Our culture also displays a lamentable prejudice toward right-handedness, a bias deeply embedded in nearly all Western languages, where right is dextrous (from the Latin *dexter*, or "right"), *Recht* (or "justice" in German), *droit* (or "law" in French), and, well, just plain right—while left is sinister (from Latin for "left") or gauche. If we overextend the theme of cerebral asymmetry, we might be tempted to trace this prejudice to our Western bias for rational over intuitive thought, since the favored left brain controls the valued right side.

Fritjof Capra makes such a claim in *The Turning Point*, his polemic against reductionist thinking in Western science. Our preferences for right-handedness, he claims, reflect "our culture's Cartesian bias in favor of rational thought." Yet this proposal, superficially attractive, makes no sense on further reflection. The originators of our language had no notion of neurological crossover and, if they thought about it at all, would probably have figured that each brain controlled its own side (a right-minded view)—if they even knew about divided brains. The obvious reason for our prejudice lies in the simple frequencies of handedness and our unfortunate tendency to despise, and even to fear, the uncommon. For some unknown reason, right-handedness prevails overwhelmingly in all human cultures—and most of these cultures have tried to convert their deviants to the path of righteousness. My grandmother, a natural lefty—I am a righty by the way—wrote haltingly with her right hand because her left had been tied behind her back in turn-of-the-century Hungarian schools. Common sense dictates that the source of our pro-right prejudice lies in simple frequency nurtured by xenophobia—not in neurological knowledge that our ancestors could not have possessed. Jesus sits at the right hand of the Father because most of us skewer our enemies and write our Bibles with the same hand.

Right-handedness is so much more common that we might ask whether lefties follow the usual distinction of right and left brains—or whether their cerebral hemispheres might not be reversed as well. In fact, we find both patterns. Most lefties show the standard distinction, with language in the left brain and most spatial patterning in the right, but some display the reversed difference, with language in their right brains. Lefties often exhibit another interesting distinction from righties—and mark this point well, as the source of the bogus claim we shall soon discuss: their brains are often less lateralized than those of righties; that is, the two hemispheres of lefties are often more similar in their performance, with much overlap of function and less distinction between linear and integrative skills. Thus lefties are often more imperfectly handed, and closer to ambidextrous in their performance, than righties. (Handedness, by the way, also extends beyond the human species. Cats and dogs show paw preferences, and rats tend to turn one way or the other.)

We love fads, none more these days than overextensions of legitimate differences between right and left brains. We hear that women are right-brained, that Chinese are right-brained, that we'd all be better off if we heeded our neglected right brains. I suppose that the argument had to spill over into baseball some day, where the oldest of ancient observations proclaims that left-handed hitters have a small but certain edge over righties. Aha, it must be those right brains that critics of Western culture are trying so hard to cultivate. But wait, before we get too intrigued with another extension of a hot fad, let's consider the equally ancient and obvious commonsense explanation for the edge that lefties enjoy. It is also well known that batters do better against pitchers of the opposite hand—for the obvious reason that balls served from the opposite side are more clearly seen. Righties do better against left-handed pitchers; switch-hitters invariably face their oponents from the opposite side. (I would also not discount the equally old argument that lefties gain a slight advantage from standing closer to first base—that must be good for beating out a few infield hits per season.)

The standard explanation for higher batting averages among lefties invokes the same argument about frequency that invalidated Capra's claim. Since most people are righties, most pitching comes from the right side and lefties gain their traditional edge. I counted the first 1,000 pitchers listed in *The Baseball Encyclopedia*, and 77 percent of them are or were righties. This explanation is so commonsensical and, well, right-minded that I can't imagine any other serious contender. But challenged it was, and, of all places, in the staid *New England Journal of Medicine* for November 11, 1982, in a note by John M. McLean, M.D., and Francis M. Ciurczak, Ed.D., titled "Bimanual Dexterity in Major League Baseball Players: A Statistical Study."

McLean and Ciurczak first found that lefties are overrepresented among baseball players; the well-known edge is clearly exploited. Among current major league players, they count 324 righties and 177 lefties, or 35 percent lefties (in contrast with the 23 percent I calculated for pitchers). When we consider the top hitters of all time, lefties are in the majority, 76 to 63.

New York Giant Mel Ott hits left-handed in the 1936 World Series against the Yankees. *Credit: AP/Wide World Photos*

McLean and Ciurczak then considered batting averages, but first they divided left-handed batters into "pure" lefties, who both bat and throw with their left hands and "mixed" lefties, who bat left but throw right. The pure lefties had higher batting averages, while mixed lefties neatly match the righties in both categories. For all players active in 1980, righties average .264, lefties who throw right .260, and pure lefties .281. For the top hitters of all time, righties average .314, lefties who throw right also .314, and pure lefties .322.

McLean and Ciurczak reason that since lefties who throw right apparently enjoy no advantage in hitting, the traditional explanation must be abandoned—for these mixed lefties also face as much right-handed pitching and stand as close to first base as their pure colleagues. As an alternative, they probe the current fad and come up with a hypothesis based on right and left brains. Only the pure lefties, they argue, display the relative weakness of lateralization discussed above—that is, pure lefties do not have as strong a dominant hand as either pure righties or lefties who throw right. Thus lack of a strongly dominant hand must confer some advantage, since bats are held with both hands. They conclude, in typically dense, but decipherable, scientific prose: "This relative but pervasive lack of lateralization in left-handers may in some manner contribute to the motor function of the nondominant hand, thereby enhancing a dexterity that clearly requires the concert of both hands."

I reject this explanation and believe I can show, from McLean and Ciurczak's data, and from some of my own compilation, that the commonsense explanation based on greater frequency of right-handed pitching still holds. If I am correct, I must provide an explanation for why lefties who throw right do not bat as well as pure lefties.

Forgive the appeal to philistinism. I well remember that on my stickball court all us righties were incessantly experimenting and trying to hit left-handed, while the few natural lefties among our friends remained smugly content with their lot. We all knew the advantages that accrue to lefties, and we tried to avail ourselves of them, usually without much luck.

Yet some experimenters did enjoy success and did manage to convert themselves into left-handed hitters. Most of these people continued to throw right. Thus many left-handed hitters who throw right are not true lefties, but natural righties who have trained themselves to bat left. This must exact some toll upon batting averages. I also assume that most people who both bat left and throw left are natural lefties. Therefore, lefties who throw right tend to bat more poorly than pure lefties because many of them are not natural lefties and they balance the edge that they enjoy swinging left with the disadvantage of playing against a natural bent. Thus pure lefties do better not because their brains are less lateralized, but for the traditional reason: they see more right-handed than left-handed pitching and, as natural lefties, suffer no compensating disadvantage of playing against an inborn disposition.

My traditional explanation would gain some support if I could show that large numbers of players really do force themselves to hit lefty against a natural inclination. McLean and Ciurczak's own data supply such a hint. I was surprised by the high frequency of lefties who throw right in their study—they actually outnumber the pure lefties in all categories. Among all recorded players, 1,069 bat left but throw right, while only 694 are pure lefties. Among active players, 91 are mixed, 86 pure, while for top hitters, 45 are mixed and 31 pure. By comparison, righties who throw left are rare birds. Among top hitters, we find only 2, in contrast with 45 lefties who throw right.

But McLean and Ciurczak also counted some controls—high school and grammar school students not headed toward the major leagues. In these data, two items support my claim. First, pure lefties now outnumber those who hit left but throw right (25 to 10 for high school students and 11 to 3 for grammar school students). Second, lefties who throw right are no longer more common than righties who throw left (10 vs. 12 for high schools and 3 vs. 5 for grammar schools). It seems that non-baseball players are not struggling to bat left, and that the exaggerated number of mixed lefties among major league players must therefore represent, largely, a group of natural righties who have forced a change upon themselves and must pay for it with lower batting averages than pure lefties.

I was able to corroborate this conclusion by my own compilation of pitchers. I reasoned that since pitchers do not pay much attention to their own hitting (where absence of a designated hitter rule still permits them to bat), we would not find the same concentration of lefties who throw right among pitchers. On counting the first 1,000 pitchers listed in *The Baseball Encyclopedia*, I found 686 pure righties, 171 pure lefties, 84 who bat left and throw right, and 59 who throw left and bat right. The differences between batters and pitchers are much greater than I would have imagined and must, I believe, be explained as I propose—by the argument that many batters who are natural righties have trained themselves to bat left, and pay a price for it.

To reiterate, among all players, 694 are pure lefties, while 1,069 bat left but throw right; but among pitchers, 171 are pure lefties, while only 84 bat left and throw right. Moreover, among pitchers, lefties who throw right are about as common as righties who throw left, while among hitters, lefties who throw right seem to be about ten times as common as righties who throw left.

I won't close with the yahoo's blare of gimme that old-time religion, the traditional way has triumphed over newfangled science. Rather, simple common sense about handedness seems to edge out a faddist proposal based on overextended reasoning, just as pure lefties continue to edge out us poor, dextrous, ordinary, right-minded, northpaws.

Why No One Hits .400 Any More

C omparisons may be odious, but we cannot avoid them in a world that prizes excellence and yearns to know whether current pathways lead to progress or destruction. We are driven to contrast past with present and use the result to predict an uncertain future. But how can we make fair comparison since we gaze backward through the rose-colored lenses of our most powerful myth—the idea of a former golden age?

Nostalgia for an unknown past can elevate hovels to castles, dung heaps to snow-clad peaks. I had always conceived Calvary, the site of Christ's martyrdom, as a lofty mountain, covered with foliage and located far from the hustle and bustle of Jerusalem. But I stood on its paltry peak last year. Calvary lies inside the walls of Old Jerusalem (just barely beyond the city borders of Christ's time). The great hill is but one staircase high; its summit lies *within* the Church of the Holy Sepulchre.

I had long read of Ragusa, the great maritime power of the medieval Adriatic. I viewed it at grand scale in my mind's eye, a

First published as "Entropic Homogeneity Isn't Why No One Hits .400 Any More" in *Discover*, August 1986.

vast fleet balancing the powers of Islam and Christendom, sending forth its elite to the vanguard of the "invincible" Spanish Armada. Medieval Ragusa has survived intact—as Dubrovnik in Yugoslavia. No town (but Jerusalem) can match its charm, but I circled the battlements of its city walls in fifteen minutes. Ragusa, by modern standards, is a modest village at most.

The world is so much bigger now, so much faster, so much more complex. Must our myths of ancient heroes expire on this altar of technological progress? We might dismiss our deep-seated tendency to aggrandize older heroes as mere sentimentalism—and plainly false by the argument just presented for Calvary and Ragusa. And yet, numbers proclaim a sense of truth in our persistent image of past giants as literally outstanding. Their legitimate claims are relative, not absolute. Great cities of the past may be villages today, and Goliath would barely qualify for the NBA. But, compared with modern counterparts, our legendary heroes often soar much farther above their own contemporaries. The distance between commonplace and extraordinary has contracted dramatically in field after field.

Baseball provides my favorite examples. Few systems offer better data for a scientific problem that evokes as much interest, and sparks as much debate, as any other: the meaning of trends in history as expressed by measurable differences between past and present. This article uses baseball to address the general question of how we may compare an elusive past with a different present. How can we know whether past deeds matched or exceeded current prowess? In particular, was Moses right in his early pronouncement (Genesis 6:4): "There were giants in the earth in those days"?

Baseball has been a bastion of constancy in a tumultuously changing world, a contest waged to the same purpose and with the same basic rules for one hundred years. It has also generated an unparalleled flood of hard numbers about achievement measured every which way that human cleverness can devise. Most

other systems have changed so profoundly that we cannot meaningfully mix the numbers of past and present. How can we compare the antics of Larry Bird with basketball as played before the
twenty-four-second rule or, going further back, the center jump
after every basket, the two-handed dribble, and finally nine-man
teams tossing a lopsided ball into Dr. Naismith's peach basket?
Yet while styles of play and dimensions of ballparks have altered
substantially, baseball today is the same game that "Wee Willie"
Keeler and Nap Lajoie played in the 1890s. Bill James, our premier
guru of baseball stats, writes that "the rules attained essentially
their modern form after 1893" (when the pitching mound
retreated to its current distance of sixty feet six inches). The numbers of baseball can be compared meaningfully for a century of
play.

When we contrast these numbers of past and present, we
encounter the well-known and curious phenomenon that inspired
this article: great players of the past often stand further apart from
their teammates. Consider only the principal measures of hitting
and pitching: batting average and earned run average. No one has
hit .400 since Ted Williams reached .406 nearly half a century ago
in 1941, yet eight players exceeded .410 in the fifty years before
then. Bob Gibson had an earned run average of 1.12 in 1968. Ten
other pitchers have achieved a single season ERA below 1.30, but
before Gibson we must go back a full fifty years to Walter Johnson's 1.27 in 1918. Could the myths be true after all? Were the
old guys really better? Are we heading toward entropic homogeneity and robotic sameness?

These past achievements seem paradoxical because we know
perfectly well that all historical trends point to a near assurance
that modern athletes must be better than their predecessors.
Training has become an industry and obsession, an upscale profession filled with engineers of body and equipment, and a separate branch of medicine for the ills of excess zeal. Few men now
make it to the majors just by tossing balls against a barn door dur-

ing their youth. We live better, eat better, provide more opportunity across all social classes. Moreover, the pool of potential recruits has increased fivefold in one hundred years by simple growth of the American population.

Numbers affirm this ineluctable improvement for sports that run against the absolute standard of a clock. The Olympian powers-that-be finally allowed women to run the marathon in 1984. Joan Benoit won it in 2:24:54. In 1896, Spiridon Loues had won in just a minute under three hours; Benoit ran faster than any male Olympic champion until Emil Zatopek's victory at 2:23:03 in 1952. Or consider two of America's greatest swimmers of the 1920s and 1930s, men later recruited to play Tarzan (and faring far better than Mark Spitz in his abortive commercial career). Johnny Weissmuller won the one-hundred-meter freestyle in 59.0 in 1924 and 58.6 in 1928. The women's record then stood at 1:12.4 and 1:11.0, but Jane had bested Tarzan by 1972 and the women's record has now been lowered to 54.79. Weissmuller also won the four-hundred-meter freestyle in 5:04.2 in 1924, but Buster Crabbe had cut off more than fifteen seconds by 1932 (4:48.4). Female champions in those years swam the distance in 6:02.2 and 5:28.5. The women beat Johnny in 1956, Buster in 1964, and have now (1984) reached 4:07.10, half a minute quicker than Crabbe.

Baseball, by comparison, pits batter against pitcher and neither against a constant clock. If everyone improves as the general stature of athletes rises, then why do we note any trends at all in baseball records? Why do the best old-timers stand out above their modern counterparts? Why don't hitting and pitching continue to balance?

The disappearance of .400 hitting becomes even more puzzling when we recognize that *average* batting has remained relatively stable since the beginning of modern baseball in 1876. The chart on the next page displays the history of mean batting averages since 1876. (I only include men with an average of at least two at-

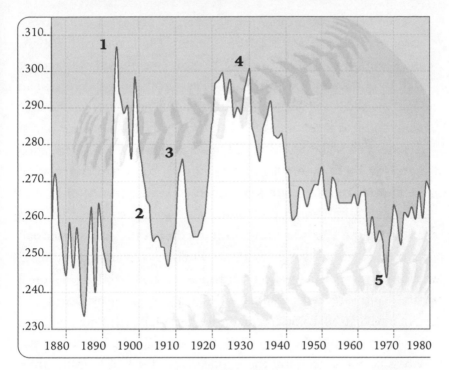

Averages rose after the pitching mound was moved back (1); declined after adoption of the foul-strike rule (2); rose again after the invention of the cork-center ball (3) and during the "lively ball" era (4). The dip in the 1960s (5) was "corrected" in 1969 by lowering the pitching mound and decreasing the strike zone.

bats per game since I wish to gauge trends of regular players. Nineteenth-century figures [National League only] include 80 to 100 players for most years [a low of 54 to a high of 147]. The American League began in 1901 and raised the average to 175 players or so during the long reign of two eight-team leagues, and to above 300 for more recent divisional play.) Note the constancy of mean values: the average ballplayer hit about .260 in the 1870s, and he hits about .260 today. Moreover, this stability has been actively promoted by judicious modifications in rules whenever hitting or pitching threatened to gain the upper hand and provoke a runaway trend of batting averages either up or down. Consider all the major fluctuations:

After beginning around .260, averages began to drift downward, reaching the .240s during the late 1880s and early 1890s. Then, during the 1893 season, the pitching mound was moved back to its current sixty feet six inches from home plate (it had begun at forty-five feet, with pitchers delivering the ball underhand, and had moved steadily back during baseball's early days). The mean soared to its all-time high of .307 in 1894 and remained high (too high, by my argument) until 1901, when adoption of the foul-strike rule promoted a rapid downturn. (Previously, foul balls hadn't influenced the count.) But averages went down too far during the 1900s until the introduction of the cork-center ball sent them abruptly up in 1911. Pitchers accommodated, and within two years, averages returned to their .260 level—until Babe Ruth wreaked personal havoc on the game by belting 29 homers in 1919 (more than entire teams had hit many times before). Threatened by the Black Sox scandal, and buoyed by the Babe's performance (and the public's obvious delight in his free-swinging style), the moguls introduced—whether by conscious collusion or simple acquiescence we do not know—the greatest of all changes in 1920. Scrappy one-run, savvy-baserunning, pitcher's baseball fell from fashion; big offense and swinging for the fences was in. Averages rose abruptly, and this time they stayed high for a full twenty years, even breaking .300 for the second (and only other) time in 1930. Then in the early 1940s, after war had siphoned off the best players, averages declined again to their traditional .260 level.

The causes behind this twenty-year excursion have provoked one of the greatest unresolved debates in baseball history. Conventional wisdom attributes these rises to the introduction of a "lively ball." But Bill James, in his masterly *Historical Baseball Abstract*, argues that no major fiddling with baseballs can be proved in 1920. He attributes the rise to coordinated changes in rules (and pervasive alteration of attitudes) that imposed multiple and simultaneous impediments upon pitching, upsetting the traditional balance for a full twenty years. Trick pitches—the spitball, shine ball, and emery ball—were all banned. More important, umpires now supplied shiny new balls any time the slightest scruff or spot appeared. Previously, soft, scratched, and darkened balls remained in play as long as possible (fans were even expected to throw back "souvenir" fouls). The replacement of discolored and scratched with shiny and new, according to James, would be just as effective for improving hitting as any mythical lively ball. In any case averages returned to the .260s by the 1940s and remained quite stable until their marked decline in the mid-1960s. When Carl Yastrzemski won the American League batting title with a paltry .301 in 1968, the time for redress had come again. The moguls lowered the mound, restricted the strike zone, and averages promptly rose again—right back to their time-honored .260 level, where they have remained ever since.

This exegetical detail shows how baseball has been maintained, carefully and consistently, in unchanging balance since its inception. Is it not, then, all the more puzzling that downward trends in best performances go hand in hand with constancy of average achievement? Why, to choose the premier example, has .400 hitting disappeared, and what does this erasure teach us about the nature of trends and the differences between past and present?

We can now finally explicate the myth of ancient heroes—or, rather, we can understand its partial truth. Consider the two ingredients of our puzzle and paradox: (1) admitting the profound and general improvement of athletes (as measured in clock sports with absolute standards), star baseball players of the past probably didn't match today's leaders (or, at least, weren't notably better); (2) nonetheless, top baseball performances have declined while averages are actively maintained at a fairly constant level. In short, the old-timers did soar farther above their contemporaries, but must have been worse (or at least no better) than modern leaders. The .400 hitters of old were relatively better, but absolutely worse (or equal).

How can we get a numerical handle on this trend? I've argued several times in various articles that students of biological evolution (I am one) approach the world with a vision different from time-honored Western perspectives. Our general culture still remains bound to its Platonic heritage of pigeonholes and essences. We divide the world into a set of definite "things" and view variation and subtle shadings as nuisances that block the distinctness of real entities. At best, variation becomes a device for calculating an average value seen as a proper estimate of the true thing itself. But variation *is* the irreducible reality; nature provides nothing else. Averages are often meaningless (mean height of a family with parents and young children). There is no quintessential human being—only black folks, white folks, skinny people, little people, Manute Bol, and Eddie Gaedel. Copious and continuous variation is us.

But enough general pontification. The necessary item for this study is practical, not ideological. The tools for resolving the paradox of ancient heroes lie in the direct study of variation, not in exclusive attention to stellar achievements. We've failed to grasp this simple solution because we don't view variation as a reality itself, and therefore don't usually study it directly.

I can now state, in a few sentences, my theory about trends in general and .400 hitting in particular (sorry for the long cranking up, and the slow revving down to come, but simple ideas with unconventional contexts require some exposition if they hope to become reader-friendly). Athletes have gotten better (the world in general has become bigger, faster, and more efficient—this may not be a good thing at all; I merely point out that it has happened). We resist this evident trend by taking refuge in the myth of ancient heroes. The myth can be exploded directly for sports

Ted Williams, the last major leaguer to finish a season hitting .400, belts a home run in a 1953 Red Sox–Cleveland Indians game. *Credit: Bettmann/Corbis*

with absolute clock standards. In a system with relative standards (person against person)—especially when rules are subtly adjusted to maintain constancy in measures of average perform- ance—this general improvement is masked and cannot be recov- ered when we follow our usual traditions and interpret figures for average performances as measures of real things. We can, how- ever, grasp the general improvement of systems with relative standards by a direct study of variation—recognizing that varia- tion itself is a *decline in variation*. Paradoxically, this decline pro- duces a decrease in the difference between average and stellar performance. Therefore, modern leaders don't stand so far above their contemporaries. The "myth" of ancient heroes—the greater distance between average and best in the past—actually records the improvement of play through time.

Declining variation becomes the key to our puzzle. Hitting .400

isn't a thing in itself, but an extreme value in the distribution of batting averages (I shall present the data for this claim below). As variation shrinks around a constant mean batting average, .400 hitting disappears. It is, I think, as simple as that.

Reason one for declining variation: *Approach to the outer limits of human capacity.*

Well-off people in developed nations are getting taller and living longer, but the trend won't go on forever. All creatures have outer limits set by evolutionary histories. We're already witnessing the approach to limits in many areas. Maximum life span isn't increasing (although more and more people live long enough to get a crack at the unchanging heights). Racehorses have hardly speeded up, despite enormous efforts of breeders and the unparalleled economic incentive for shaving even a second off top performance (Kentucky Derby winners averaged 2:06.4 during the 1910s and 2:02.0 for the past ten years). Increase in human height has finally begun to level off (daughters of Radcliffe women are now no taller than their mothers). Women's sports records are declining rapidly as opportunity opens up, but some male records are stabilizing.

We can assess all these trends, and the inevitable decline in improvement as we reach the outer limits, because we measure them by absolute clock standards. Baseball players must also be improving, but the relative standard of batting averages, maintained at a mean of about .260, masks the advance. Let's assume that the wall at the right in the top diagram (opposite page) represents the outer limit, and the bell-shaped curve well to its left marks variation in batting prowess one hundred years ago. I suspect that all eras boast a few extraordinary individuals, people near the limits of body and endurance, however lower the general average. So, a few players resided near the right wall in 1880—but the average Joe stood far to their left, and variation among all players was great. Since then, everyone has improved. The best may have inched a bit toward the right wall, but average players

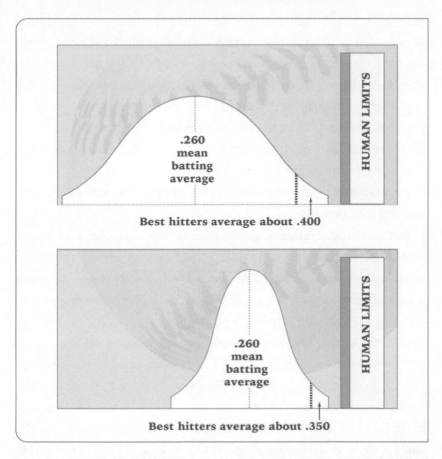

.260
mean
batting
average

HUMAN LIMITS

Best hitters average about .400

.260
mean
batting
average

HUMAN LIMITS

Best hitters average about .350

The disappearance of .400 hitters is the paradoxical result of improvement in play, even as average batters (.260) converge upon the wall of human limits.

have moved substantially in that direction. Meanwhile, increasing competition and higher standards have eliminated very weak hitters (once tolerated for their superior fielding and other skills).

So as average players approach the limiting right wall (bottom diagram), variation decreases strongly on both flanks—at the high end for simple decline in space between the average and the limit, and at the low end by decreasing tolerance as general play improves. The relative standards of baseball have masked this trend; hitting has greatly improved, but we still measure its average as .260 because pitching has gained in concert. We can, however, assess this improvement in a different way—by inevitable decline in variation as the average converges on the limiting wall. Modern stars may be an inch or two closer to the wall—they're absolutely better (or at least no worse) than ancient heroes. But the average has moved several feet closer—and the distance between ordinary (kept at .260) and best has decreased. In short, no more .400 hitters. Ironically, the disappearance of .400 hitting is a sign of improvement, not decline.

Reason two (really the same point stated differently): *Systems equilibrate as they improve.*

Baseball was feeling its way during the early days of major league play. Its rules were our rules, but scores of subtleties hadn't yet been developed or discovered; rough edges careered out in all directions from a stable center. To cite just a few examples (again from Bill James): pitchers began to cover first base in the 1890s; during the same decade, Brooklyn invented the cut-off play, while the Boston Beaneaters developed the hit-and-run and signals from runner to batter. Gloves were a joke in those early days—just a little leather over the hand, not a basket for trapping balls. In 1896 the Phillies actually experimented for seventy-three games with a lefty shortstop. Traditional wisdom applied. He stank; he had the worst fielding average and the fewest assists in the league among regular shortstops.

In an era of such experiment and indifference, truly great players could take advantage in ways foreclosed ever since. "Wee Willie" Keeler could "hit 'em where they ain't" (and bat .432 in 1897) because fielders didn't yet know where they should be. Consider the predicament of a modern Wade Boggs or a Rod Carew. Every pitch is charted, every hit mapped to the nearest square inch. Fielding and relaying have improved dramatically. Boggs and Keeler probably stood in the same place, just a few inches from the right wall of human limits, but average play has so crept up on Boggs that he lacks the space for taking advantage of suboptimality in others. All these improvements must rob great batters of ten or twenty hits a year—more than enough to convert our modern best into .400 hitters.

To summarize, variation in batting averages must decrease as improving play eliminates the rough edges that great players could exploit, and as average performance moves toward the limits of human possibility and compresses great players into an ever decreasing space between average play and the unmovable right wall.

In an article I wrote for *Vanity Fair*, I measured this decline of variation about a constant average on the cheap. I simply took the five highest and five lowest averages for regular players in each year and compared them with the league average. I found that differences between both average and highest and between average and lowest have decreased steadily through the years (see chart, next page). The disappearance of .400 hitting—the most discussed and disputed trend in the history of baseball—isn't a reflection of generally higher averages in the past (for no one hit over .400 during the second decade of exalted averages, from 1931 to 1940, and most .400 hitting in our century occurred between 1900 and 1920, when averages stood at their canonical [and current] .260 level). Nor can this eclipse of high hitting be entirely attributed to the panoply of conventional explanations that view .400 averages as a former "thing" now extinct—more grueling schedules, too many night games, better fielding, invention of the slider, and relief pitching. For .400 hitting isn't a thing to be extirpated, but an extreme value in a distribution of variation for batting averages. The reasons for declining variation, as presented above, are different from the causes for disappearance of an entity. Declining variation arises as a general property of systems that stabilize and improve while maintaining constant rules of performance through time. The extinction of .400 hitting is, paradoxically, a mark of increasingly *better* play.

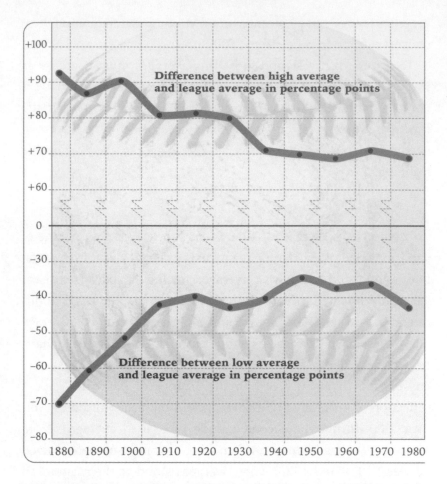

Batting averages are neither as high nor as low as they used to be.

We have now calculated the decline of variation properly, and at vastly more labor (with thanks to my research assistant Ned Young for weeks of work, and to Ed Purcell, Nobel laureate and one of the world's greatest physicists—but also a serious fan with good ideas). The standard deviation is a statistician's basic measure of variation. To compute the standard deviation, you take (in this case) each individual batting average and subtract it from the league average for that year. You then square each value (multiply it by itself) in order to eliminate negative numbers for batting averages below the mean (a negative times a negative gives a positive number). You then add up all these values and divide them by the total number of players—giving an average squared deviation of individual players from the mean. Finally, you take the square root of this number to obtain the average, or standard, deviation itself. The higher the value, the more extensive, or spread out, the variation.

We calculated the standard deviation of batting averages for each year (an improvement from my former high and low five, but much more work). The chart on page 168 plots the trend of standard deviations in batting averages year by year. Our hypothesis is clearly confirmed. Standard deviations have been dropping steadily and irreversibly. The decline itself has decelerated over the years as baseball stabilizes—rapidly during the nineteenth century, more slowly through the twentieth, and reaching a stable plateau by about 1940.

If I may make a personal and subjective comment, I was stunned and delighted (beyond all measure) by the elegance and clarity of this result. I pretty well knew what the general pattern would be because standard deviations are so strongly influenced by extreme values (a consequence of squaring each individual deviation in the calculation)—so my original cheap method of five highest and lowest produced a fair estimate. But I never dreamed that the decline would be so regular, so devoid of exception of anomaly for even a single year—so unvarying that we could even pick out such subtleties as the deceleration in decline. I've spent my entire professional career studying such statistical distributions, and I know how rarely one obtains such clean results in better behaved data of controlled experiments or natural growth in simple systems. We usually encounter some glitch, some anomaly, some funny years. But the decline of standard deviation for batting averages is so regular that it looks like a plot for a law of nature. I find this all the more remarkable because the graph of averages themselves through time shows all the noise and fluctu-

ations expected in natural systems. Yet mean batting averages
have been constantly manipulated by the moguls of baseball to
maintain a general constancy, while no one has tried to monkey
with the standard deviation. Thus, while mean batting averages
have gone up and down to follow the whims of history and the
vagaries of invention, the standard deviation has marched steadily
down at a decreasing pace, apparently perturbed by nothing of
note. I regard this regularity of decline as further evidence that
decreasing variation through time is the primary predictable feature of stabilizing systems.

The details are impressive in their regularity. All four beginning
years of the 1870s sport high values of standard deviation greater
than 0.050, while the last reading in excess of 0.050 occurs in
1886. Values between 0.04 and 0.05 mark the rest of the nineteenth century, with three years just below, at 0.038 to 0.040. The
last reading in excess of 0.040 occurs in 1911. Subsequently,
decline within the 0.03 and 0.04 range shows the same precision
of detail by even decrease with years. The last reading as high as
0.037 occurs in 1937, and of 0.035 in 1941. Only two years have
exceeeded 0.034 since 1957. Between 1942 and 1980, values
remained entirely within the restricted range of 0.0285 to 0.0348.
I'd thought that at least one unusual year would upset the pattern
—that one nineteenth-century value would achieve late-twentieth-
century lows, or one more recent year soar to ancient highs—but
we find no such result. All measures from 1906 back to the beginning are higher than every reading from 1938 to 1980. We find no
overlap at all. This—take it from an old trooper—is regularity
with a vengeance. Something general is going on here, and I think
I know what.

The decadal averages show continuous decline before stabilization in the 1940s. (A note for statistically minded readers:
standard deviations are expressed in their own units of measure-

ment—mouse tails in millimeters, mountains in megatons. Thus, as mean values rise and fall, standard deviations may go up and down to track the mean rather than record exclusively the amount of spread. This poses no problem for most of our chart, because averages have been so stable through time at about .260. But the twenty-point rise in averages during the 1920s and 1930s might entail artificially elevated standard deviations. We can correct for this effect by computing the coefficient of variation—one hundred times the standard deviation divided by the mean—for each year. Also listed are decadal averages for coefficients of variation—and we now see that apparent stabilization between the 1910s and 1920s was masking a continuing decline in coefficient of variation, as the 1920s rise in averages canceled out decline in variation when measured by the standard deviation.)

If my editors were more indulgent, I could wax at distressing length about more details and different measures. Just one final hint of a more interesting pattern revealed by finer dissection: the chart on the next page amalgamates the two leagues, but their trends are somewhat different. In the National League, variation declined during the nineteenth century, but stabilized early in the twentieth. In the American League, founded in 1901, variation dropped steadily right through the 1940s. Thus, each league followed the same pattern—the time of origin setting a pattern of decline for decades to come. Can we use existence or stabilization of declining variation as a mark of maturity? Did the leagues differ fundamentally during the early years of our century—the National already mature, the American still facing a few decades of honing and trimming the edges?

No one has invested more time and energy in the study of numbers than baseball aficionados. We have measures and indices for everything imaginable—from simple lists of at-bats to number of times a black shortstop under six feet tall has been caught stealing third on pitchouts by righties to left-handed catchers. Yet I don't think that this most basic pattern in the standard deviation of batting averages has been properly noted, or its significance assessed. As I argued above, the biases of our upbringing force a focus on averages treated as things, and virtually preclude proper attention to variation considered as irreducible reality. The standard deviation is our base-level tool for studying variation—as fundamental as milk for babies and cockroaches for New York apartments. Yet, after decades of loving attention to minutiae of averages, we can still gain insights from an unexplored pattern in the very simplest kiddie measure of variation. What better illustration for my claim that our culture undervalues variation at its peril?

After this detail, I've earned the right to end with a bit of philosophical musing, ostensibly in the great decline-of-civilization tra-

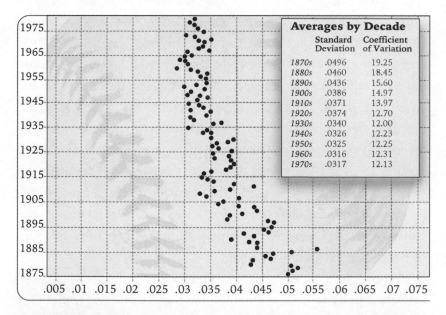

Averages by Decade		
	Standard Deviation	Coefficient of Variation
1870s	.0496	19.25
1880s	.0460	18.45
1890s	.0436	15.60
1900s	.0386	14.97
1910s	.0371	13.97
1920s	.0374	12.70
1930s	.0340	12.00
1940s	.0326	12.23
1950s	.0325	12.25
1960s	.0316	12.31
1970s	.0317	12.13

Each dot represents the standard deviation of batting averages for one year. While the mean has gone up and down with the whims of history and the vagaries of invention, the standard deviation has marched steadily downward at a decreasing pace, as shown by its ever slower drift to the left.

dition, but really a sneaky bit of optimism from the depth of my sanguine soul.

The message of this study in variation might seem glum, almost cosmically depressing in its paradox—that general improvement clips the wings of true greatness. No one soars above the commonplace any more. General advance brings declining variation in its wake; heroes are extinct. The small population of Europe yielded both a Bach and a Mozart in just one hundred years; where shall we find such transcendent geniuses to guide (or at least enlighten) our uncertain and perilous present?

I wish to propose, in closing, a more general framework for understanding trends in time as an interaction between the location of bell-shaped curves in variation and the position (and potential for mobility) of the limiting right wall for human excellence. This theme transcends sports (or any particular example), and our model should include mind work as well as body work. I suggest three rough categories, with a fundamental example for each, ranging from high to low potential for future accomplishment.

Consider science as a system of knowledge. In most areas, our ignorance is abysmal compared with our sense of what we might learn and know. The curve of knowledge, in other words, stands far from the right wall. Moreoever, the wall itself (or at least our perception of it) seems flexible before the growth of knowledge, as new theories suggest pathways to insight never considered previously. Science seems progressive since current ignorance provides so much space to its right, and since the wall itself can be pushed back by the very process that signals our approach. Still, one cannot avoid—with that special sadness reserved for recognizing a wonderful thing gone forever—the conviction that certain seminal discoveries established truths so central and so broad in import that we cannot hope to win insight in such great gulps again, for the right wall moves slowly and with limits, and we may never again open up space for jumps so big. Plate tectonics has revolutionized geology, but we cannot match the thrill of those who discovered that time comes in billions, not thousands—for deep time, once discovered, set the root of a profession forever. These are exciting days for biology, but no one will taste the intellectual power of a man alone at Downe—Charles Darwin reformulating all nature with the passkey of evolution.

I would place most sports, as well as musical performance, in a second category, where the best have long stood near an inflexible right wall. When we remove impediments imposed by custom (women's sports) or technology (certain musical instruments), improvement may be rapid. But progress comes in inches of milliseconds for goals long sought and unimpeded (I doubt that Stern plays notably better than Paganini, Horowitz than Liszt, E. Power Biggs than Bach—and neither horse nor human male is shaving much off the mile run these days). The small contribution of this article lies in this second domain—in showing that decline in variation will measure improvement when relative standards mask progress measured against such absolute criteria as clocks.

Lest we lament this second category for its limited licenses in improvement, consider the painful plight of a third domain where success in striving depletes the system itself. The right wall of our first domain was far away and somewhat flexible, near and rigid (but still stable) in our second. In this third domain, success hits the wall and consumes it—as if the mile run had disappeared as a competitive sport as soon as one hundred people ran the distance in less than four minutes. Given an ethic that exalts perennial originality in artistic composition, the history of music (and many other arts) may fall into this domain. One composer may exploit a basic style for much of a career, but successors may not follow this style in much detail, or for very long. Such striving for newness may grant us joy forever if a limitless array of potential styles awaits discovery and exploitation. But perhaps the world is not so bounteous; perhaps we've already explored most of what even a highly sophisticated audience can deem accessible. Perhaps the wall of an intelligible vanguard has been largely consumed. Perhaps there is a simple solution to the paradox of why we now generate no Bach or Mozart in a world far larger, with musical training provided for millions more. Perhaps they reside among us, but we've consumed all styles of expression so deeply tuned to the human soul. If so, I might timidly advance a truly reactionary proposal. The death of Mozart at thirty-five may have been the deepest tragedy of our cultural history (great scientists have died even younger, but their work can be done by others). We perform his handful of operas over and over again. We might be enjoying a dozen more—some counted as the most sublime of all musical works—if he had survived even to fifty. Suppose a composer now lived who could master his style and write every bit as well. The ethic of originality forbids it absolutely, but would the integrity of art collapse forever if this person wrote just a few more great pieces in that genre? Not a hundred, just three or four to supplement *Don Giovanni* and *Die Zauberflöte*. Would such an addition not be esteemed a public service beyond all others?

Enough. I'm waxing lugubrious, despite promises to the contrary. For while I may yearn to hear Beethoven's Tenth Symphony, I don't lament a lost past or decry a soft present. In sport, and art, and science (how I wish it were so in politics as well), we live in the best world we've ever known, though not in the best of all possible worlds. So be it that improvement must bury in its wake the myth of ancient heroes. We've exposed the extinction of .400 hitting as a sign of progress, not degradation—the paradoxical effect of declining variation as play improves and stabilizes, and as average contestants also approach the right wall of human limits.

Do not lament the loss of literally outstanding performance (largely a figment, in any case, of failings among the ordinary, not a mark of greater prowess among the best). Celebrate instead the immense improvement of average play. (I rather suspect that we would regard most operatic performances of 1850, and most baseball games of 1900, as sloppy and amateurish—not to mention the village squabbles that enter history as epic battles.) Do not lament our past ease in distinguishing the truly great. Celebrate instead the general excellence that makes professional sports so exciting today. And appreciate the need for subtlety and discernment that modern fans must develop to make proper asessments; we must all now be connoisseurs to appreciate our favorite games fully. Above all, remember that the possibility for transcendence never dies. We live for that moment, the truly unpredictable performance that shatters all expectation. We delight all the more in Dwight Gooden and Larry Bird because they stand out among a panoply of true stars. Besides, I really wrote this article only because I have a hunch that I want to share (and we professor types need to set context before we go out on a limb): Wade Boggs is gonna hit .400 this year.

The Streak of Streaks

Book reviewed:

Streak: Joe DiMaggio and the Summer of '41 by Michael Seidel

My father was a court stenographer. At his less than princely salary, we watched Yankee games from the bleachers or high in the third deck. But one of the judges had season tickets, so we occasionally sat in the lower boxes when hizzoner couldn't attend. One afternoon, while DiMaggio was going 0 for 4 against, of all people, the lowly St. Louis Browns (now the even lowlier Baltimore Orioles), the great man fouled one in our direction. "Catch it, Dad," I screamed. "You never get them," he replied, but stuck up his hand like the Statue of Liberty—and the ball fell right in. I mailed it to DiMaggio, and, bless him, he actually sent the ball back, signed and in a box marked "insured." Insured, that is, to make me the envy of the neighborhood, and DiMaggio the model and hero of my life.

I met DiMaggio a few years ago on a small playing field at the Presidio of San Francisco. My son, wearing DiMaggio's old number 5 on his Little League jersey, accompanied me, exactly one generation after my father caught that ball. DiMaggio gave him a pointer or two on batting and then signed a ball for him. One generation passeth away, and another generation cometh: but the earth abideth forever.

My son, uncoached by Dad, and given the chance that comes but once in a lifetime, asked DiMaggio as his only query about life and career: "Suppose you had walked every time up during one game of your fifty-six-game hitting streak? Would the streak have been over?" DiMaggio replied that, under 1941 rules, the streak would have ended, but that this unfair statute has since been revised, and such a game would not count today.

My son's choice for a single question tells us something vital about the nature of legend. A man may labor for a professional lifetime, especially in sport or in battle, but posterity needs a single transcendent event to fix him in permanent memory. Every hero must be a Wellington on the right side of his personal Waterloo; generality of excellence is too diffuse. The unambiguous factuality of a single achievement is adamantine. Detractors can argue forever about the general tenor of your life and works, but they can never erase a great event.

In 1941, as I gestated in my mother's womb, Joe DiMaggio got at least one hit in each of fifty-six successive games. Most records are only incrementally superior to runners-up; Roger Maris hit sixty-one homers in 1961, but Babe Ruth hit sixty in 1927 and fifty-nine in 1921, while Hank Greenberg (1938) and Jimmy Foxx (1932) both hit fifty-eight. But DiMaggio's fifty-six-game hitting streak is ridiculously and almost unreachably far from all challengers ("Wee Willie" Keeler and Peter Rose, both with forty-four, come second). Among sabremetricians (a happy neologism based on an acronym for members of the Society for American Baseball

Research, and referring to the statistical mavens of the sport)—a contentious lot not known for agreement about anything—we find virtual consensus that DiMaggio's fifty-six-game hitting streak is the greatest accomplishment in the history of baseball, if not all modern sport.

The reasons for this respect are not far to seek. Single moments of unexpected supremacy—Johnny Vander Meer's back-to-back no-hitters of 1938, Don Larsen's perfect game in the 1956 World Series—can occur at any time to almost anybody, and have an irreducibly capricious character. Achievements of a full season—Maris's sixty-one homers, Ted Williams's batting average of .406, also posted in 1941 and not equaled since—have a certain overall majesty, but they don't demand unfailing consistency every single day; you can slump for a while, so long as your average holds. But a streak must be absolutely exceptionless; you are not allowed a single day of subpar play, or even bad luck. You bat only four or five times in an average game. Sometimes two or three of these efforts yield walks, and you get only one or two shots at a hit. Moreover, as tension mounts and notice increases, your life becomes unbearable. Reporters dog your every step; fans are even more intrusive than usual (one stole DiMaggio's favorite bat right in the middle of his streak). You cannot make a single mistake.

Thus Joe DiMaggio's fifty-six-game hitting streak is both the greatest factual achievement in the history of baseball and a principal icon of American mythology. What shall we do with such a central item of our cultural history? Michael Seidel's happy response is a book devoted not to generalities or implications of the streak   many have done this, too many times—but to day-by-day details of how a man gets from one to fifty-six with no misses in between. This book chronicles the intricate factual events of DiMaggio's achievement, and pays the best kind of proper respect, while providing the right sort of description. I shall return to Seidel, but first let me illustrate another approach to such an icon.

Statistics and mythology may seem the most unlikely bedfellows. How can we quantify Caruso or measure *Middlemarch*? But if God could mete out heaven with the span (Isaiah 40:12), perhaps we can say something useful about hitting streaks. The statistics of "runs," defined as continuous series of good or bad results (including baseball's streaks and slumps), is a well-developed branch of the profession, and can yield clear—but wildly counterintuitive—results. (The fact that we find these conclusions so surprising is the key to appreciating DiMaggio's achievement, the point of this article, and the gateway to an important insight about the human mind.)

Start with a phenomenon that nearly everyone both accepts and considers well understood—"hot hands" in basketball. Now and then, someone just gets hot, and can't be stopped. Basket after basket falls in—or out as with "cold hands," when a man can't buy a bucket for love or money (choose your cliché). The reason for this phenomenon seems clear enough; it lies embodied in the maxim: "When you're hot, you're hot; and when you're not, you're not." You get that touch, build confidence; all nervousness fades, you find your rhythm; swish, swish, swish. Or you miss a few, get rattled, endure the booing, experience despair; hands start shaking, and you realize that you shoulda stood in bed.

Everybody knows about hot hands. The only problem is that no such phenomenon exists. The Stanford psychologist Amos Tversky studied every basket made by the Philadelphia 76ers for more than a season. He found, first of all, that probabilities of making a second basket did not rise following a successful shot. Moreover, the number of "runs," or baskets in succession, was no greater than what a standard random, or coin-tossing, model would predict. (If the chance of making each basket is 0.5, for example, a reasonable value for good shooters, five hits in a row will occur, on average, once in thirty-two sequences—just as you can expect to toss five successive heads about once in thirty-two times, or 0.55.)

Of course Larry Bird, the great forward of the Boston Celtics, will have more sequences of five than Joe Airball—but not because he has greater will or gets in that magic rhythm more often. Larry has longer runs because his average success rate is so much higher, and random models predict more frequent and longer sequences. If Larry shoots field goals at 0.6 probability of success, he will get five in a row about once every thirteen sequences (0.6⁵). If Joe, by contrast, shoots only 0.3, he will get his five straight only about once in 412 times. In other words, we need no special explanation for the apparent pattern of long runs. There is no ineffable "causality of circumstance" (if I may call it that), no definite reason born of the particulars that make for heroic myths—courage in the clinch, strength in adversity, etc. You only have to know a person's ordinary play in order to predict his sequences. (I rather suspect that we are convinced of the contrary not only because we need myths so badly, but also because we remember the successes and simply allow the failures to fade from memory. More on this later.) But how does this revisionist pessimism work for baseball?

My colleague Ed Purcell, Nobel laureate in physics but, for purposes of this subject, just another baseball fan,[1] has done a comprehensive study of all baseball streak and slump records. His firm conclusion is easily and swiftly summarized. Nothing ever happened in baseball above and beyond the frequency predicted by coin-tossing models. The longest runs of wins or losses are as long as they should be, and occur about as often as they ought to. Even the hapless Orioles, at 0 and 21 to start this season, only fell

[1] Richard Sisk of the *New York Daily News Sunday* magazine (March 27, 1988) wrote a funny article about the sabremetric studies of three Harvard professors—Purcell, Dudley Herschbach, and myself. It ran with the precious title: "Buncha Pointyheads Sittin' Around Talkin' Baseball."

victim to the laws of probability (and not to the vengeful God of racism, out to punish major league baseball's only black manager).

But "treasure your exceptions," as the old motto goes. One major exception does exist, absolutely only one—one sequence so many standard deviations above the expected distribution that it should not have occurred at all: Joe DiMaggio's fifty-six-game hitting streak in 1941. The intuition of baseball aficionados has been vindicated. Purcell calculated that to make it likely (probability greater than 50 percent) that a run of even fifty games will occur once in the history of baseball up to now (and fifty-six is a lot more than fifty in this kind of league), baseball's rosters would have to include either four lifetime .400 batters or fifty-two lifetime .350 batters over careers of one thousand games. In actuality, only three men own lifetime batting averages in excess of .350, and no one is anywhere near .400 (Ty Cobb at .367, Rogers Hornsby at .358, and Shoeless Joe Jackson at .356). DiMaggio's streak is the most extraordinary thing that ever happened in American sports. He sits on the shoulders of two bearers— mythology and science. For Joe DiMaggio accomplished what no other ballplayer has done. He beat the hardest taskmaster of all, a woman who makes Nolan Ryan's fastball look like a cantaloupe in slow motion—Lady Luck.

Seidel's book succeeds with a simple and honorable premise. The streak itself is such a good story, such an important event in our cultural history, that the day-by-day chronicle will shape a bare sequence into a wonderful drama with beginning, middle, and end. And so we move from the early days of DiMaggio's streak, when no one realized that anything of interest was happening; through the excruciating middle games when George Sisler's modern record of forty-one, then Keeler's all-time mark of forty-four, were approached and broken; to later times of pleasure and coasting when DiMaggio was only smashing his own record, set the day before; and to the final, fateful game fifty-seven, when Ken Keltner made two great plays at third base and lost DiMaggio the prospect of a lifetime advertising contract with the Heinz ketchup company.

But just as baseball, at least in our metaphors, is so much more than a game, Seidel has written more than a sports book. Seidel is professor of literature at Columbia University, and *Streak* belongs to a growing genre of baseball books written by, if you will pardon my citation of the last footnote, "pointyheads" (no offense intended since I, alas, am one). Baseball has long enjoyed a distinguished literature, from Ring Lardner to the incomparable Roger Angell—and I have seen no satisfactory resolution for the old puzzle of why baseball, but no other sport, has attracted some of America's finest writers. But the new genre is quite different— serious, scholarly books treating baseball as something that might even get you tenure at a major university (as something other than athletic coach): Jules Tygiel's *Baseball's Great Experiment*, on Jackie Robinson and the racial integration of the game; or Charles C. Alexander's *Ty Cobb*, a sociology of a time as well as a biography of the greatest and nastiest player of them all.

Seidel has tried to place DiMaggio's feat in a larger setting of history and culture by weaving in and around his fifty-six-game saga the chronicle of other events during the summer of 1941. There is no tendentiousness here, no attempt to find deep meaning, no theory about baseball imitating or reflecting anything about "real" life. Instead, Seidel presents a sensitive and judicious selection of surrounding events simply, I think, to provide the background for a genuine legend. (As my only mild criticism of the book: I felt that this strategy sometimes smacks a bit of reading old newspapers and listing the main events in order.) While DiMaggio hit away, Rudolf Hess parachuted into Scotland, Hitler

Joe DiMaggio singles against the Cleveland Indians on July 16, 1941, in the fifty-sixth game of his consecutive hitting streak. *Credit: AP/Wide World Photos*

invaded Russia, and Roosevelt maneuvered America toward its inevitable involvement, as Charles Lindbergh toured the country in the losing cause of an isolationism that, for his part at least, conveyed more than a faint odor of pro-German sympathy. On the evening after DiMaggio hit safely in game twelve, the nighttime contest between the New York Giants and the Boston Braves was halted for forty-five minutes to broadcast FDR's "unlimited emergency" speech over the loudspeakers. (After paying ransom to the aforementioned thief, DiMaggio auctioned off his streak bat to benefit the USO.) In the meantime, *Citizen Kane* played its initial run, commercial television made its first broadcasts in New York City, and the Grand Central Red Cap Barbershop Quartet won the citywide contest sponsored by the New York Parks Department, only to face the indignity of disqualification at the nationals in St. Louis. The Red Caps were black.

With apologies to Seidel (for he was probably sandbagged by

his publishers on this), I must mention one funny error. The caption to a photo reads: "Ted Williams as he looked in 1941 when he hit .406." But the picture, unless I need a very peculiar pair of glasses, shows Phil Rizzuto. Now you couldn't find two more different people. Williams was tall, thin, taciturn, cold, the finest hitting machine since Ty Cobb, but not exactly perfect in the outfield. Rizzuto was just the opposite: short, stocky, convivial, not much with the stick, but the finest shortstop in the league. Moreover, Rizzuto played with DiMaggio on the Yankees, Williams for their archrivals, the Boston Red Sox. But then, an even more amusing mix-up once appeared in the "errata" section of the *New York Times*: "The photo that appeared yesterday on page forty-one, labeled as the sun, was the moon."

Seidel's book will help us to treasure DiMaggio's achievement by bringing together the details of a genuine legend. But a larger issue lies behind basic documentation and simple appreciation. For we don't understand the truly special character of DiMaggio's record because we are so poorly equipped, whether by habits of culture or by our modes of cognition, to grasp the workings of random processes and patterning in nature.

That old Persian tentmaker, Omar Khayyám, understood the quandary of our lives:

> *Into this Universe, and* Why *not knowing,*
> *Nor* Whence, *like Water willy-nilly flowing; And out of it, as Wind*
>   *along the Waste,*
> *I know not* Whither, *willy-nilly blowing.*

But we cannot bear these conclusions. We must have comforting answers. We see pattern, for pattern surely exists, even in a purely random world. (Only a highly nonrandom universe could possibly cancel out the clumping that we perceive as pattern. We think we see constellations because the stars are dispersed at random in the heavens, and therefore clump in our sight.) Our error lies not in the perception of pattern but in automatically imbuing pattern with meaning, especially with meaning that can bring us comfort, or dispel confusion. Again, Omar took the more honest approach:

> *Ah, love! could you and I with Fate conspire*
> *To grasp this sorry Scheme of Things entire, Would not we shatter it to*
>   *bits—and then*
> *Re-mould it nearer to the Heart's Desire!*

We, instead, have tried to impose that "heart's desire" on the actual earth and its largely random patterns:

> *All Nature is but Art, unknown to thee;*
> *All Chance, Direction, which thou canst not see;*
> *All Discord, Harmony not under-stood;*
> *All partial Evil, universal Good.*
>   (Alexander Pope, *Essay on Man*, end of Epistle 1)

Sorry to wax so poetic and tendentious about something that leads back to DiMaggio's hitting streak (pointyheadedness in action, I suppose), but this broader setting is the source of our misinterpretation. We believe in "hot hands" because we must impart meaning to a pattern—and we like meanings that tell stories about heroism, valor, and excellence. We believe that long streaks and slumps must have direct causes internal to the sequence itself, and we have no feel for the frequency and length of sequences in random data. Thus, while we understand that DiMaggio's hitting streak was the longest ever, we don't appreciate its truly special character because we view all the others as equally patterned by cause, only a little shorter. We distinguish DiMaggio's feat merely by quantity along a continuum of courage;

we should, instead, view his fifty-six-game hitting streak as a unique assault on the otherwise unblemished record of Dame Probability.

Amos Tversky, who studied "hot hands," has performed a series of elegant psychological experiments with Daniel Kahneman. These long-term studies have provided our finest insight into "natural reasoning" and its curious departure from logical truth. To cite an example, they construct a fictional description of a young woman: "Linda is thirty-one years old, single, outspoken, and very bright. She majored in philosophy. As a student, she was deeply concerned with issues of discrimination and social justice, and also participated in antinuclear demonstrations." Subjects are then given a list of hypothetical statements about Linda: they must rank these in order of presumed likelihood, most to least probable. Tversky and Kahneman list eight statements, but five are a blind, and only three make up the true experiment:

> Linda is active in the feminist movement.
> Linda is a bank teller.
> Linda is a bank teller and is active in the feminist movement.

Now it simply must be true that the third statement is least likely, since any conjunction has to be less probable than either of its parts considered separately. Everybody can understand this when the principle is explained explicitly and patiently. But all groups of subjects, sophisticated students who ought to understand logic and probability as well as folks off the street corner, rank the last statement as more probable than the second. (I am particularly fond of this example because I know that the third statement is least probable, yet a little homunculus in my head continues to jump up and down, shouting at me—"but she can't just be a bank teller; read the description.")

Why do we so consistently make this simple logical error? Tversky and Kahneman argue, correctly I think, that our minds are not built (for whatever reason) to work by the rules of probability, though these rules clearly govern our universe. We do something else that usually serves us well, but fails in crucial instances: we "match to type." We abstract what we consider the "essence" of an entity, and then arrange our judgments by their degree of similarity to this assumed type. Since we are given a "type" for Linda that implies feminism, but definitely not a bank job, we rank any statement matching the type as more probable than another that only contains material contrary to the type. This propensity may help us to understand an entire range of human preferences, from Plato's theory of form to modern stereotyping of race or gender.

We might also understand the world better, and free ourselves of unseemly prejudice, if we properly grasped the workings of probability and its inexorable hold, through laws of logic, upon much of nature's pattern. "Matching to type" is one common error; failure to understand random patterning in streaks and slumps is another—hence Tversky's study of both the fictional Linda and the 76ers' baskets. Our failure to appreciate the uniqueness of DiMaggio's streak derives from the same unnatural and uncomfortable relationship that we maintain with probability. (If we understood Lady Luck better, Las Vegas might still be a roadstop in the desert, and Nancy Reagan might not have a friend in San Francisco.)

My favorite illustration of this basic misunderstanding, as applied to DiMaggio's hitting streak, appeared in a recent article by baseball writer John Holway, "A Little Help from His Friends," and subtitled "Hits or Hype in '41" (*Sports Heritage*, November/December 1987). Holway points out that five of DiMaggio's successes were narrow escapes and lucky breaks. He received two benefits of the doubt from official scorers on plays that might have been judged as errors. In each of two games, his only hit was a cheapie. (In game sixteen, a ball dropped untouched in the out-field and had to be ruled a hit, even though the ball could have been caught, had it not been misjudged; in game fifty-four, DiMaggio dribbled one down the third baseline, easily beating the throw because the third baseman, expecting the usual, was play-ing far back.) The fifth incident is an ofttold tale, perhaps the most interesting story of the streak. In game thirty-eight, DiMag-gio was 0 for 3 going into the last inning. Scheduled to bat fourth, he might have been denied a chance to hit at all. Johnny Sturm popped up to begin the inning, but Red Rolfe then walked. Slug-ger Tommy Henrich, up next, was suddenly swept with a pre-monitory fear: suppose I ground into a double play and end the inning? An elegant solution immediately occurred to him: why not bunt (an odd strategy for a power hitter)? Henrich laid down a beauty; DiMaggio, up next, promptly drilled a double to left.

Holway's account is interesting, but his premise is entirely, almost preciously, wrong. First of all, none of the five incidents represents an egregious miscall. The two hits were less than ele-gant, but they were undoubtedly legitimate; the two boosts from official scorers were close calls on judgment plays, not gifts. As for Henrich, I can only repeat manager Joe McCarthy's comment when Tommy asked him for permission to bunt: "Yeah, that's a good idea." Not a terrible strategy either—to put a man into scor-ing position for an insurance run when you're up 3–1.

But these details do not touch the main point—Holway's premise is false because he accepts the conventional mythology about long sequences. He believes that streaks are unbroken runs of causal courage—so that any prolongation by hook or crook is an outrage against the deep meaning of the phenomenon. But extended sequences are no such thing. Long streaks always are, and must be, a matter of extraordinary luck imposed upon great skill. Please don't make the vulgar mistake of thinking that Purcell or Tversky or I or anyone else would attribute a long streak to "just luck"—as though everyone's chances are exactly the same, and streaks represent nothing more than the lucky atom that kept moving in one direction. Long hitting streaks happen to the greatest players—Sisler, Keeler, DiMaggio, Rose—because their general chance of getting a hit is so much higher than average. Just as Joe Airball cannot match Larry Bird for runs of baskets, Joe's cousin Bill Ofer, with a lifetime batting average of .184, will never have a streak to match DiMaggio's with a lifetime average of .325. The statistics show something else, and something fascinating: there is no "causality of circumstance," no "extra" that the great can draw from the soul of their valor to extend a streak beyond the ordinary expectation of coin-tossing models for a series of unconnected events, each occurring with the characteristic probability for that particular player. Good players have higher characteristic probabilities, hence longer streaks.

Of course DiMaggio had a little luck during his streak. That's what streaks are all about. No long sequence has ever been entirely sustained in any other way (the Orioles almost won several of those twenty-one games). DiMaggio's remarkable achievement—its uniqueness, in the unvarnished literal sense of that word—lies in whatever he did to extend his success well beyond the reasonable expectations of random models that have governed every other streak or slump in the history of baseball.

Probability does pervade the universe—and in this sense, the old chestnut about baseball imitating life really has validity. The statistics of streaks and slumps, properly understood, do teach an important lesson about epistemology, and life in general. The history of a species, or any natural phenomenon that requires unbroken continuity in a world of trouble, works like a batting streak. All are games of a gambler playing with a limited stake against a house with infinite resources. The gambler must eventually go bust. His aim can only be to stick around as long as possible, to have some fun while he's at it, and, if he happens to be a moral agent as well, to worry about staying the course with honor. The best of us will try to live by a few simple rules: do justly, love mercy, walk humbly with thy God, and never draw to an inside straight.

DiMaggio's hitting streak is the finest of legitimate legends because it embodies the essence of the battle that truly defines our lives. DiMaggio activated the greatest and most unattainable dream of all humanity, the hope and chimera of all sages and shamans: he cheated death, at least for a while.

January 3, 1985

Joe DiMaggio
2150 Beach Street
San Francisco, CA 94123

Dear Joe,

My best wishes to you for a happy 1985. I hope you had a chance to see the *NOVA* show in which you so kindly participated. I have received so many favorable comments, with unanimous agreement that your appearance made the show.

I mentioned to you in San Francisco that my colleague Ed Purcell, a Nobel Laureate and one of the world's greatest physicists, had determined that your fifty-six-game hit streak was, statistically, the most unusual and unexpected great event in the history of baseball. Ed recently sent me the enclosed note in which he derives the reason for his statement. The mathematical details need not be pursued, but the chart on the back of the second page will give you some idea of how remarkable and unpredictable your achievement was in statistical terms. The top row labeled b represents lifetime batting averages of .400, .380, and .300. The first column labeled n at the left indicates the number of games in a hitting streak—40, 50, and 60 in this example. The nine numbers in the chart itself give you the probability that a batter with a lifetime batting average of b will have a hit streak of number of games n over a career of one thousand games. Just consider the .0096 value for a .350 lifetime average and a fifty-game hitting streak. This means that a lifetime .350 batter has only nine chances in a thousand to have a fifty-game hitting streak in a career of one thousand games. To make it more likely than unlikely that such a hitting streak would exist, the number in the chart must be greater than .5—for a probability of greater than one-half. Thus, there would have to be fifty-two lifetime .350 hitters in order to make the probability of a fifty-game hit streak more than likely (.0086 times 52 equals the crucial value of one-half). I don't have my encyclopedia handy, but I think that only three or four people actually have lifetime averages exceeding .350 (Cobb, Hornsby, perhaps Shoeless Joe Jackson). But your streak went for fifty-six games, a value that would only become more likely to happen than not to happen if baseball included more than one hundred lifetime .350 hitters.

You asked me jokingly if this analysis meant that your record would never be broken. Even us pompous academics wouldn't dare to make a statement like that. But Ed Purcell's analysis does suggest that of all baseball records, your hit streak is surely the one least likely to be broken.

Thanks again for your time and, especially, for your kindness to my son Ethan.

Sincerely,
Stephen Jay Gould
/ap
Encl.

The Creation Myths
of Cooperstown

You may either look on the bright side and say that hope springs eternal or, taking the cynic's part, you may mark P. T. Barnum as an astute psychologist for his proclamation that suckers are born every minute. The end result is the same: you can, Honest Abe notwithstanding, fool most of the people all of the time. How else to explain the long and continuing compendium of hoaxes—from the medieval shroud of Turin to Edwardian Piltdown Man to an ultramodern array of flying saucers and astral powers—eagerly embraced for their consonance with our hopes or their resonance with our fears?

Some hoaxes make a sufficient mark on history that their products acquire the very status initially claimed by fakery—legitimacy (although as an object of human or folkloric, rather than natural, history. I once held the bones of Piltdown Man and felt that I was handling an important item of Western culture).

The Cardiff Giant, the best American entry for the title of paleontological hoax turned into cultural history, now lies on display in a shed behind a barn at the Farmer's Museum in Cooperstown,

Reprinted with permission from *Natural History* (November 1989). Copyright the American Museum of Natural History (1989).

New York. This gypsum man, more than ten feet tall, was "discovered" by workmen digging a well on a farm near Cardiff, New York, in October 1869. Eagerly embraced by a gullible public, and ardently displayed by its creators at fifty cents a pop, the Cardiff Giant caused quite a brouhaha around Syracuse, and then nationally, for the few months of its active life between exhumation and exposure.

The Cardiff Giant was the brainchild of George Hull, a cigar manufacturer (and general rogue) from Binghampton, New York. He quarried a large block of gypsum from Fort Dodge, Iowa, and shipped it to Chicago, where two marble cutters fashioned the rough likeness of a naked man. Hull made some crude and minimal attempts to give his statue an aged appearance. He chipped off the carved hair and beard because experts told him that such items would not petrify. He drove darning needles into a wooden block and hammered the statue, hoping to simulate skin pores. Finally, he dumped a gallon of sulfuric acid all over his creation to simulate extended erosion. Hull then shipped his giant in a large box back to Cardiff.

Hull, as an accomplished rogue, sensed that his story could not hold for long and, in that venerable and alliterative motto, got out while the getting was good. He sold a three-quarter interest in the Cardiff Giant to a consortium of highly respectable businessmen, including two former mayors of Syracuse. These men raised the statue from its original pit on November 5 and carted it off to Syracuse for display.

The hoax held on for a few more weeks, and Cardiff Giant fever swept the land. Debate raged in newspapers and broadsheets between those who viewed the giant as a petrified fossil and those who regarded it as a statue wrought by an unknown and wondrous prehistoric race. But Hull had left too many tracks—at the gypsum quarries in Fort Dodge, at the carver's studio in Chicago, along the roadways to Cardiff (several people remembered seeing an awfully large box passing on a cart just days before the supposed discovery). By December, Hull was ready to recant, but held his tongue a while longer. Three months later, the two Chicago sculptors came forward, and the Cardiff Giant's brief rendezvous with fame and fortune ended.

The common analogy of the Cardiff Giant with Piltdown Man works only to a point (both were frauds passed off as human fossils) and fails in one crucial respect. Piltdown was cleverly wrought and fooled professionals for forty years, while the Cardiff Giant was preposterous from the start. How could a man turn to solid gypsum, while preserving all his soft anatomy, from cheeks to toes to penis? Geologists and paleontologists never accepted Hull's statue. O. C. Marsh, later to achieve great fame as a discoverer of dinosaurs, echoed a professional consensus in his unambiguous pronouncement: "It is of very recent origin and a decided humbug."

Why, then, was the Cardiff Giant so popular, inspiring a wave of interest and discussion as high as any tide in the affairs of men during its short time in the sun? If the fraud had been well executed, we might attribute this great concern to the dexterity of the hoaxers (just as we grant grudging attention to a few of the most accomplished art fakers for their skills as copyists). But since the Cardiff Giant was so crudely done, we can only attribute its fame to the deep issue, the raw nerve, touched by the subject of its fakery—human origins. Link an absurd concoction to a noble and mysterious subject and you may prevail, at least for a little while. My opening reference to P. T. Barnum was not meant sarcastically; he was one of the great practical psychologists of the nineteenth century—and his motto applies with special force to the Cardiff Giant: "No humbug is great without truth at the bottom." (Barnum made a copy of the Cardiff Giant and exhibited it in New York City. His mastery of hype and publicity assured that his model far outdrew the "real" fake when the original went on display at a rival establishment in the same city.)

For some reason (to be explored, but not resolved, in this

essay), we are powerfully drawn to the subject of beginnings. We yearn to know about origins, and we readily construct myths when we do not have data (or we suppress data in favor of legend when a truth strikes us as too commonplace). The hankering after an origin myth has always been especially strong for the closest subject of all—the human race. But we extend the same psychic need to our accomplishments and institutions—and we have devised origin myths and stories for the beginning of hunting, of language, of art, of kindness, of war, of boxing, bowties, and brassieres. Most of us know that the Great Seal of the United States pictures an eagle holding a ribbon reading *e pluribus unum*. Fewer would recognize the motto on the other side (check it out on the back of a dollar bill): *annuit coeptis*—"he smiles on our beginnings."

Cooperstown may house the Cardiff Giant, but the fame of this small village in central New York does not rest on its celebrated namesake, author James Fenimore, or its lovely Lake Otsego or the Farmer's Museum. Cooperstown is "on the map" by virtue of a different origin myth—one more parochial, but no less power-ful, for many Americans, than the tales of human beginnings that gave life to the Cardiff Giant. Cooperstown is the sacred founding place in the official myth about the origin of baseball.

Origin myths, since they are so powerful, can engender enor-mous practical problems. Abner Doubleday, as we shall soon see, most emphatically did not invent baseball at Cooperstown in 1839 as the official tale proclaims; in fact, no one invented base-ball at any moment or in any spot. Nonetheless, this creation myth made Cooperstown the official home of baseball, and the Hall of Fame, with its associated museum and library, set its roots in this small village, inconveniently located near nothing in the way of airports or accommodations. We all revel in bucolic imagery on the field of dreams, but what a hassle when tens of thousands line the roads, restaurants, and port-a-potties during the annual Hall of Fame weekend, when new members are enshrined and two major league teams arrive to play an exhibition game at Abner Doubleday Field, a sweet little ten-thousand-seater in the middle of town. Put your compass at Cooperstown, make your radius at Albany—and you'd better reserve a year in advance if you want any accommodation within the enormous resulting circle.

After a lifetime of curiosity, I finally got the opportunity to witness this annual version of forty students in a telephone booth or twenty circus clowns in a Volkswagen. Since Yaz (former Boston star Carl Yastrzemski) was slated to receive baseball's Nobel in 1989, and his old team was playing in the Hall of Fame game, and since I'm a transplanted Bostonian, Tom Heitz, chief of the wonderful baseball library at the Hall of Fame, kindly invited me to join the sardines in this most lovely of all cans.

The silliest and most tendentious of baseball writing tries to wrest profundity from the spectacle of grown men hitting a ball with a stick by suggesting linkages between the sport and deep issues of morality, parenthood, history, lost innocence, gentleness, and so on, seemingly ad infinitum. (The effort reeks of silliness because baseball is profound all by itself and needs no excuses; people who don't know this are not fans and are therefore unreachable anyway.) When people ask me how baseball imitates life, I can only respond with what the more genteel newspapers used to call a "barnyard epithet," but now, with growing bravery, usually render as "bullbleep." Nonetheless, baseball is a major item of our culture, and it does have a long and interesting history. Any item or institution with these two properties must generate a set of myths and stories (perhaps even some truths) about its beginnings. And the subject of beginnings is the bread and butter of this column on evolution in the broadest sense. I shall make no woolly analogies between baseball and life; this is an essay on the origins of baseball, with some musings on why beginnings of all sorts hold such fascination for us. (I thank Tom Heitz not only for the invitation to Cooperstown at its yearly

acme but also for drawing the contrast between creation and evolution stories of baseball, and for supplying much useful information from his unparalleled storehouse.)

Stories about beginnings come in only two basic modes. An
entity either has an explicit point of origin, a specific time and
place of creation, or else it evolves and has no definable moment
of entry into the world. Baseball provides an interesting example
of this contrast because we know the answer and can judge
received wisdom by the two chief criteria, often opposed, of exter-
nal fact and internal hope. Baseball evolved from a plethora of previous stick-and-ball games. It has no true Cooperstown and no
Doubleday. Yet we seem to prefer the alternative model of origin
at a moment of creation—for then we can have heroes and sacred
places. By contrasting the myth of Cooperstown with the fact of
evolution, we can learn something about our cultural practices
and their frequent disrespect for truth.

The official story about the beginning of baseball is a creation
myth, and a review of the reasons and circumstances of its fabri-
cation may give us insight into the cultural appeal of stories in
this mode. A. G. Spalding, baseball's first great pitcher during his
early career, later founded the sporting goods company that still
bears his name and became one of the great commercial moguls
of America's gilded age. As publisher of the annual *Spalding's Official Base Ball Guide*, he held maximal power in shaping both public and institutional opinion on all facets of baseball and its
history. As the sport grew in popularity, and the pattern of two
stable major leagues coalesced early in our century, Spalding and
others felt the need for clarification (or merely for codification) of
opinion on the hitherto unrecorded origins of an activity that
truly merited its common designation as America's "national pastime."

In 1907, Spalding set up a blue ribbon committee to investigate
and resolve the origins of baseball. The committee, chaired by
A. G. Mills and including several prominent businessmen and two

senators who had also served as presidents of the National League, took much testimony but found no smoking gun for a beginning. Then, in July 1907, Spalding himself transmitted to the committee a letter from Abner Graves, then a mining engineer in Denver, who reported that Abner Doubleday had, in 1839, interrupted a marbles game behind the tailor's shop in Cooperstown, New York, to draw a diagram of a baseball field, explain the rules of the game, and designate the activity by its modern name of "base ball" (then spelled as two words).

Such "evidence" scarcely inspired universal confidence, but the commission came up with nothing better—and the Doubleday myth, as we shall soon see, was eminently functional. Therefore, in 1908, the Mills Commission reported its two chief findings: first, "that base ball had its origins in the United States"; and second, "that the first scheme for playing it, according to the best evidence available to date, was devised by Abner Doubleday, at Cooperstown, New York, in 1839." This "best evidence" consisted only of "a circumstantial statement by a reputable gentleman"— namely Graves's testimony as reported by Spalding himself.

When cited evidence remains so laughably insufficient, one must seek motivations other than concern for the truth value. The key to underlying reasons stands in the first conclusion of Mills's committee: hoopla and patriotism (cardboard version) decreed that a national pastime must have an indigenous origin. The idea that baseball had evolved from a wide variety of English stick-and-ball games—although true—did not suit the mythology of a phenomenon that had become so quintessentially American. In fact, Spalding had long been arguing, in an amiable fashion, with Henry Chadwick, another pioneer and entrepreneur of baseball's early years. Chadwick, born in England, had insisted for years that baseball had developed from the British stick-and-ball game called "rounders"; Spalding had vociferously advocated a purely American origin, citing the colonial game of "one old cat" as a distant precursor, but holding that baseball itself represented something

so new and advanced that a pinpoint of origin—a creation myth—
must be sought.

Chadwick considered the matter of no particular importance,
arguing (with eminent justice) that an English origin did not
"detract one iota from the merit of its now being unquestionably
a thoroughly American field sport, and a game too, which is fully
adapted to the American character." (I must say that I have grown
quite fond of Mr. Chadwick, who certainly understood evolutionary change and its chief principle that historical origin need not
match contemporary function.) Chadwick also viewed the committee's whitewash as a victory for his side. He labeled the Mills
report as "a masterful piece of special pleading which lets my dear
old friend Albert [Spalding] escape a bad defeat. The whole matter was a joke between Albert and myself."

We may accept the psychic need for an indigenous creation
myth, but why Abner Doubleday, a man with no recorded tie to
the game and who, in the words of Donald Honig, probably
"didn't know a baseball from a kumquat"? I had wondered about
this for years, but only ran into the answer serendipitously during
a visit to Fort Sumter in the harbor of Charleston, South Carolina.
There, an exhibit on the first skirmish of the Civil War points out
that Abner Doubleday, as captain of the Union artillery, had per-
sonally sighted and given orders for firing the first responsive vol-
ley following the initial Confederate attack on the fort. Doubleday
later commanded divisions at Antietam and Fredericksburg,
became at least a minor hero at Gettysburg, and retired as a brevet
major general. In fact, A. G. Mills, head of the commission, had
served as part of an honor guard when Doubleday's body lay in
state in New York City, following his death in 1893.

If one requires an American hero, could anyone be better than
the man who fired the first shot (in defense) of the Civil War?
Needless to say, this point was not lost on the members of Mills's
committee. Spalding, never one to mince words, wrote to the
committee when submitting Graves's dubious testimony: "It cer-

Abner Doubleday in 1865. *Credit: Corbis*

tainly appeals to an American pride to have had the great national
game of base ball created and named by a Major General in the
United States Army." Mills then concluded in his report: "Perhaps
in the years to come, in view of the hundreds of thousands of people who are devoted to base ball, and the millions who will be,
Abner Doubleday's fame will rest evenly, if not quite as much,
upon the fact that he was an inventor . . . as upon his brilliant and
distinguished career as an officer in the Federal Army."

And so, spurred by a patently false creation myth, the Hall of
Fame stands in the most incongruous and inappropriate locale of
a charming little town in central New York. Incongruous and
inappropriate, but somehow wonderful. Who needs another
museum in the cultural maelstroms (and summer doldrums) of
New York, Boston, or Washington? Why not a major museum in
a beautiful and bucolic setting? And what could be more fitting
than the spatial conjunction of two great American origin

myths—the Cardiff Giant and the Doubleday Fable? Thus, I too
am quite content to treat the myth gently, while honesty requires
'fessing up. The exhibit on Doubleday in the Hall of Fame
Museum sets just the right tone in its caption: "In the hearts of
those who love baseball, he is remembered as the lad in the pas-
ture where the game was invented. Only cynics would need to
know more." Only in the hearts; not in the minds.

Baseball evolved. Since the evidence is so clear (as epitomized
below), we must ask why these facts have been so little appreciated for so long, and why a creation myth like the Doubleday story
ever gained a foothold. Two major reasons have conspired: first,
the positive block of our attraction to creation stories; second, the
negative impediment of unfamiliar sources outside the usual
purview of historians. English stick-and-ball games of the nineteenth century can be roughly classified into two categories along
social lines. The upper and educated classes played cricket, and
the history of this sport has been copiously documented because
the literati write about their own interests, and because the activities of men in power are well recorded (and constitute virtually
all of history, in the schoolboy version). But the ordinary pastimes
of rural and urban working people can be well nigh invisible in
conventional sources of explicit commentary. Working people
played a different kind of stick-and-ball game, existing in various
forms and designated by many names, including "rounders" in
western England, "feeder" in London, and "base ball" in southern
England. For a large number of reasons, forming the essential difference between cricket and baseball, cricket matches can last up
to several days (a batsman, for example, need not run after he hits
the ball and need not expose himself to the possibility of being
put out every time he makes contact). The leisure time of working people does not come in such generous gobs, and the lower-
class stick-and-ball games could not run more than a few hours.

Several years ago, at the Victoria and Albert Museum in London, I learned an important lesson from an excellent exhibit on

the late-nineteenth-century history of the British music hall. This is my favorite period (Darwin's century, after all), and I consider myself tolerably well informed on cultural trends of the time. I can sing any line from any of the Gilbert and Sullivan operas (a largely middle-class entertainment), and I know the general drift of high cultural interests in literature and music. But here was a whole world of entertainment for millions, a world with its heroes, its stars, its top forty songs, its gaudy theaters—and I knew nothing, absolutely nothing, about it. I felt chagrined, but my ignorance had an explanation beyond personal insensitivity (and the exhibit had been mounted explicitly to counteract the selective invisibility of certain important trends in history). The music hall was the chief entertainment of Victorian working classes, and the history of working people is often invisible in conventional written sources. It must be rescued and reconstituted from different sorts of data; in this case, from posters, playbills, theater accounts, persistence of some songs in the oral tradition (most were never published as sheet music), recollections of old-timers who knew the person who knew the person. . . .

The early history of baseball—the stick-and-ball game of working people—presents the same problem of conventional invisibility, and the same promise of rescue by exploration of unusual sources. Work continues and intensifies as the history of sport becomes more and more academically respectable, but the broad outlines (and much fascinating detail) are now well established. As the upper classes played a codified and well-documented cricket, working people played a largely unrecorded and much more diversified set of stick-and-ball games ancestral to baseball. Many sources, including primers and boys' manuals, depict games recognizable as precursors to baseball well into the early eighteenth century. Occasional references even spill over into high culture. In *Northanger Abbey*, written at the close of the eighteenth century, Jane Austen remarks: "It was not very wonderful that Catherine . . . should prefer cricket, base ball, riding on horseback,

and running about the country, at the age of fourteen, to books."
As this quotation illustrates, the name of the game is no more
Doubleday's than the form of play.

These ancestral styles of baseball came to America with early
settlers and were clearly well established by colonial times. But
they were driven ever further underground by Puritan proscrip-
tions of sport for adults. They survived largely as children's games
and suffered the double invisibility of location among the poor
and the young. But two major reasons brought these games into
wider repute and led to a codification of standard forms quite
close to modern baseball between the 1820s and the 1850s. First,
a set of social reasons, from the decline of Puritanism to increased
concern about health and hygiene in crowded cities, made sport
an acceptable activity for adults. Second, middle-class and professional people began to take up these early forms of baseball, and
with this upward social drift came teams, leagues, written rules,
uniforms, stadiums, guidebooks: in short, all the paraphernalia of
conventional history.

I am not arguing that these early games could be called baseball with a few trivial differences (evolution means substantial
change, after all), but only that they stand in a complex lineage,
better called a nexus, from which modern baseball emerged, eventually in a codified and canonical form. In those days before
instant communication, every region had its own version, just as
every set of outdoor steps in New York City generated a different
form of stoopball in my youth, without threatening the basic
identity of the game. These games, most commonly called town
ball, differed from modern baseball in substantial ways. In the
Massachusetts Game, a codification of the late 1850s drawn up by
ballplayers in New England towns, four bases and three strikes
identify the genus, but many specifics are strange by modern standards. The bases were made of wooden stakes projecting four feet
from the ground. The batter (called the striker) stood between
first and fourth base. Sides changed after a single out. One hun-

dred runs (called tallies), not a higher score after a specified number of innings, spelled victory. The field contained no foul lines, and balls hit in any direction were in play. Most importantly, runners were not tagged out but were retired by "plugging," that is, being hit with a thrown ball while running between bases. Consequently, since baseball has never been a game for masochists, balls were soft—little more than rags stuffed into leather covers—and could not be hit far. (Tom Heitz had put together a team of Cooperstown worthies to re-create town ball for interested parties and prospective opponents. Since few other groups are well schooled in this lost art, Tom's team hasn't been defeated in ages, if ever. "We are the New York Yankees of town ball," he told me. His team is called, quite appropriately in general but especially for this essay, the Cardiff Giants.)

Evolution is continual change, but not insensibly gradual transition; in any continuum some points are always more interesting than others. The conventional nomination for the most salient point in this particular continuum goes to Alexander Joy Cartwright, leader of a New York team that started to play in Lower Manhattan, eventually rented some changing rooms and a field in Hoboken (just a quick ferry ride across the Hudson), and finally drew up a set of rules in 1845, later known as the New York Game. Cartwright's version of town ball is much closer to modern baseball, and many clubs followed his rules—for standardization became ever more vital as the popularity of modern baseball grew and opportunity for play between regions increased. In particular, Cartwright introduced two key innovations that shaped the disparate forms of town ball into a semblance of modern baseball. First, he eliminated plugging and introduced tagging in the modern sense; the ball could now be made harder, and hitting for distance became an option. Second, he introduced foul lines, again in the modern sense as his batter stood at a home plate and had to hit the ball within the lines defined from home through first and third bases. The game could now become a spectator sport because areas close to the field but out of action could, for the first time, be set aside for onlookers.

The New York Game may be the highlight of a continuum, but it provides no origin myth for baseball. Cartwright's rules were followed in various forms of town ball. His New York Game still included many curiosities by modern standards (twenty-one runs, called aces, won the game, and balls caught on one bounce were outs). Moreover, our modern version is an amalgam of the New York Game plus other town ball traditions, not Cartwright's baby grown up by itself. Several features of the Massachusetts Game entered the modern version in preference to Cartwright's rules. Balls had to be caught on the fly in Boston, and pitchers threw overhand, not underhand as in the New York Game (and in professional baseball until the 1880s).

Scientists often lament that so few people understand Darwin and the principles of biological evolution. But the problem goes deeper. Too few people are comfortable with evolutionary modes of explanation in any form. I do not know why we tend to think so fuzzily in this area, but one reason must reside in our social and psychic attraction to creation myths in preference to evolutionary stories—for creation myths, as noted before, identify heroes and sacred places, while evolutionary stories provide no palpable, particular thing as a symbol for reverence, worship, or patriotism. Still, we must remember—and an intellectual's most persistent and nagging responsibility lies in making this simple point over and over again, however noxious and bothersome we render ourselves thereby—that truth and desire, fact and comfort, have no necessary, or even preferred, correlation (so rejoice when they do coincide).

To state the most obvious example in our current political turmoil: human growth is a continuum, and no creation myth can define an instant for the origin of an individual life. Attempts by antiabortionists to designate the moment of fertilization as the beginning of personhood makes no sense in scientific terms (and also violate a long history of social definitions that traditionally focused on the quickening, or detected movement, of the fetus in the womb). I will admit—indeed, I emphasized as a key argument in this essay—that not all points on a continuum are equal. Fertilization is a more interesting moment than most, but it no more provides a clean definition of origin than the most interesting moment of baseball's continuum—Cartwright's codification of the New York Game—defines the beginning of our national pastime. Baseball evolved and people grow; both are continua without definable points of origin. Probe too far back and you reach absurdity, for you will see Nolan Ryan on the hill when the first ape hit a bird with a stone; or you will define both masturbation and menstruation as murder—and who will then cast the first stone? Look for something in the middle, and you find nothing but continuity—always a meaningful "before," and always a more modern "after." (Please note that I am not stating an opinion on the vexatious question of abortion—an ethical issue that can only be decided in ethical terms. I only point out that one side has rooted its case in an argument from science that is not only entirely irrelevant to the proper realm of resolution but also happens to be flat-out false in trying to devise a creation myth within a continuum.)

And besides, why do we prefer creation myths to evolutionary stories? I find all the usual reasons hollow. Yes, we may need heroes and shrines, but is there not grandeur in the sweep of continuity? Shall we revel in a story for all humanity that may include the sacred ball courts of the Aztecs, and perhaps, for all we know, a group of *Homo erectus* hitting rocks or skulls with a stick or femur? Or shall we halt beside the mythical Abner Doubleday, standing behind the tailor's shop in Cooperstown, and say "behold the man"—thereby violating truth and, perhaps even worse, extinguishing both thought and wonder?

The Brain of Brawn

I can only beg indulgence for opening a sporting commentary with the most venerable of professorial conceits: a quotation from the classics. Nearly twenty-five hundred years ago, long before Mr. Doubleday didn't invent baseball in 1839, Protagoras characterized our lamentable tendency to portray all complex issues as stark dichotomies of us against them: "There are two sides to every question, exactly opposite to each other."

Often, we highlight these caricatures by pairing the poles of our dichotomies in rhyme or alliteration as well—as in nature vs. nurture for the origin of our behaviors, or brain vs. brawn for the sources of manly success. Strength for the warrior and the athlete; smarts for the scholar and the tycoon.

Discerning sports fans do not carry this dichotomy to the extreme of regarding their athletic heroes as pervasively deficient in mind—as if God gave each person just so much "oomph," thus requiring that an ounce of intellect be rendered back for each ounce of muscle added on. Rather, we tend to characterize the mental skill of athletes as an intuitive grasp of bodily movement

First published in the *New York Times*, June 25, 2000. Reprinted with permission of the *New York Times*.

and position, a "physical intelligence," if you will. Thus, we do recognize a mental component in DiMaggio's grace, in the beautiful and devastatingly effective motions of Michael Jordan or Muhammad Ali, and even in the sheer force of Shaq pushing through to the basket. (Perhaps no one can stop three hundred pounds of acceleration, but the big man still has to know where he should end up.)

This fallacious belief in the intuitive and physical nature of athletic mentality may best be summarized in the common sports term for a player on a roll of successive triumphs at bat or basket: "He's unconscious!"

On the other side of the same misconception, we often blame the intrusion of unwanted consciousness when a fine player, after many years of professional success, encounters a glitch in performing the ordinary operations of his trade. Thus, when Chuck Knoblauch "freezes," and suddenly cannot execute the conventional flip from second to first base, we say that his conscious brain has intruded upon a bodily skill that must be honed by practice into a purely automatic and virtually infallible reflex.

I do not regard this conventional view as entirely wrong, but I do think that, for two major reasons, we seriously undervalue the mental side of athletic achievement when we equate the intellectual aspect of sports with unverbalizable bodily intuition and regard anything overtly conscious as "in the way."

First, one of the most intriguing, and undeniable, properties of great athletic performance lies in the impossibility of regulating certain central skills by overt mental deliberation: the required action simply doesn't grant sufficient time for the sequential processing of conscious decisions. The defining paradox, and delicious fascination, of hitting a baseball lies most clearly within this category.

Batters just don't have enough time to judge a pitch from its initial motion and then to decide whether and how to swing. Batters must "guess," from the depths of their study and experience, before a pitcher launches his offering; and a bad conjecture can make even the greatest hitters look awfully foolish, as when Pedro Martinez throws his change-up with the exact same arm motion as his fastball, and the batter, guessing heat, has already completed his swing before the ball ever lollygags across the plate.

Indeed, such mental operations cannot proceed consciously and sequentially. But these skills do not therefore become a lesser form of intellect confined to the bodily achievements of athletes. Many of the most abstract and apparently mathematical feats of mind fall into the same puzzling category.

For example, several of history's greatest mental calculators have been able to specify the algorithms, or rules of calculation, that they claim to use in performing effectively instantaneous feats, like specifying the day of the week for any date in any year, no matter how many centuries past or future. But extensive studies show that these calculators work too quickly to achieve their results by any form of conscious and sequential figuring.

Second, the claim that Knoblauch's distress arises from the imposition of brain upon feeling (or mind upon matter) represents the worst, and most philistine, of mischaracterizations. Yes, one form of unwanted, conscious mentality may be intruding upon a different and required style of unconscious cognition. But we encounter mentality in either case, not body against mind. Knoblauch's problem takes the same form as many excruciating impediments in purely mental enterprises with writer's block as the most obvious example, when obsession with learned rules of style and grammar impedes the flow of good prose. And we surely cannot designate our unblocked mode as less intellectual merely because we cannot easily describe its delights or procedures.

I don't deny the differences in style and substance between athletic and conventional scholarly performance, but we surely err in regarding sports as a domain of brutish intuition (dignified, at

Yankee Chuck Knoblauch, in happier times, hits a home run in game three of the 1999 World Series against the Atlanta Braves. In the 2000 World Series against the Mets, Knoblauch would bat 1 for 10 as the designated hitter but would not play a single inning at second base. *Credit: Reuters New-Media Inc./Corbis*

best, with some politically correct euphemism like "bodily intelligence") and literature as the rarefied realm of our highest mental acuity. The greatest athletes cannot succeed by bodily gifts alone. They must also perform with their heads, and they study, obsess, rage against their limitations, and practice and perfect with the same dedication and commitment that all good scholars apply to their Shakespeare.

Mark McGwire, endlessly studying the videos of every pitch for every pitcher he will ever face, surely matches a careful scholar's checking every last footnote for his monograph of a lifetime.

McGwire's mental skill may be harder to verbalize, but not because athletes are stupid or intrinsically less articulate than writers. Rather, this style of unconscious mentality gropes for verbal description in all domains of its operation. In my admittedly limited personal experience, I have found great performers of classical music even less able than ballplayers to articulate the bases for their success.

And so, to Chuck Knoblauch, a truly fine ballplayer, we can only say: This too will pass. I look forward to seeing you at the stadium on a cool day in late October. Top of the ninth, two outs, game seven of the World Series. Some National League victim hits a grounder to second, and you flip the ball deftly to first for the final out. Yanks win the Series, four games to three. And, following the conventions for scoring plays in baseball, this last out goes down in history with the code for a second baseman's assist followed by a first baseman's putout—4–3.

Baseball's Reliquary: The Oddly Possible Hybrid of Shrine and University

B aseball did not win its central place in America's heart and culture because the sport, in a silliness of common parlance, "imitates life" or stands as a symbol for larger truths and trends of human existence. Rather, baseball became America's defining sport for the far more ordinary and concrete reasons of simple persistence and pervasiveness. One would have to inhabit a particularly tall ivory tower, or a particularly deep cave, to deny the status of sport as a central institution of human culture.

Baseball, as the codified form of a large variety of basically similar stick-and-ball games, has, like the poor, always been with us. Teams, leagues, and various lists of "official" rules had coalesced by the mid-nineteenth century, but Jane Austen refers to something called "base ball" in her 1797 novel *Northanger Abbey*, and various contests based on hitting a ball with a stick and scoring by running around bases came to America in the early days of European colonization, and then grew, diversified, and coalesced as the nation expanded and knit together.

Reprinted with permission from *Natural History* (March 2002). Copyright the American Museum of Natural History (2002).

One might assume, given the current popularity of football and basketball among Americans of all social classes, that these sports, rather than baseball, should carry (or at least share) the status of "national pastime." But these games are neophytes in popular acclaim, as anyone of my generation will remember. They do boast a reasonably long following, but mainly as college sports. During my childhood, professional basketball and football were distinctly minor enterprises with short seasons and limited followings. Baseball, however, known to every sentient fan, and played with enthusiasm by farmers, street urchins, and swells (or whatever prosperous young men have been called at various times), has been keeping us together from our beginnings.

If I may offer just one person's testimony, I am enmeshed in four generations of serious rooting. My immigrant grandfather acclimatized to America by watching Jack Chesbro win forty-one games for the New York Highlanders in 1904. My father regaled me with tales of Ruth and Gehrig, the ultimate secular gods of his world. I have been a passionate Yankee fan from the tears of joy at age eight for victory over the Brooklyn Dodgers in the 1949 World Series to bitter tears in November 2001 at a gruesomely painful ending in Phoenix—that is, from DiMaggio to Jeter. My son, a native of Boston, has switched to the Red Sox; he rises by the bashed dreams and plunges into the despairs of that particularly painful form of rooting. (I was especially touched when he interviewed me last year for a paper in his college sociology course on baseball as a mode of bonding between fathers and sons—though daughters will now be commonly included as well—especially in past generations when fathers, culturally restrained to far greater emotional distance, could use this opportunity for forging ties otherwise hard to establish.)

Baseball's status as both a secular religion and an embodiment of important themes in American history imposes a common, yet paradoxical, problem for any exhibit dedicated to conveying the essence and vitality of the enterprise. How can a museum display two apparently different, even contradictory, aspects of a single subject at the same time, especially when both embody primary responsibilities of museums in general: the role of the reliquary (reverent displays of sacred objects, whose importance lies in their very being), and the role of the teacher (instructive display of informative objects, whose importance lies in their ability to inspire questions)? How can the awe of reverence mix with the skepticism of learning?

In my observations, only two museums have ever managed to solve this common dilemma in a consistent, even triumphant way: the Ellis Island Immigration Museum (where I can pay homage to my grandfather's courage, as embodied in full walls devoted to respectful display of such humble but noble items as battered traveling bags and lockets of loved ones left behind, and also study the history of American immigration in any desired degree of detail) and the National Baseball Hall of Fame and Museum in Cooperstown, New York (where I can immerse myself among the actual relics of our primary secular religion and also trace nearly any desired detail or generality about the history of baseball and its linkages to American life).

The wonderful selection from Cooperstown, on temporary display at the American Museum of Natural History starting this month, epitomizes this duality to near perfection and therefore gives us a lesson in how to hybridize these two greatest potential excellences of museums, despite their apparently irreconcilable disparity. In other (and more specific) words, we can learn a ton about baseball, while feeling both the spine shivers of contact with "holy" items and the touch of *genius loci*, the magic of real and special places.

To cash out my claims by examples on display, consider just five categories where the object as both relic and item for instruction forges potential synergy rather than frustrating contradiction:

1. *The embodiment of mythology*. As a supreme irony, the Cooperstown museum, as argued above, has covered itself in deserved

glory, but still occupies an utterly inappropriate turf for the weird-est of perfectly reasonable circumstances—the very antithesis of *genius loci*. I say this not primarily for the practical reason that this tiny and isolated town in central New York State cannot find enough hotel rooms within fifty miles to house the crowds of peo-ple wishing to attend the annual induction ceremonies for the Hall of Fame, but simply because Cooperstown can stake no legit-imate claim as a shrine for baseball. As argued above, baseball experienced no eureka of origin, but just grew, evolved, and even-tually coagulated from a host of precursors. But humans need ori-gin myths, so when baseball became enshrined as a national pastime, an official commission, established early in the twenti-eth century, was charged with the task of discovering baseball's origins. For a set of complex reasons, the members of the com-mission allowed themselves to be persuaded that Abner Double-day had effectively invented the game in Cooperstown in 1839. No even remotely plausible evidence links Doubleday to baseball. But Doubleday was certainly a sufficiently adequate American hero to embody an origin myth, for he had fired the first Union shots of the Civil War, as artillery officer at Fort Sumter, and he later served as one of the generals at Gettysburg.

In any case, myths require relics, so you may see on display the famous Doubleday ball—submitted as corroboration for the founding legend, perhaps discovered in Cooperstown, probably a bit younger than 1839, and surely possessing no plausible tie to Mr. Doubleday himself. I have also been told that enough nails from the true cross exist in European cathedral reliquaries to affix a hundred of Spartacus's soldiers to their crosses on the Appian Way. Thank God that the human mind can embrace contradiction by acknowledging reality in the head yet respectfully allowing an imposter to stand for a symbol in the heart. (In a funny and recur-sive sense, moreover, once frauds achieve sufficient fame, they become legitimate objects of history in their own right!)

2. *Relics and icons*. If a reliquary really preserved a nail of the

true cross, any Christian (I am not one) would bow in reverent awe, and any decent person (as I am) would stand respectfully before such an important item of history and symbol of human cruelty and hope. Well, this exhibit includes many true relics of a secular church that admittedly cannot claim similar importance but does mean one helluva lot to many quite sane and even reasonably perceptive people. Hey folks, I mean you're really going to see the Babe's bat from 1927 (the year he hit those sixty dingers for an "unbeatable" record), Roger Maris's bat from 1961 when he broke the record, and Mark McGwire's bat from when the record fell again in 1998. And because failure can be as sublime as hope (the raised Lazarus versus that nail of the true cross, although I know that Christian theology does not regard the Crucifixion as a dud), you will also see Michael Jordan's bat from the year he tried baseball, discovered that he really couldn't hit a curve ball despite being the world's greatest athlete, batted about .225 in a year of minor league play, but stayed the course (and played the full season) with honor.

3. *Records of sacred events.* Churches and shrines not only boast general heroes, they also feature parables and stories of canonical import. Baseball revels in poignant, heroic, and defining stories by the dozen, and many items in this exhibition embody such crucial moments. But just as you need a scorecard to tell the players (an adage with baseball origins), so too do you need a tale to explain each of these items. So let me tell you just two stories of ultimate pain from two generations of Yankee worship in my family. (I suspect that cleansing drafts of pain match ecstatic quaffs of joy in any religion.) First, the 1926 World Series ring of Grover Cleveland Alexander. So what? Well (and you can see the scene yourself in an old film, with none other than Ronald Reagan playing the inebriated pitcher), here's the setting: October 10, the deciding seventh game of the World Series, Cardinals against Yankees. The Yanks, just slightly behind in the score, load the bases in the seventh, and the Cardinals' manager brings in his aged hero, the

dipsomaniacal Alexander, who had pitched a full game (and won) the day before and then got stinking drunk, never expecting a call for the final contest. Tony Lazzeri at the plate, and my dad (age eleven) at the radio. Lazzeri hits one headed for the seats, a homer, and a Yankee victory, but the ball goes foul by a few feet. Alexander then strikes Lazzeri out and later wins the game. My father thought he would never again be happy but recovered two days later. Second, a ball used by Johnny Podres in the 1955 World Series. Well, I was walking home from school with my friend (and Dodger fan) Steve Cole, listening to the seventh and last game of the World Series. Podres won for the Dodgers, the only time (in their Brooklyn incarnation) that the Bums ever beat the Yanks in the World Series. I'm not sure that I've ever been truly happy since then. But wiser—and that's more important, I suppose.

4. *Linkage to general culture.* Religion wouldn't do much for us as a sanitized shrine, fully divorced from the spaces and realities of surrounding life. And as I noted to open this piece, baseball does not stand for America because the sport imitates life in some metaphorical way; rather, baseball illustrates nearly all aspects of America because the institution has been so central and important in our life and culture (and also because the basic rules of play have not changed for more than a century, so we can truly understand and feel the import of old happenings). Consider just two cardinal (if tragic) realities of our lives. First, war. The exhibition includes the most famous icon of all, the ultimate sign of baseball's importance to the fabric of America: President Franklin D. Roosevelt's 1942 letter to the baseball commissioner, urging that play continue during World War II so that symbols of normalcy might boost our morale. For other items, one needs a bit more explanation. I love the pairing of Moe Berg's ID Card for the Office of Strategic Services with Bob Feller's military goggles, both from World War II. Berg, baseball's great raconteur and quite mediocre catcher, always claimed that he spoke at least half a dozen languages and had worked as a spy, tracking Werner

Heisenberg and the German nuclear program during the war. His tales were widely disbelieved, but several recent studies have confirmed the basic story after all. Feller, the fastest pitcher of his generation, a rootin' tootin' midwestern conservative and a fighting man from day one, was a genuine military hero—never doubted for a moment, always honored, and God bless. Another item needs no explanation for its searing into recent memory: a baseball found in the rubble of the World Trade Center.

Second, the sad history of racism, where baseball has ever so much to answer for but finally responded well, albeit so belatedly. Again, humble items, easily bypassed, tell deep tales once one knows the context. Consider, for example, the baseball cards for Pumpsie Green and Larry Doby: Green, a utility infielder of no special merit as a player, wins his poignant role in this sad history as the first black player on the last team to integrate—shameful to say, the Boston Red Sox, from New England's bastion of liberty. Doby, a truly great player for the Cleveland Indians, has never received his proper due because he came second, and our culture remembers only front-runners: Jackie Robinson, as everyone knows, integrated baseball with the Brooklyn Dodgers of the National League in 1947; Doby entered just after Robinson, as the first black player in the American League.

5. *Social spreadings and meanings*. Baseball has become so enmeshed within our general culture that I can only feel sorry for Europeans who, in watching American movies, have to be mystified by the young stud's lament, "I didn't even get to first base with her," or who cannot appreciate the poignancy of a great moment in the history of tear-jerkery—when Gary Cooper, playing Lou Gehrig in *The Pride of the Yankees*, asks a physician who has just diagnosed the fatal illness that now officially bears his name, "Doc, is this strike three?"

Yes, you can use baseball to understand general culture. But the process can also work in the less-appreciated reverse direction by citing cultural norms to understand baseball's peculiarities. To choose two examples, both auditory rather than visual this time: Everyone knows the ritual of singing "Take Me Out to the Ball-game" during the seventh-inning stretch, but where did this ditty—second in inanity and frequency only to "Happy Birthday" as an American universal—come from? The piece sounds like a pop song from the Gay Nineties or the early twentieth century—an entirely correct inference, by the way. But, as the Edison cylinder in the Museum's exhibition shows, the words that we know and sing comprise only the chorus for a standard pop tune that has several verses as well. And the verses record the pleas of a young woman trying to convince her boyfriend to "take me out . . ."!

As a second example, I could never understand why such abominable and silly doggerel as "Casey at the Bat" ever became the canonical poem of both American baseball and the normalcy of failure in general. That is, until I *heard* the poem in an ancient film of a vaudeville performer (as the Victor disc in this exhibition illustrates). Then I understood. The poem was written to be declaimed, not to be read silently. Declamation of poetry in the nineteenth century represented a standard social recreation in American life, a fixture of nearly every party, and the doggerel succeeds marvelously in this intended aural context.

Finally, if we need any more proof for the vitality of baseball, and the power of *genius loci*, just stare in reverence at the center-piece of this exhibition: a pile of dirt from Ebbets Field, home of the Brooklyn Dodgers (and the greatest ballpark I ever knew—an admission, remember, that comes from a Yankee fan!). I mean, folks, it's just a pile of dirt. And dirt is dirt. Yeah, and nails are nails. But a nail from the true cross and dirt from Ebbets Field— need I say more? We cannot dedicate, we cannot consecrate, we cannot hallow such ground. Robbie did, and Campy, and Duke, and PeeWee, and also the Preacher—and what poor power do we have to add or detract? So of course I don't care if I ever get back,

Brooklyn's Ebbetts Field in 1956. *Credit: Bettmann/Corbis*

because I'm there already, and there's no other place to go. Truly we are all in this particular game together; and if we play our collective cards right (after all, my family's going on four generations and still counting), we may ward off strike three for the evolutionary equivalent of forever.

Jim Bowie's Letter and
Bill Buckner's Legs

Charlie Croker, former football hero of Georgia Tech and recently bankrupted builder of the new Atlanta—a world of schlock and soulless office towers, now largely unoccupied and hemorrhaging money—seeks inspiration, as his world disintegrates, from the one item of culture that stirs his limited inner self: a painting, originally done to illustrate a children's book ("the only book Charlie could remember his father and mother ever possessing") by N. C. Wyeth of "Jim Bowie rising up from his deathbed to fight the Mexicans at the Alamo." On "one of the happiest days of his entire life," Charlie spent $190,000 at a Sotheby's auction to buy this archetypal scene for a man of action. He then mounted his treasure in the ultimate shrine for successful men of our age—above the ornate desk on his private jet.

Tom Wolfe describes how his prototype for redneck moguls (in his novel *A Man in Full*) draws strength from his inspirational painting:

From *I Have Landed* by Stephen Jay Gould, copyright © 2002 by Turbo, Inc. Used by permission of Harmony Books, a division of Random House, Inc.

And so now, as the aircraft roared and strained to gain alti-
tude, Charlie concentrated on the painting of Jim Bowie
. . . as he had so many times before. . . . Bowie, who was
already dying, lay on a bed. . . . He had propped himself up
on one elbow. With his other hand he was brandishing his
famous Bowie knife at a bunch of Mexican soldiers. . . . It
was the way Bowie's big neck and his jaws jutted out
towards the Mexicans and the way his eyes blazed defiant
to the end, that made it a great painting. Never say die,
even when you're dying, was what that painting said. . . .
He stared at the indomitable Bowie and waited for an infu-
sion of courage.

Nations need heroes, and Jim Bowie did die in action at the
Alamo, along with Davy Crockett and about 180 fighters for Texian independence (using the "i" then included in the name),
under the command of William B. Travis, an articulate twenty-six-
year-old lawyer with a lust for martyrdom combined with a fear-
lessness that should not be disparaged, whatever one may think
of his judgment. In fact, I have no desire to question Bowie's legitimate status as a hero at the Alamo at all. But I do wish to explicate his virtues by debunking the legend portrayed in Charlie
Croker's painting, and by suggesting that our admiration should
flow for quite different reasons that have never been hidden, but
that the legend leads us to disregard.

The debunking of canonical legends ranks as a favorite intellectual sport for all the usual and ever-so-human reasons of one-
upmanship, aggressivity within a community that denies itself the
old-fashioned expression of genuine fisticuffs, and the simple
pleasure of getting details right. But such debunking also serves a
vital scholarly purpose at the highest level of identifying and correcting some of the most serious pitfalls in human reasoning. I
make this somewhat grandiose claim for the following reason:

The vertebrate brain works primarily as a device tuned to the recognition of patterns. When evolution grafted consciousness in human form upon this organ in a single species, the old inherent search for patterns developed into a propensity for organizing these patterns as stories, and then for explaining the surrounding world in terms of the narratives expressed in these tales. For universal reasons that probably transcend the cultural particulars of individual groups, humans tend to construct their stories along a limited number of themes and pathways, favored because they grant both useful sense and satisfying meaning to the confusion (and often to the tragedy) of life in our complex surrounding world.

Stories, in other words, only "go" in a limited number of strongly preferred ways, with the two deepest requirements invoking, first, a theme of directionality (linked events proceeding in an ordered sequence for definable reasons, and not as an aimless wandering—back, forth, and sideways—to nowhere); and second, a sense of motivation, or definite reasons propelling the sequence (whether we judge the outcomes good or bad). These motivations will be rooted directly in human purposes for stories involving our own species. But tales about nonconscious creatures or inanimate objects must also provide a surrogate for valor (or dishonorable intent for dystopian tales)—as in the virtue of evolutionary principles that dictate the increasing general complexity of life, or the lamentable inexorability of thermodynamics in guaranteeing the eventual burnout and explosion of the sun. In summary, and at the risk of oversimplification, we like to explain pattern in terms of directionality, and causation in terms of valor. The two central and essential components of any narrative—pattern and cause—therefore fall under the biasing rubric of our mental preferences.

I will refer to the small set of primal tales based upon these deep requirements as "canonical stories." Our strong propensity for expressing all histories, be they human, organic, or cosmic, in terms of canonical stories would not entail such enormous prob-

lems for science—but might be viewed, instead, as simply humor-
ous in exposing the foibles of *Homo sapiens*—if two properties of
mind and matter didn't promote a potentially harmless idiosyncrasy into a pervasive bias actively derailing our hopes for understanding events that unfold in time. (The explanation of temporal
sequences defines the primary task of a large subset among our
scientific disciplines—the so-called historical sciences of geology,
anthropology, evolutionary biology, cosmology, and many others.
Thus, if the lure of "canonical stories" blights our general understanding of historical sequences, much of what we call "science"
labors under a mighty impediment.)

As for matter, many patterns and sequences in our complex
world owe their apparent order to the luck of the draw within random systems. We flip five heads in a row once every thirty-two
sequences on average. Stars clump into patterns in the sky
because they are distributed effectively at random (within con-
traints imposed by the general shape of our Milky Way galaxy)
with respect to the earth's position in space. An absolutely even
spacing of stars, yielding no perceivable clumps at all, would
require some fairly fancy, and obviously nonexistent, rules of
deterministic order. Thus, if our minds obey an almost irresistible
urge to detect patterns, and then to explain these patterns in the
causal terms of a few canonical stories, our quest to understand
the sources (often random) of order will be stymied.

As for mind, even when we can attribute a pattern to conventional nonrandom reasons, we often fail to apprehend both the
richness and the nature of these causes because the lure of canonical stories leads us to entertain only a small subset among legitimate hypotheses for explaining the recorded events. Even worse,
since we cannot observe everything in the blooming and buzzing
confusion of the world's surrounding richness, the organizing
power of canonical stories leads us to ignore important facts readily within our potential sight, and to twist or misread the information that we do manage to record. In other words, and to

summarize my principal theme in a phrase, canonical stories predictably "drive" facts into definite and distorted pathways that validate the outlines and necessary components of these archetypal tales. We therefore fail to note important items in plain sight, while we misread other facts by forcing them into preset mental channels, even when we retain a buried memory of actual events.

This essay illustrates how canonical stories have predictably relegated crucial information to misconstruction or invisibility in two great folk tales of American history: Bowie's letter and Buckner's legs, as oddly (if euphoniously) combined in my title. I will then extend the general message to argue that the allure of canonical stories acts as the greatest impediment to better understanding throughout the realm of historical science—one of the largest and most important domains of human intellectual activity.

Jim Bowie's Letter

How the canonical story of "all the brothers were valiant, and all the sisters virtuous," has hidden a vital document in plain sight. (This familiar quotation first appears on the tomb of the Duchess of Newcastle, who died in 1673 and now lies in Westminster Abbey.)

The Alamo of San Antonio, Texas, was not designed as a fortress, but as a mission built by eighteenth-century Spaniards. Today, the Alamo houses exhibits and artifacts, most recalling the death of all Texian defenders in General Santa Anna's assault, with a tenfold advantage in troops and after nearly two weeks of siege, on March 6, 1836. This defeat and martyrdom electrified the Texian cause, which triumphed less than two months later when Sam Houston's men captured Santa Anna at the Battle of San Jacinto on April 21, and then forced the Mexican general to barter Texas for his life, his liberty, and the return of his opium bottle.

The Alamo's exhibits, established and maintained by the

Daughters of the Republic of Texas, and therefore no doubt more partisan than the usual (and, to my mind, generally admirable) fare that the National Park Service provides in such venues, tells the traditional tale, as I shall do here. (Mexican sources, no doubt, purvey a different but equally traditional account from another perspective.) I shall focus on the relationship of Bowie and Travis, for my skepticism about the canonical story focuses on a fascinating letter, written by Bowie and prominently displayed in the Alamo, but strangely disregarded to the point of invisibility in the official presentation.

In December 1835, San Antonio had been captured by Texian forces in fierce fighting with Mexican troops under General Cos. On January 17, 1836, Sam Houston ordered Jim Bowie and some thirty men to enter San Antonio, destroy the Alamo, and withdraw the Texian forces to more defendable ground. But Bowie, after surveying the situation, disagreed for both strategic and symbolic reasons, and decided to fortify the Alamo instead. The arrival, on February 3, of thirty additional men under the command of William B. Travis strengthened Bowie's decision.

But tension inevitably developed between two such different leaders, the forty-year-old, hard-drinking, fearlessly independent, but eminently practical and experienced Bowie, and the twenty-six-year-old troubled and vainglorious Travis, who had left wife and fortune in Alabama to seek fame and adventure on the Texian frontier. (Mexico had encouraged settlement of the Texian wilderness by all who would work the land and swear allegiance to the liberal constitution of 1824, but the growing Anglo majority had risen in revolt, spurred by the usual contradictory motives of lust for control and love of freedom, as expressed in anger at Santa Anna's gradual abrogation of constitutional guarantees.)

Bowie commanded the volunteers, while Travis led the "official" army troops. A vote among the volunteers overwhelmingly favored Bowie's continued leadership, so the two men agreed upon an uneasy sharing of authority, with all orders to be signed by both. This arrangement became irrelevant, and Travis assumed full command, when Bowie fell ill with clearly terminal pneumonia and a slew of other ailments just after the siege began on February 23. In fact, Charlie Croker's painting notwithstanding, Bowie may have been comatose, or even already dead, when Mexican forces broke through on March 6. He may have made his legendary last "stand" (in supine position), propped up in his bed with pistols in hand, but he could not have mounted more than a symbolic final defense, and his legendary knife could not have reached past the Mexican bayonets in any case.

The canonical story of valor at the Alamo features two incidents, both centered upon Travis, with one admitted as legendary by all serious historians, and the other based upon a stirring letter, committed to memory by nearly all Texas schoolchildren ever since. As for the legend, when Travis realized that no reinforcements would arrive, and that all his men would surely die if they defended the Alamo by force of arms (for Santa Anna had clearly stated his terms of no mercy or sparing of life without unconditional surrender), he called a meeting, drew a line in the sand, and then invited all willing defenders of the Alamo to cross the line to his side, while permitting cowards and doubters to scale the wall and make their inglorious exit (as one man did). In this stirring legend, Jim Bowie, now too weak to stand, asks his men to carry his bed across the line.

Well, Travis may have made a speech at the relevant time, but no witness and survivor (several women and one slave) ever reported the story. (The tale apparently originated about forty years later, supposedly told by the single man who had accepted Travis's option to escape.)

As for the familiar letter, few can read Travis's missive with a dry eye, while even the most skeptical of Alamo historians heaps honor upon this document of February 24, carried by a courier (who broke through the Mexican lines) to potential reinforcements, but addressed to "The People of Texas and All Americans in the World." (For example, Ben H. Proctor describes Travis as "egotistical, proud, vain, with strong feelings about his own destiny, about glory and personal mission . . . trouble in every sense of the word," but judges this missive as "one of the truly remarkable letters of history, treasured by lovers of liberty everywhere." See Proctor's pamphlet, *The Battle of the Alamo* [Texas State Historical Association, 1986].)

> I am besieged, by a thousand or more of the Mexicans under Santa Anna—I have sustained a continual bombardment & cannonade for 24 hours & have not lost a man—The enemy has demanded a surrender at discretion, otherwise, the garrison are to be put to the sword, if the fort is taken—I have answered the demand with a cannon shot, & our flag still waves proudly from the walls—*I shall never surrender or retreat*. Then, I call on you in the name of Liberty, of patriotism & everything dear to the American character, to come to our aid, with all dispatch—The enemy is receiving reinforcements daily & will no doubt increase to three or four thousand in four or five days. If this call is neglected, I am determined to sustain myself as long as possible & die like a soldier who never forgets what is due to his own honor & and that of his country—
> VICTORY OR DEATH.

Although a small group of thirty men did arrive to reinforce the Alamo, their heroic presence as cannon and bayonet fodder could not alter the course of events, while a genuine force that could have made a difference, several hundred men stationed at nearby Goliad, never came to Travis's aid, for complex reasons still under intense historical debate. Every Texian fighter died in Santa Anna's attack on March 6. According to the usual legend, all the men fell in action. But substantial, if inconclusive, evidence indicates that six men may have surrendered at the hopeless end, only to be summarily executed by Santa Anna's direct order. The probable presence of Davy Crockett among this group accounts for the disturbing effect and emotional weight of this persistent tale.

As something of an Alamo buff, and a frequent visitor to the site in San Antonio, I have long been bothered and intrigued by a crucial document, a letter by the Alamo's other leader, Jim Bowie, that seems to provide quite a different perspective upon the siege, but doesn't fit within the canonical legend and hardly receives a mention in any official account at the shrine itself. Bowie's letter thus remains "hidden in plain sight"—sitting in its own prominent glass case, right in the main hall of the on-site exhibition. This curious feature of "prominently displayed but utterly passed over" has fascinated me for twenty years. I have, in three visits to the Alamo, bought every popular account of the battle for sale at the extensive gift shop. I have read these obsessively and can assert that Bowie's letter, while usually acknowledged, receives short shrift in most conventional descriptions.

Let us return to a phrase in Travis's celebrated letter and fill in some surrounding events: "the enemy has demanded a surrender . . . I have answered the demand with a cannon shot." The basic outline has not been disputed: When Santa Anna entered San Antonio with his army and began his siege on February 23, he unfurled a blood-red flag—the traditional demand for immediate surrender, with extermination as the consequence of refusal— from the tower of the Church of San Fernando. Travis, without consulting his co-commander, fired the Alamo's largest cannon, an eighteen-pounder, in defiant response—just as he boasted in his famous letter, written the next day.

The complexities that threaten the canonical story now intrude. Although Santa Anna had issued his uncompromising and blustering demand in a public display, many accounts, filled with different details but all pointing in the same credible direction, indicate that he also proposed a parley for negotiation with the Alamo defenders. (Even if Santa Anna didn't issue this call, the canonical story takes its strong hit just from the undisputed fact that Bowie, for whatever reason, thought the Mexicans had suggested a parley. Among the various versions, Santa Anna's forces also raised a white flag—the equally traditional signal for a parley—either accidentally or purposefully, and either before or after Travis's cannon shot; or else that a Mexican soldier sounded the standard bugle call for an official invitation to negotiations.)

In any case, Bowie, who by most accounts was furious at Travis for the impetuous bravado and clearly counterproductive nature of his purely symbolic cannon shot, grabbed a piece of paper and wrote, in Spanish signed with a faltering hand (for Bowie was already ill, but not yet prostrate and still capable of leadership), the "invisible" letter that just won't mesh with the canonical story, and therefore remains hidden on prominent display at the Alamo (I cite the full text of Bowie's letter, in the translation given in C. Hopewell's biography, *James Bowie* [Eakin Press, 1994]):

> Because a shot was fired from a cannon of this fort at the time a red flag was raised over the tower, and soon afterward having been informed that your forces would parley, the same not having been understood before the mentioned discharge of cannon, I wish to know if, in effect, you have called for a parley, and with this object dispatch my second aide, Benito James, under the protection of a white flag, which I trust will be respected by you and your forces. God and Texas.

I don't want to exaggerate the meaning of this letter. I cannot assert a high probability for a different outcome if Bowie had remained strong enough to lead, and if Santa Anna had agreed to negotiations. Some facts dim the force of any speculation about a happier outcome that would have avoided a strategically senseless slaughter with an inevitable military result, and would thus have spared the lives of 180 Texians (and probably twice as many Mexicans). For example, Bowie did not display optimal diplomacy in his note, if only because he had originally written "God and the Mexican Federation" in his signatory phrase (indicating his support for the constitution of 1824, and his continued loyalty to this earlier Mexican government), but, in a gesture that can only be termed defiant, crossed out "The Mexican Federation" and wrote "Texas" above.

More important, Santa Anna officially refused the offer of Bowie's courier, and sent back a formal response promising extermination without mercy unless the Texians surrendered unconditionally. Moreover, we cannot be confident that Texian lives would have been spared even if the Alamo's defenders had surrendered without a fight. After all, less than a month after the fall of the Alamo, Santa Anna executed several hundred prisoners—the very men who might have come to Travis's aid—after their surrender at Goliad.

In the confusion and recrimination between the two commands, Travis then sent out his own courier and received the same response, but, according to some sources, with the crucial addition of an "informal" statement that, if the Texians laid down their arms within an hour, their lives and property would be spared, even though the surrender must be technically and officially "unconditional." Such, after all, has always been the way of war, as good officers balance the need for inspirational manifestos with their even more important moral and strategic responsibility to avoid a "glory trap" of certain death. Competent leaders have always understood the crucial difference between public proclamations and private bargains.

Thus, I strongly suspect that if Bowie had not become too ill to lead, some honorable solution would eventually have emerged through private negotiations, if only because Santa Anna and Bowie, as seasoned veterans, maintained high mutual regard beneath their strong personal dislike—whereas I can only imagine what Santa Anna thought of the upstart and self-aggrandizing Travis. In this alternate and unrealized scenario, most of the brothers would have remained both valiant and alive. What resolution fits best with our common sensibilities of morality and human decency: more than four hundred men slaughtered in a battle with an inevitable result, thus providing an American prototype for a claptrap canonical story about empty valor over honorable living; or an utterly nonheroic, tough-minded, and practical solution that would have erased a great story from our books, but restored hundreds of young men to the possibilities of a full life, complete with war stories told directly to grandchildren?

Finally, one prominent Alamo fact, though rarely mentioned in this context, provides strong support for the supposition that wise military leaders usually reach private agreements to avoid senseless slaughter. Just three months earlier, in December 1835, General Cos had made his last stand against Texian forces at exactly the same site—within the Alamo! But Cos, as a professional soldier, raised a white flag and agreed to terms with the Texian conquerors: he would surrender, disarm, withdraw his men, retreat southwestward over the Rio Grande, and not fight again. Cos obeyed the terms of his bargain, but when he had crossed the Rio Grande to safety, Santa Anna demanded his return to active duty. Thus, the same General Cos—alive, kicking, and fighting—led one of the companies that recaptured the Alamo on March 6. Travis would have cut such a dashing figure at San Jacinto!

Bill Buckner's Legs

How the canonical story of "but for this" has driven facts that we can all easily recall into a false version dictated by the needs of narrative.

Any fan of the Boston Red Sox can recite chapter and verse of a woeful tale, a canonical story in the land of the bean and the cod, called "the curse of the Bambino." The Sox established one of major league baseball's most successful franchises of the early twentieth century. But the Sox won their last World Series way back in 1918. A particular feature of all subsequent losses has convinced Boston fans that their team labors under an infamous curse, initiated in January 1920, when Boston owner Harry Frazee simply and cynically sold the team's greatest player—the best left-handed pitcher in baseball, but soon to make his truly indelible mark on the opposite path of power hitting—for straight cash needed to finance a flutter on a Broadway show, and not for any advantages or compensation in traded players. Moreover, Frazee sold Boston's hero to the hated enemy, the New York Yankees. This man, of course, soon acquired the title of Sultan of Swat, the Bambino, George Herman "Babe" Ruth.

The Red Sox have played in four World Series (1946, 1967, 1975, and 1986) and several playoff series since then, and they have always lost in the most heartbreaking manner—by coming within an inch of the finish line and then self-destructing. Enos Slaughter of the rival St. Louis Cardinals scored from first on a single in the decisive game of the 1946 World Series. In 1975, the Sox lost game seven after a miraculous victory in game six, capped by Bernie Carbo's three-run homer to tie the score and won, in extra innings, by Carlton Fisk, when he managed to overcome the laws of physics by body English, and cause a ball that he had clearly hit out of bounds to curve into the left-field foul pole for a home run.

And so the litany goes. But all fans will tell you that the worst moment of utter incredibility—the defeat that defies all belief in natural causality, and must therefore record the operation of a true curse—terminated game six in the 1986 World Series. (Look, I'm not even a Sox fan, but I still don't allow anyone to mention this event in my presence; the pain remains too great!) The Sox, leading the Series three games to two and requiring only this victory for their first Ring since 1918, entered the last inning with a comfortable two-run lead. Their pitcher quickly got the first two outs. The Sox staff had peeled the foil off the champagne bottles (but, remembering the curse, had not yet popped the corks). The Mets management had already, and graciously, flashed "congratulations Red Sox" in neon on their scoreboard. But the faithful multitude of fans, known as "Red Sox Nation," remained glued to their television sets in exquisite fear and trembling.

And the curse unfolded, with an intensity and cruelty heretofore not even imagined. In a series of scratch hits, bad pitches, and terrible judgments, the Mets managed to score a run. (I mean, even a batting-practice pitcher, even you or I, could have gotten someone out for the final victory!) Reliever Bob Stanley, a good man dogged by bad luck, came in and threw a wild pitch to bring the tying run home. (Some, including yours truly, would have scored the pitch as a passed ball, but let's leave such contentious irrelevancies aside for the moment.) And now, with two outs, a man on second and the score tied, Mookie Wilson steps to the plate.

Bill Buckner, the Sox's gallant first baseman, and a veteran with a long and truly distinguished career, should not even have been playing in the field. For weeks, manager John McNamara had been benching Buckner for defensive purposes during the last few innings of games with substantial Red Sox leads—for, after a long and hard season, Buckner's legs were shot, and his stride gimpy. In fact, he could hardly bend down. But the sentimental McNamara wanted his regular players on the field when the great, and seemingly inevitable, moment arrived—so Buckner stood at first base.

I shudder as I describe the outcome that every baseball fan knows so well. Stanley, a great sinkerball pitcher, did exactly what he had been brought in to accomplish. He threw a wicked sinker that Wilson could only tap on the ground toward first base for an easy out to cap the damage and end the inning with the score still tied, thus granting the Sox hitters an opportunity to achieve a

Mookie Wilson's ground ball bounces between Bill Buckner's legs. *Credit: Republished with permission of Globe Newspaper Company, Inc.*

comeback and victory. But the ball bounced right through Buckner's legs into the outfield as Ray Knight hurried home with the winning run. Not to the side of his legs, and not under his lunging glove as he dived to the right or left for a difficult chance—but right through his legs! The seventh and concluding game hardly mattered. Despite brave rhetoric, no fan expected the Sox to win (hopes against hope to be sure, but no real thoughts of victory). They lost.

This narration may drip with my feelings, but I have presented the straight facts. The narrative may be good and poignant enough in this accurate version, but this factual tale cannot satisfy the lust of the relevant canonical story for an evident reason. The canonical story of Buckner's travail must follow a scenario that might be called "but for this." In numerous versions of "but for this," a large and hugely desired result fails to materialize— and the absolutely opposite resolution, both factually and morally, unfolds instead—because one tiny and apparently inconsequential piece of the story fails to fall into place, usually by human error or malfeasance. "But for this" can brook no nuancing, no complexity, no departure from the central meaning and poignant tragedy that an entire baleful outcome flows absolutely and entirely from one tiny accident of history.

"But for this" must therefore drive the tale of Bill Buckner's legs into the only version that can validate the canonical story. In short, poor Bill must become the one and only cause and focus of ultimate defeat or victory. That is, if Buckner fields the ball properly, the Sox win their first World Series since 1918 and eradicate the curse of the Bambino. But if Buckner bobbles the ball, the Mets win the Series instead, and the curse continues in an even more intense and painful way. For Buckner's miscue marks the unkindest bounce of all, the most improbable, trivial little error sustained by a good and admired man. What hath God wrought?

Except that Buckner's error did *not* determine the outcome of the World Series for one little reason, detailed above but all too easily forgotten. When Wilson's grounder bounced between Buckner's legs, the score was already tied! (Not to mention that this game was the sixth and, at worst for the Sox, the penultimate game of the Series, not the seventh and necessarily final contest. The Sox could always have won game seven and the entire Series, no matter how the negotiations of God and Satan had proceeded over Bill Buckner as the modern incarnation of Job in game six.) If Buckner had fielded the ball cleanly, the Sox would not have won the Series at that moment. They would only have secured the opportunity to do so, if their hitters came through in extra innings.

We can easily excuse any patriotic American who is not a professional historian, or any casual visitor for that matter, for buying into the canonical story of the Alamo—all the brothers were valiant—and not learning that a healthy and practical Bowie might have negotiated an honorable surrender at no great cost to the Texian cause. After all, the last potential eyewitness has been underground for well over a century. We have no records beyond the written reports, and historians cannot trust the account of any

eyewitness, for the supposed observations fall into a mire of contradiction, recrimination, self-interest, aggrandizement, and that
quintessentially human propensity for spinning a tall tale.

But any baseball fan with the legal right to sit in a bar and argue
the issues over a mug of the house product should be able to
recall the uncomplicated and truly indisputable facts of Bill Buckner's case with no trouble at all, and often with the force of eyewitness memory, either exulting in impossibly fortuitous joy, or
groaning in the agony of despair and utter disbelief, before a television set. (To fess up, I should have been at a fancy dinner in
Washington, but I "got sick" instead and stayed in my hotel room.
In retrospect, I should not have stood in bed.)

The subject attracted my strong interest because, within a year
after the actual event, I began to note a pattern in the endless
commentaries that have hardly abated, even fifteen years later—
for Buckner's tale can be made relevant by analogy to almost any
misfortune under a writer's current examination, and Lord only
knows we experience no shortage of available sources for pain.
Many stories reported, and continue to report, the events accurately—and why not, for the actual tale packs sufficient punch,
and any fan should be able to extract the correct account directly
from living and active memory. But I began to note that a substantial percentage of reports had subtly, and quite unconsciously
I'm sure, driven the actual events into a particular false version—
the pure "end member" of ultimate tragedy demanded by the
canonical story "but for this."

I keep a growing file of false reports, all driven by requirements
of the canonical story—the claim that, but for Buckner's legs, the
Sox would have won the Series, forgetting the inconvenient complexity of a tied score at Buckner's ignominious moment, and
sometimes even forgetting that the Series still had another game
to run. This misconstruction appears promiscuously, both in hurried daily journalism and in rarefied books by the motley crew of
poets and other assorted intellectuals who love to treat baseball

as a metaphor for anything else of importance in human life or the history of the universe. (I have written to several folks who made this error, and they have all responded honorably with a statement like: "Omigod, what a jerk I am! Of course the score was tied. Jeez [sometimes bolstered by an invocation of Mary and Joseph as well], I just forgot!")

For example, a front-page story in *USA Today* for October 25, 1993, discussed Mitch Williams's antics in the 1993 Series in largely unfair comparison with the hapless and blameless Bill Buckner:

> Williams may bump Bill Buckner from atop the goat list, at least for now. Buckner endured his nightmare Oct. 25, 1986. His Boston Red Sox were one out away from their first World Series title since 1918 when he let Mookie Wilson's grounder slip through his legs.

Or this from a list of Sox misfortunes, published in the *New York Post* on October 13, 1999, just before the Sox met the Yanks (and lost of course) in their first full series of postseason play:

> Mookie Wilson's grounder that rolled through the legs of Bill Buckner in Game 6 of the 1986 World Series. That happened after the Red Sox were just one out away from winning the World Series.

For a more poetic view between hard covers, consider the very last line of a lovely essay written by a true poet and devoted fan to introduce a beautifully illustrated new edition of the classic poem about failure in baseball, *Casey at the Bat*:

> Triumph's pleasures are intense but brief; failure remains with us forever, a mothering nurturing common humanity. With Casey we all strike out. Although Bill Buckner won

a thousand games with his line drives and brilliant fielding, he will endure in our memories in the ninth inning of
the sixth game of a World Series, one out to go, as the ball
inexplicably, ineluctably, and eternally rolls between his
legs.[1]

But the nasty little destroyer of lovely canonical stories then
pipes up in his less mellifluous tones: "But I don't know how many
outs would have followed, or who would have won. The Sox had
already lost the lead; the score was tied." Factuality embodies its
own form of eloquence; and gritty complexity often presents an
even more interesting narrative than the pure and archetypal "end
member" version of our canonical stories. But something deep
within us drives accurate messiness into the channels of canonical stories, the primary impositions of our minds upon the world.

To any reader who now raises the legitimate issue of why a scientist should write an essay about two stories in American history
that bear no evident relevance to any overtly scientific question, I
simply restate my opening and general argument: human beings
are pattern-seeking, story-telling creatures. These mental propen-
sities generally serve us well enough, but they also, and often,
derail our thinking about all kinds of temporal sequences—in the
natural world of geological change and the evolution of organ-
isms, as well as in human history—by leading us to cram the real
and messy complexity of life into simplistic channels of the few
preferred ways that human stories "go." I call these biased pathways "canonical stories"—and I argue that our preferences for
tales about directionality (to explain patterns), generated by motivations of valor (to explain the causal basis of these patterns)
have distorted our understanding of a complex reality where different kinds of patterns and different sources of order often pre-
dominate.

[1]In fact, it was the tenth inning. [Ed.]

I chose my two stories on purpose—Bowie's letter and Buckner's legs—to illustrate two distinct ways that canonical stories distort our reading of actual patterns: first, in the tale of Jim Bowie's letter, by relegating important facts to virtual invisibility when they cannot be made to fit the canonical story, even though we do not hide the inconvenient facts themselves, and may even place them on open display (as in Bowie's letter at the Alamo), and second, in the tale of Bill Buckner's legs, where we misstate easily remembered and ascertainable facts in predictable ways because these facts did not unfold as the relevant canonical stories dictate.

These common styles of error—hidden in plain sight, and misstated to fit canonical stories—arise as frequently in scientific study as in historical inquiry. To cite, in closing, the obvious examples from our standard misreadings of the history of life, we hide most of nature's diversity in plain sight when we spin our usual tales about increasing complexity as the central theme and organizing principle of both evolutionary theory and the actual history of life. In so doing, we unfairly privilege the one recent and transient species that has evolved the admittedly remarkable invention of mental power sufficient to ruminate upon such questions.

This silly and parochial bias leaves the dominant and most successful products of evolution hidden in plain sight—the indestructible bacteria that have represented life's mode (most common design) for all 3.5 billion years of the fossil record (while *Homo sapiens* hasn't yet endured for even half a million years—and remember that it takes a thousand million to make a single billion). Not to mention that if we confine our attention to multicellular animal life, insects represent about 80 percent of all species, while only a fool would put money on us, rather than them, as probable survivors a billion years hence.

For the second imposition of canonical stories upon different and more complex patterns in the history of life—predictable distortion to validate preferred tales about valor—need I proceed any further than the conventional tales of vertebrate evolution that we all have read since childhood, and that follow our Arthurian mythology about knights of old and men so bold? I almost wince when I find the first appearance of vertebrates on land, or of insects in the air, described as a "conquest," although this adjective retains pride of place in our popular literature.

And we still seem unable to shuck the image of dinosaurs as born losers vanquished by superior mammals, even though we know that dinosaurs prevailed over mammals for more than 130 million years, starting from day one of mammalian origins. Mammals gained their massively delayed opportunity only when a major extinction, triggered by extraterrestrial impact, removed the dinosaurs—for reasons that we do not fully understand, but that probably bear no sensible relation to any human concept of valor or lack thereof. This cosmic fortuity gave mammals their chance, not because any intrinsic superiority (the natural analog of valor) helped them to weather this cosmic storm, but largely, perhaps, because their small size, a side-consequence of failure to compete with dinosaurs in environments suited for large creatures, gave mammals a lucky break in the form of ecological hiding room to hunker down.

Until we abandon the silly notion that the first amphibians, as conquerors of the land, somehow held more valor, and therefore embody more progress, than the vast majority of fishes that remained successfully in the sea, we will never understand the modalities and complexities of vertebrate evolution. Fish, in any case, encompass more than half of all vertebrate species today, and might well be considered the most persistently successful class of vertebrates. So should we substitute a different canonical story called "there's no place like home" for the usual tale of conquest on imperialistic models of commercial expansion?

If we must explain the surrounding world by telling stories— and I suspect that our brains do force us into this particular rut— let us at least expand the range of our tales beyond the canonical to the quirky, for then we might learn to appreciate more of the richness out there beyond our pale and usual ken, while still honoring our need to understand in human terms. Robert Frost caught the role and necessity of stories—and the freedom offered by unconventional tales—when he penned one of his brilliant epitomes of deep wisdom for a premature gravestone in 1942:

And were an epitaph to be my story
I'd have a short one ready for my own.
I would have written of me on my stone:
I had a lover's quarrel with the world.

CRITICISM

Diamonds Are a Fan's Best Friend

Books reviewed:

Ball Four Plus Ball Five by Jim Bouton

Mr. October: The Reggie Jackson Story by Maury Allen

Ttrue innovation carries within itself the seeds of its own obsolescence. Our urges to copy when unimaginative, or to improve and extend when more inspired, convert yesterday's rebel into today's ho-hum.

Jim Bouton shined during the closing days of the great Yankee dynasty. He won two games in the 1964 World Series, but could not stop the Cardinals and their Gibson machine single-handedly. He pitched so hard that his cap, obeying Newton's third law, often flew off as his body lunged forward. Mickey Mantle called him the "bulldog." But his arm went bad and he won only nine games during his last four years as a Yankee. In 1969, he tried to come back as a marginally effective knuckleballer, barely holding on in the bullpen of the hapless Seattle Pilots (now the respectable Milwaukee Brewers), an expansion team that spent its single year of life mired deep in the cellar of the American League West. There

First published in *Washington Post Book World*, June 21, 1981.

he composed *Ball Four*, an honest and irreverent daily account of a baseball season viewed from within and below. Its candor scandalized a profession that expected to keep its secrets and come before the reading public with traditional books about sexless, Coke-drinking, cardboard heroes. Bouton's book was so successful that honest confession replaced myth-making as a preferred literary genre of the field.

Ten years later, Bouton has reissued *Ball Four* with a forty-page update, inevitably titled *Ball Five*. In rereading classics, I am always struck by the contrast between memory and reality. Many of the famous scenes of *Ball Four* have not lost their impact, but I remembered them as chapters, while they actually appear as paragraphs. Although *Ball Four* does recount the flaky antics of grown men, such as an unbeauty contest conducted to pick Yogi Berra's successor on the "all-ugly nine" among active players, its real focus is on the anxieties and frustrations of a sore-armed athlete on a third-rate team. Its strength, in retrospect, lies not in its exposés—tame stuff compared with later works modeled upon it, and notoriously silent on race and real sex, while reasonably explicit about drinking and pill popping. Rather its relentless, even tedious, rendition of daily hopes, pettinesses, and pains— why did they yank me, why didn't they pitch me—displays a human side of sports that we never discern in baseball books of the pre-Bouton era.

Ball Four is a permanent antidote to the common view that ballplayers are hunks of meat, naturally and effortlessly displaying the talents that nature provided. Excellence in anything is a single-minded struggle, to be valued if only for its rarity. The honest struggles of winners *and* losers are our sustaining hopes for a species mired in mediocrity—whether the struggle be expressed in relentless search for the perfect knuckleball, the holy grail, or the Great American Novel.

Ball Five recounts Bouton's last decade as a broadcaster, actor, divorcé, and even comeback pitcher for the Atlanta Braves. It is

studded with quotable one-liners. On Billy Martin's reaction to
Ball Four (before he wrote his own book in the Boutonian tradition): "Billy Martin . . . came running across the field hollering for
me to get the hell out. . . . Because I've grown accustomed to the
shape of my nose, I got the hell out." On the high salaries that
Bouton never enjoyed: "My position is that while the players
don't deserve all that money, the owners don't deserve it even
more." Still, *Ball Five* is too sketchy to merit purchase on its own
strength; for it is only a little less insubstantial than its title. Yet
if *Ball Five* served as a vehicle for bringing *Ball Four* back into print,
then it has done its part.

Today, Bouton's book as exposé seems almost quaint in comparison with those that followed. Indeed, we will never again see
books in the style of *Lucky to Be a Yankee*, the heroic account of Joe
DiMaggio that set such an unrealistic pattern for my own youth.
Maury Allen, author of a fine post-Boutonian book on the hero of
my childhood (*Where Have You Gone, Joe DiMaggio?*), has now written *Mr. October*, a perfectly adequate, though uninspired, biography of Reggie Jackson. *Mr. October* is a sports book in the old style.
It contains much hackneyed writing in the heroic tradition: "Har-
nessing all the power in his 205-pound twenty-five-year-old body,
Jackson exploded in a flash as the ball moved toward the plate."
It tells the heartwarming stories of Reggie's visits to dying cancer
patients, old and young. One picture caption reads: "Reggie has
extraordinary demands on his time but always finds time for kids.
Here he makes a handicapped lad one happy fellow." Allen even
puts in a good word for George Steinbrenner, citing his charitable
contributions to underprivileged kids. It purveys quick and dirty
conclusions as profundity—including the psychobabble interpretation of Jackson's relationship with Billy Martin offered by "a
leading Bellevue psychiatrist" who requested anonymity because
he had never met either men, but only read about them.

Yet, through all this hasty conventionality, *Mr. October* contains
some honestly forthright and controversial material. Its discus-

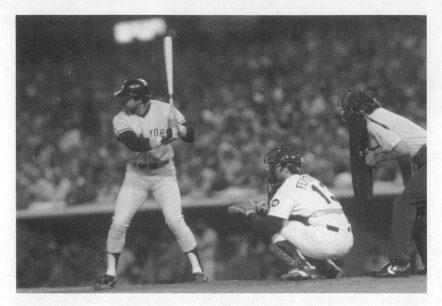

Reggie Jackson, playing for the Yankees, bats against the Los Angeles Dodgers in the 1978 World Series. *Credit: Neil Preston/Corbis*

sions about the sex lives of players on the road is far more extensive than Bouton's was. Allen's account of persistent racism at both ends of the hierarchy—how many black owners and utility infielders do you see?—is as serious an indictment of modern baseball as anyone could raise. To make it in the majors, a black man had still better be a star—like Reggie Jackson. It is Jim Bouton's legacy that even the most ordinary of sports books now outdoes *Ball Four* in candor.

Yet I wonder. Surely we don't want dishonest books that misrepresent real people. Yet the ballplayer as unadorned hero has a legitimate place in American mythology. To me, Joe DiMaggio looks as elegant selling Mr. Coffee today as he did swinging a bat when I was a kid. As a nation, we are too young to have true mythic heroes, and we must press real human beings into service. Honest Abe Lincoln the legend is quite a different character from Abraham Lincoln the man. And so should they be. And so should both be treasured, as long as they are distinguished. In a complex and confusing world, the perfect clarity of sports provides a focus for legitimate, utterly unambiguous support of disdain. The Dodgers are evil, the Yankees good. They really are, and have been for as long as anyone in my family can remember.

So Reggie, I am happy to know you a bit better as a man. But I will always remember you most for a glorious day in 1977— in October, of course—when you destroyed the enemy with three homers on three pitches. And I'll keep eating those Reggie bars, even though the taste leaves something to be desired, and even though the Baby Ruth was named for Grover Cleveland's daughter.

Angell Hits a Grand Slam with Collected Baseball Essays

Book reviewed:

Late Innings: A Baseball Companion by Roger Angell

P eople buy *The New Yorker* for the damnedest of reasons. Sophisticated vulgarians like the cartoons; social climbers fancy the rarefied ads. Some people, for all I know, might even read the immensely long and uncompromisingly literate articles. I happily pay my yearly subscription just to read Roger Angell's occasional essays on baseball. *Late Innings* collects Angell's essays of the past five years and proves once and for all that wholes can be more than the sum of their admirable parts.

Angell devotes the bulk of *Late Innings* to the pair of essays he writes each year to sandwich the season—his musings on spring training, and his post-Series summary. More topical essays on people and events lie interspersed amidst this recurrent format. These include his masterful portrait of Bob Gibson (who single-handedly punctured the Impossible Dream of 1967), his account of life in the semipros, where people still play for love (and in frustration), and the finest essay of all—a beautiful, understated

First published in the *Boston Sunday Globe*, 1982.

account of a single college game that explains and justifies the deep affection so many of us feel for baseball.

On the eve of the 1981 baseball strike, Angell is in New Haven attending a game between Yale and St. John's. He is propelled by an ulterior motive, not an abiding passion for college ball. He has just learned that Smokey Joe Wood is still alive (at ninety-one) and as much a fan as ever. Since Wood coached the Yale team from the 1920s through the 1940s, Angell arranges through an intermediary to meet him at the game.

(Wood compiled a 34–5 record pitching for the Red Sox in 1912, perhaps the greatest performance for a single season in baseball history. Some people say he was faster than Walter Johnson, and the argument still rages among aficionados. But he lost his niche in baseball's Pantheon at Cooperstown because he injured his pitching arm the next year and never recouped. Still, he would not quit and retooled himself as a better than average outfielder for five seasons with the Indians.)

Angell chats with Wood and gets a good flow of baseball reminiscences: pitching against Johnson, eating fried chicken cooked by Tris Speaker, Cobb at bat. But something is wrong, and Angell begins to fear that he is exploiting an old man who played for fourteen years and, by God's grace, has lived to repeat the tales for sixty years. So he stops probing and begins to watch the game, which, unexpectedly, becomes riveting.

Ron Darling of Yale pitches eleven innings of no-hit ball and loses 1–0 in the twelfth. And suddenly we realize that, in Angell's literary web, this contest has become Wood's greatest game, his 1–0 victory over Walter Johnson, extending his own winning streak to fourteen games, and ending Johnson's at sixteen. The continuity that he tried to establish directly with Wood (and, as a sensitive man, could not) is cemented indirectly through the act that unites them with the players on the field through nearly one hundred years of history—a well-played game.

This extraordinary climax leads Angell to a discourse on the controlling simile that captures his love of baseball and his belief that it is important. Baseball is like a river, both in the steady pace of its own action, permitting talk and a leisurely approach to beer and peanuts along the way, and in the continuity it establishes with our past through the isolation of individual performance (we can compare Wood's 1912 season with Guidry's in 1978, but how do you keep score during a football game?).

The simile also captures his anger and sadness at current developments that may destroy the game from within: subservience to media revenues that alienate players from fans by turning them into celebrities for their salaries rather than their performances, and that destroy the game's pace by devaluing the primacy of a long regular season and encouraging such hokey hype as the additional round of playoffs that further cheapened the disastrous, strike-shortened 1981 season.

Angell is a baseball conservative in the best, dynamic sense of understanding the game's inner strength and source of its continuity. "What compensation," he asks in reference to last year's strike, "can ever be made to us, the fans, who are the true owners and neighbors and keepers of the game for this dry, soundless summer and for the loss of our joy?"

The twice-yearly regular pieces are just as riveting and, by judicious editing, have not been tarnished by age. His account of the excruciating or exhilarating 1978 season (depending upon whether you favor the Sox or the Yanks) remains the premier essay of its genre. It also contains the greatest one-liner in the history of sports literature—his pugnacious insistence that Yaz's final pop to third was not a divinely inevitable outcome, as the protracted history of Boston misery might lead us to suspect: "I still don't see why it couldn't have been arranged for him to single to right center. . . . I think God was shelling a peanut."

It is an old truism that baseball has captured the attention of many eminent literati, while other sports have not. Angell is the finest of them all, but the source of his success does not lie primarily with his powerful writing or with his deep understanding of baseball's general appeal. It resides instead in the source of his continuity with Joe Wood—his love for the details of a well-played game. He is no literary rip-off artist, but a real fan who follows hundreds of games each year. His simile of the river is arresting literature, but look for his primary success in a three-page disquisition—written with as much literary power, by the way—on all the pros, cons, details, and implications of Reggie Jackson's famous right-hip rhumba that deflected the ball, broke up a double play, and probably saved the 1978 Series. The power of baseball lies in its daily details. If the moguls who pander to TV revenues ever remember this, we may save the game and, as a substantial benefit on the side, guarantee a few more decades of Angell's prose and insight.

The Black Men Who
Integrated Big League Ball

Book reviewed:

Baseball's Great Experiment: Jackie Robinson and His Legacy by Jules Tygiel.

The American League won the 1983 All-Star Game, but only following an extended and substantial drought before this year's drubbing (thirty losses in thirty-six games since 1950), compared with exemplary success before then (twelve wins in sixteen games). About the only explanation for this stunning reverse in fortunes that makes any sense to me is the greater willingness of the National League to avail itself, early and with less hesitation, of the great pool of untapped talent—black players who, before Jackie Robinson's debut in 1947, had been systematically excluded from major league baseball. And, as we contemplate the fading fortunes of our beloved Sox, we must face honestly (for all the legitimate veneration of Tom Yawkey) the fact that part of their persistent failure must lie in their slowness (as the very last major league team to integrate) to exploit this pool.

First published in the *Boston Sunday Globe*, August 28, 1983.

To this day, the Sox field but one black in their starting line-up—
and where would they be without him?

The integration of major league baseball in the late 1940s is
both a microcosm of the most important American social transformation of modern times and a wonderful human drama in
itself. It is not merely the tale of one enlightened, if complex,
executive—Branch Rickey—bringing one highly talented young
player, Jackie Robinson, to the Brooklyn Dodgers in 1947. The
story stretches back to the nineteenth century when the great Cap
Anson led a shameful movement to drum out from major league
baseball the few blacks then precariously accepted. And the story
then extends forward through the history of the Negro Leagues to
a wide ranging struggle involving numerous unsung heroes (like
black sports writers for the Negro press) to drive white America
from its hypocrisy.

Speaking of hypocrisy, the "official" position of major league
baseball, so often expressed by former commissioner Kenesaw
Mountain Landis, held that blacks were welcome but that none of
sufficient quality had presented themselves—a patently risible bit
of nonsense with the likes of Satchel Paige and Josh Gibson toil-
ing for pittances in the Negro Leagues. (My father often told me
a story of Paul Robeson's in camera plea for integration before the
annual meeting of baseball executives in the mid-1940s—where
Dad, as a freelance stenographer, had been hired to record the
secret proceedings for private use. Robeson, replete with flowing
beard from his triumph, then under way, as Othello on Broadway,
made a stirring statement that brought tears to my father's eyes.
Robeson finished and left, and Kenesaw Mountain Landis moved
on to the next item of business without a single word of discussion or commentary.)

Tygiel succeeds in this fine book primarily because he casts his
net so broadly in time, place, and status. He captures all the dignity of the great Negro League players who never had a chance,

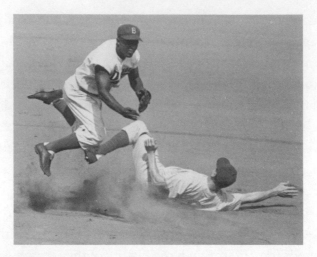

Jackie Robinson attempts to turn a double play in a game against the Chicago Cubs, 1952. *Credit: Bettmann/Corbis*

but who loved the game so much that they still predominantly mix tales of pleasure with their disappointment. He portrays the main act as the high drama it was, with its two so different principals—Branch Rickey, a contradictory mixture of humbug and ideals, profit seeking, and genuine commitment to equality; and Jackie Robinson, bristling with talent and with legitimate anger, but forced by his agreement with Rickey to mute his assertive personality and win acceptance by "good" example. (As a primary measure of white hypocrisy, caucasian supporters of integration took it for granted that blacks would have to be better behaved and more talented than their white contemporaries to "better their race" and win, by exemplary conduct, what was really no more than a birthright—a chance to compete according to their talents!)

But Tygiel does not confine himself to Robinson and Rickey. He ranges as widely as possible, discussing the fates and experiences of all black pioneers in the major and minor leagues. The tales of Larry Doby, Roy Campanella, Don Newcombe, and Luke Easter, the first black pathbreakers in the majors, are well documented—

but Tygiel gives as much space to the struggles of aging Negro
League stars caught and placed in the low minor leagues and
never given a chance in the majors. He also documents the tra-
vails of black players during spring training in the segregated
South, and he discusses the integration of the southern minor
leagues—what should have been the most difficult battle, but
often proceeded without great distress (given the economic
power of blacks as potential spectators), in an age of official seg-
regation.

If the book has any faults, I must mention a slight schizophre-
nia of intent. Tygiel, a history professor by trade, can't quite
decide whether he is writing a sports book or a scholarly disser-
tation. Thus, the book is replete—absolutely chockfull—with
those annoying and irrelevant footnotes that you have to look up
in the back, and with the kind of scholarly documentation that
can disrupt the flow of popular writing. When he switches gears
and tries to write in the vernacular sports idiom, the effect is
sometimes embarrassing—full of an overblown adjectivitis that,
too many times, casts Robinson as the "broad-shouldered black
athlete," and Campy as the "stocky catcher." I didn't find these
phrases too offensive, but when a home run becomes a "prodigious projectile," then I do cringe.

Still, the importance of the subject so far transcends a simple
ball game that the scholar's approach certainly seems justified.
The integration of baseball was no self-contained tale, or just a
minor incident within a social movement. It formed a major chapter of America's most important domestic story of the mid-
twentieth century. We are grateful to Tygiel for such a fine and
sensitive documentation.

The general importance of the subject might best be documented by a quote from Don Newcombe, the black Dodger
pitcher who could be so good that I hated him (as a Giant and
Yankee fan), and who also often hit over .300 to boot (he was fre-

quently used as a pinch hitter). Newcombe recounts a visit from Martin Luther King: "We were paying our dues long before the civil rights marches. Martin Luther King told me in my home one night, 'You'll never know what you and Jackie and Roy do to make it possible to do my job.'"

Baseball and the
Two Faces of Janus

Books reviewed:

  Baseball: The People's Game by Harold Seymour
  Men At Work: The Craft of Baseball by George F. Will
  When the Cheering Stops: Former Major Leaguers and Their Lives
by Lee Heiman, Dave Weiner, and Bill Gutman

C onsider baseball as Janus, the double-visaged god of our
beginnings. One face looks beyond our everyday world
into the realm of myth. I went to a game at Fenway Park
last month, accompanied by a professional sociologist and budding, but unsophisticated, baseball fan. She delighted in observing the few forms of joint action indulged in by fans of this most
individualistic sport—the wave and the seventh-inning stretch in
particular—referring to these displays, in her jargon, as "social
organization." But in the ninth inning, with Carlton Fisk at the plate
for the visiting White Sox, another apparent ritual puzzled her
greatly. Several dozen fans, dispersed throughout our vicinity, stood
up, raised their arms above their heads, and gyrated in an odd lit-

tle motion. What could this mean? My friend was utterly stumped.

I explained that this behavior fell outside the generalities of rules for human conduct in crowds, and that she would have to learn the specific mythology of baseball. The gyrating fans were enacting a ritual to be sure—by imitating, in the presence of the hero himself, a cardinal moment of baseball's history. In the bottom of the twelfth inning of the sixth game of the 1975 World Series, probably the greatest baseball game ever played, Carlton Fisk, then a catcher for the Red Sox, hit a long ball toward left field in Fenway Park. It seemed to curve foul, but Fisk gyrated his body, put some English on the air space between home plate and the arching ball, and bent its trajectory right into the left-field foul pole—thus winning the game as he jigged around the bases. It was past midnight in the little New Hampshire town of Fisk's birth, but someone ran to the church and set the bells ringing. Meanwhile, the Fenway Park organist played the Hallelujah Chorus as Fisk made his circuit. (I am also assured that the laws of physics preclude Fisk's action at a distance, but facts cannot be denied.) The fans were simply re-creating a treasured moment of legendary official history.

The other face looks back into our quotidian world of ordinary work and play. When I grew up on the streets of New York City in the late forties and early fifties, we found a hundred ways to improvise and vary the game of baseball. I particularly enjoyed the two-man versions—rubber balls bounced against stoops or pitched from one sidewalk square across a second and into the batter's box of a third in line, where the hitter slapped the ball back toward the pitcher (we called it boxball-baseball). The canonical playground version for school recesses was punchball —played with fist against that same ubiquitous pink rubber sphere. After school, we grabbed the old mop handle and played stickball.

Mythology is wondrous, a balm for the soul. But its problems cannot be ignored. At worst, it buys inspiration at the price of physical impossibility (as my initial story of churchbells and action at a distance testifies). At best, it purveys the same myopic view of history that made this most fascinating subject so boring and misleading in grade school as a sequential tale of monarchs and battles.

Most baseball books continue to bask in the mythology—tales of heroics in that tiny pinnacle of activity known as major league baseball. We have tales of unforgettable seasons; sagas of dynasties (the once-proud Yankees, the current Athletics), or disasters (Cubbies, Phillies, and Sox); and, above all, ghost-written autobiographies, now a bit more confessional than the old cardboard, but still basically hagiographical.

But the Janus face of our daily lives peeks through often enough, and even sets the theme of several contemporary baseball books. When the *New York Review* sent me this year's crop for the new season—to receive during spring training, read during a lazy summer, and report just in time for the World Series—I decided to select the three items that treated this neglected, ordinary face. These three otherwise disparate books share the common property of their allegiance to *Annales* history vs. kings and battles. Seymour tells us the explicit story of the largely undocumented mountain supporting the pinnacle (and leaves us wondering whether we should use such a metaphor at all). George Will and Heiman, Weiner, and Gutman adopt the other tactic of demythologizing from within the pinnacle—Will by displaying the workaday quality of manifest excellence in performance, Heiman et al. by tracing the heroes after they pass from the limelight into the invisibility of later life.

Baseball: The People's Game is the third volume of a distinguished series by the doyen of baseball historians, former Dodger batboy and history professor, Dr. Harold Seymour (the first two entries, *The Early Years* and *The Golden Age*, treat official history, but this magisterial compendium makes up for any previous neglect of Janus's other face). Aristotle invoked the house in a venerable and celebrated metaphor for his theory of causality (bricks and mortar as material causes, masons as efficient causes, blueprints as formal causes, and inhabitants as final causes). Seymour uses the same structure for ordering his chapters on the history of baseball up to the Second World War, as played by nonprofessionals, from kiddie toss-up games on the street to well-organized industrial and semipro leagues. In "the house of baseball," Seymour treats, sequentially, the foundation (boys' baseball), the ground floor (organized men's leagues from colleges, to towns, to industries, to the armed forces), the basement (baseball in prisons, reformatories, and Indian schools and reservations), the annex (women's baseball), and the outbuilding (black baseball).

Seymour's book, all six-hundred-plus pages of it, revels in intimate detail, often reading more like a list, filled out in prose style, than a narrative. Seymour is the leading professional in a small but growing field of sports history, yet he writes with the most admirable zeal of a hobbyist and amateur in the fine (not the pejorative) sense of a word that means "to love." I can well imagine Seymour's mode of composition. He must have hundreds of thousands of index cards (for this project surely began decades before our modern electronic shortcuts), each with the history of baseball in a particular state prison, prairie town, or military outpost. He then ordered them by time or concept and disgorged this great labor of love. Any fan must rejoice and greatly admire the results; the less committed may be forgiven for occasionally feeling that some details might be less important than others, and perhaps justifiably excludable. (Must we know, for example, that everyone became seasick during a return steamer ride from California to the Chemawa Indian School in Oregon following a pre–World War I trip by the school baseball team and band?)

Still, as the saying goes, baseball is a game of inches and an enterprise awash in particulars, statistical and otherwise; and Seymour's densely detailed account will rivet any enthusiast's attention. Since baseball is truly our "national pastime" (however trite the phrase), the various arms of the establishment that have sponsored the game have invoked utility or defense against subversion for a plethora of purposes: the promotion of "American" values in wayward boys, the suppression of unionism through fostering paternalism in factories, the spread of imperialism, and the undermining of Indian culture.

Yet just as one can't blame science, as an institution, for misuse in the service of racism, baseball was valued and enjoyed, whatever misappropriation took place. Moreover, means are not causes; and instruments remain available to both sides. The ILGWU and other major unions formed their own leagues, and the *Daily Worker* had a crackerjack sports section; Albert "Chief" Bender began his march to the Hall of Fame from an Indian boarding school, and Babe Ruth learned his baseball in a Catholic charity home for orphans and wayward children in Baltimore. Some beneficiaries admitted that the real influence flowed from baseball to the sponsoring institution, and not vice versa. An Illinois pastor gloated in 1912 about the success of his church team: "There is many a one who comes to play and remains to pray."

As for Seymour's stories, thousands upon thousands of them, I was most intrigued by two features. First, the comprehensiveness in detail (I doubt that I could even envisage many of the topics Seymour discusses, much less ferret out the information). In a dizzying few pages on small-town baseball before World War I, we learn about the purchasing of uniforms (Sears needed longer notice for delivery by July 4 than at other times); the practice of lining basepaths with buggies and then with automobiles (windshields often removed); the playing of bands; hiring of "ringers" as fraudulent substitutes in the lineup; the influence of betting; and endless arguments about the propriety of Sunday ball. Among the taller tales, we learn that during a game in Utah, with two on and none out, the batter hit a ball high into a tree (located in fair territory). The runners all circled the bases, but the opposing fielder shook the tree, dislodged the ball, caught it before it hit the ground, and turned a three-run homer into a triple play! (The innocent and bucolic wraps around the urban and commercial. A few years ago, Dave Kingman hit a high pop fly into the ceiling meshwork of the indoor stadium in Minneapolis. It never came down and was proclaimed a ground-rule double.)

Second, consider the sheer delight of a good tale (combined with instruction in broader aspects of American culture): Did you know that a baseball game once had to be interrupted at Fort Apache so that soldiers could saddle up to chase the escaped Geronimo? That several leagues operated in Panama during the building of the Canal, and that a Marine squad lost to a group of civilian players in a game staged at the bottom of the Culebra Cut, perhaps our greatest engineering triumph before the Apollo program? That a factory owner in a western city sent a note to a rival in 1883, with a gentle protest against baseball played by industrial squads on the rooftops?

> It is creditably reported to us that some of our employees frequently use the roofs of buildings extending from yours to ours to play base ball thereon. We are ever desirous to help elevate the national game, and this altitude seems to be about as high as it ever will get, yet there are also a few objections to this special location.

The details mount. A nineteenth-century drug company league included teams named the Hop Bitters, the Home Comforts, and the Paregorics (who, I trust, got many runs of one sort, and none of another). A touring women's softball team of the 1930s was called Slapsie Maxie Rosenbloom's Curvaceous Cuties (some things do change for the better). On a similar theme of prejudice, a 1908 league of the United States Steel Company formed a white squad called the "big team," and a black group called the "little jive team." In 1905, the first recorded game between two different nonwhite races occurred when a visiting Japanese team played at an Indian boarding school in California. The patronizing reporter for *Sporting News* observed: "The Orientals . . . had it over the Aborigines during all stages of the game, with the exception of the sixth inning, when the Sherman braves with a whoop broke from the reservation and went tearing madly about until six of them had scored."

President Eliot of Harvard discouraged baseball and considered a curve ball a "low form of cunning," and the pitcher's practice of looking home and then trying to pick a runner off first base as "ungentlemanly." A 1907 league at the Massachusetts State Prison featured teams by occupation (Weavers, Lasters, Carpenters, Kitchen, and Band), but the Lifers had to play the Smokes (a black team). Another game at the same prison featured the Children of Israel vs. the Sons of Italy, at least the first time around. At their second game, the prison newspaper referred only to the "Jews vs. Wops." We read that a game at Sing Sing prison had to be called off in 1916 because all balls had been fouled into the Hudson River (now pretty foul itself). Finally, Patrick Casey, a condemned man at the state prison in Carson City, Nevada, asked to umpire a game as his last request. His wish was granted as the warden arranged a match between two convict teams. Casey was executed the next day; "kill the umpire" indeed!

Seymour tells the tale of his own role as umpire, during the 1930s, for a twilight (after working hours) industrial league in

Brooklyn, dominated by Brooklyn Edison. One evening, Seymour
called out an Edison runner on a close play and was summarily
fired. If getting even marks the ultimate triumph over getting
mad, then Seymour has certainly made his mark as the recorder
and arbiter of vernacular baseball. I trust that we are past the academic elitism that would brand such a subject as peripheral or
unimportant in American history. Any activity that has comman-
deered the time and devotion of so many Americans, and that
found a place for itself at the heart of so many American institutions, cannot be dismissed because conventional taxonomy places
it into a category of play or "leisure."

George Will's *Men at Work* has led the best-seller league
throughout the summer, and for good reason. Will has pursued an
opposite tactic for illuminating the less visible face of Janus. He
has examined the pinnacle itself, the citadel known as Organized
Baseball, and tried to demythologize the institution from within.
Will's subtitle, *The Craft of Baseball*, epitomizes his thesis. Since
"baseball is a game of normal human proportions and abnormally
small margins," tiny advantages win ball games. Luck is important, and raw skill never hurts, but over a season of 162 games
and daily play, the accumulation of minuscule edges, wrought by
continual practice, obsessive watchfulness, and keen intelligence,
marks the difference between a pennant and a .500 season. "Most
games," Will rightly notes, "are won by small things executed in
a professional manner."

Will ridicules the common notion, particularly among insecure
intellectuals who don't understand the subtlety of the game, that
success in baseball rests upon sheer brawn tempered by good
instinct, because activities of the body cannot demand much of
the mind. Will quotes Tony La Russa, baseball's most intellectual
manager:

La Russa says, with a fine sense of semantic tidiness, that what are called baseball "instincts" are actually the result of "an accumulation of baseball information. They are uses of that information as the basis of decision making as game situations develop."

Will advances his unexceptionable thesis by concentrating upon the daily work and cogitation of four particularly thoughtful and industrious men at the top of their specialties within the profession—Tony La Russa for managing, Orel Hershiser for pitching, Tony Gwynn for batting, and Cal Ripken Jr. for defense. (By the way, Will's thesis, if ever properly grasped, would forthwith and forever end the silly discussion about the supposed anomaly of why so many intellectuals love baseball, and why baseball, alone among major sports, has a distinguished literature [with Will's book as the latest entry]. We who have loved and lived with the game all our lives feel no need to mount a defense against such ignorance.)

I most admire Will's success in resolving a structural problem inherent in his excellent choice of procedure. Having made a key decision to stress the incremental, repetitive honing of skills by practice, the tiny advantages that accrue with eternal vigilance to detail, and the minute edges gained from your thoughtfulness and someone else's slack, how can Will make these workaday themes lively and continuously interesting (Carlton Fisk's homer possesses an undeniable éclat compared with daily batting practice)? Will realized that his favored theme could not carry the book unaided. He has therefore created a marvel of variegated but seamless patchwork by lacing the central text with all manner of baseball lore, including statistical digressions, and hot-stove-league commentary, with a good (and entirely legitimate) sprinkling of classical tales about past and present stars from Janus's other face.

Above all, the commitment and professionalism of these splendid men shines forth, teaching us that excellence transcends any particular subject, and demands the same discipline for both body and mind. The primary value in eliminating the myth of the invincible "natural athlete" should lie in the possibility of fellowship—in the recognition that some form of excellence is accessible to anyone who can bring will and discipline to opportunity.

But I must quibble with Will's overextension of his observations on baseball to a program for American rejuvenation in general. (Of course, we all know that life imitates baseball, so I have no objection to Will's general attempt, only to this particular version.) Will actually advances two related claims in his central thesis. First, the quality of play in professional baseball has improved markedly through time, in opposition to more mythology from the other face of Janus—this time, the legend of past Golden Ages. Will writes:

> Human beings seem to take morose pleasure from believing that once there was a Golden Age, some lost Eden or Camelot or superior ancient civilization, peopled by heroes and demigods, an age of greatness long lost and irrecoverable. Piffle. Things are better than ever, at least in baseball, which is what matters most.

Second, this increasing excellence narrows the range of disparity among professional players (by relative equalization at higher summits) and makes the tiny edges supplied by obsession, practice, and intelligence all the more important. Perhaps Ruth could excel by brawn, and shun conditioning while feeding his insatiable gustatory and sexual appetites. Modern competition will not permit such laxity. Will writes:

The fundamental fact is this: For an athlete to fulfill his or her potential, particularly in a sport as demanding as baseball, a remarkable degree of mental and moral discipline is required.

We speak of such people as "driven." It would be better to say they are pulled, because what moves them is in front of them. A great athlete has an image graven on his or her imagination, a picture of an approach to perfection.

And finally, bringing both arguments together:

What spectators pay to see is a realm of excellence, in which character, work habits and intelligence—mind—make the difference between mere adequacy and excellence. The work is long, hard, exacting, and sometimes dangerous. The work is a game that men play but they do not play at it. That is why they, and their craft, are becoming better.

I am a card-carrying (dare I utter the word?) liberal, Will an equally self-identified writer of conservative bent. On baseball, however, we differ little, for most fans are deeply conservative in this jewel-like world where legacy is so precious (as Seymour shows) and where you do not die when age drops you from this realm of true and appropriate laissez-faire. I applaud Will's curmudgeonly conservatism on all issues of baseball practice. His diatribe against aluminum bats alone should inscribe him in the writer's Hall of Fame, for a deep understanding of the details that count, and the issues well worth a trip to the stake if necessary. Aluminum bats, he asserts, would destroy both the sound of baseball and the precious continuity of statistical comparability:

Allowing aluminum bats into the major leagues would constitute a serious degradation of the game, and not just for aesthetic reasons. But let us begin with them. Aesthetic reasons are not trivial. Baseball's ambiance is a complex, subtle and fragile creation. Baseball's sounds are important aspects of the game, and no sound is more evocative than that of the thwack of wood on a ball. It is particularly so when it is heard against the background sizzle of crowd noise on a radio broadcast, radio being the basic and arguably the best way to experience baseball if you can not be at the park. To a person of refined sensibilities, aluminum hitting a ball makes a sound as distressing as that of fingernails scraping a blackboard.

On the statistical point, Will notes that aluminum bats "would dilute baseball's intensely satisfying continuity and thereby would render much less interesting the comparison of player's performances. Those comparisons nourish interest in the game as it passes down from generation to generation and they sustain fans in the fallow months of the off-season."

Nor do I dispute Will's assertion that play has improved through time (especially since the evidence comes partly from my own statistical work on the history of batting averages, particularly on the elimination of .400 hitting as a paradoxical mark of improvement). I only question his upping of the ante in extending his two-part argument to a basically conservative, individualist solution of America's current social and economic ills—the dissociable and more contentious "baseball imitates life" part of his thesis. Will argues that if we, as a nation composed of individuals, could only imitate the gumption and drive of high baseball achievers who prevail by dedication and obsession more than by natural gifts, then we would regain our national power and purpose. This drive cannot be granted by governmental gift or program, but must come from within:

I believe that America's real problem is individual understretch, a tendency of Americans to demand too little of themselves, at their lathes, their desks, their computer terminals. . . . I will not belabor the point but I do assert it: If Americans made goods and services the way Ripken makes double plays, Gwynn makes hits, Hershiser makes pitches and La Russa makes decisions, you would hear no more about the nation's trajectory having passed its apogee.

I don't even dispute this claim. But I do quarrel with the premise that major league baseball, as a totality, represents an island of self-motivated excellence that could save us by extensive emulation. I think that Will has made an error in confusing parts for wholes. He has chosen four exemplary human beings at the summit of their profession—and these four share the qualities that he imputes to the entire enterprise at this level. But I doubt the validity of such a generalization. He has taken the best, but they cannot stand as surrogates for all. They are best because they have conjoined a basic intelligence and a fine body with a fierce inner drive. I don't doubt that major league baseball features more such people than you might find in your average factory or college faculty lounge. Such are the fruits of highest selectivity. But all of us who work in elite institutions of their chosen profession know that cynicism, submission, and dead wood exist at all levels. Baseball also contains its journeymen and its losers, its men of superb talent who never grow up or never catch fire. Major league baseball is not a priesthood of unflagging commitment, but an institution far more selective than most, yet still containing all kinds of folks with all manner of problems and modes of life. Major league baseball may precipitate out the losers more quickly, but we cannot so proceed in life (where consequences include death and starvation), and this oasis of unbridled laissez-faire doesn't even produce Will's universal, internally driven excellence in its own house.

My best evidence for this variety in attitude among major leaguers comes from the last of the three books reviewed here—Heiman, Weiner, and Gutman's *When the Cheering Stops*. These extended interviews with twenty-one players of the late forties through mid-seventies present a very different picture from Will's four paragons. These twenty-one include a few genuine stars, but most were journeymen who spent careers on yo-yos of trading and demotion to the minors. Some showed the obsession that has pushed Will's men to success, but most lost the drive to injury and disappointment, or never had it at all. They admired the heroes of their own age, and they recognized the zeal as well as the talent of Warren Spahn or Mickey Mantle, but could not play at this level.

These men played baseball in a different age of less intense strategy—the fifties game of "put some men on and hope for a bases-clearing homer," rather than the highly intellectual "little ball," or one-run-at-a-time (and much more exciting) baseball recaptured from the age of Cobb and Wagner and now again in vogue. These journeymen of the fifties often make too many excuses for their own abbreviated careers. (I cannot quite accept Al Weiss's argument—if only because I loved him so much after his heroics won the 1969 World Series for the Mets—that this moment of greatness wrecked his career because he could never again play to a level justifying his salary increase after his day in the sun, and he soon lost his job as a result.) They also clearly demonstrate that continuous intellectual struggle does not pervade the pinnacle at all moments. Consider these two identical assessments of Bucky Harris's managerial style, from one who loved and one who hated this successful skipper. First, from Chuck Stobbs:

> My favorite manager . . . was Bucky Harris. We'd have two
> meetings a year. On opening day he'd say, boys, you know

we're glad you're here and whathaveyou. Then, at the end of the year we'd have another meeting and he'd thank everybody for doing the best they could and say he'd hope to see us all next year.

And this, from J. W. Porter:

On opening day . . . he got everyone around him at the mound. And here's exactly what he said. He said, "Guys, you're major leaguers. If you don't know how to play this fucking game now, you never will." And he dropped the bag of balls on the mound, went and sat in the dugout and stayed there for two years until they ran him off.

I rather suspect that major league baseball imitates life pretty well—by including its share of flakes, kooks, goof-offs, and cry-babies. We can isolate a core of splendid exemplars, probably a larger core than in most professions because competition is so much stiffer. But when you probe deeply enough into the totality, all the foibles and frailties of human life emerge. Which brings me back to Janus, god of our beginnings and the "play ball" call of this essay. In his poem "A Coat," W. B. Yeats wrote of the uses of mythology:

I made my song a coat
Covered with embroideries
Out of old mythologies
From heel to throat. . . .

But others misuse his pretty covering, and he discards it:

Song, let them take it,
For there's more enterprise
In walking naked.

This review has been dedicated to defending the virtues of such nakedness—in truth value, even (for I will grant Will this) in moral instruction. This nakedness of reality is the second and less familiar face of Janus. But it's cold out there in our markedly imperfect world. So I guess we need the conventional showy face of Janus as well—the world of baseball myth and legend. And why not? In what other world is myth so harmless? Great battles kill and maim; great homers and no-hitters are pure joy or deep tragedy without practical consequence (no one, in my presence, must ever mention Bill Mazeroski's 1960 homer against my beloved Yankees). Life is inherently ambiguous; baseball games pit pure good against abject evil. Even Saddam Hussein must have committed one act of kindness in his life, but what iota of good could possibly be said for aluminum bats or the designated hitter rule?

As a skeptic and rationalist, I prefer the second face of Janus; as a fan, I acknowledge the power of his first and legendary visage. I began with a mythic home run of this first face, and I end, for symmetry's sake, with another, perhaps even more famous, as described by the hitter himself in *When the Cheering Stops*. The New York Giants (my National League club in my youth) stood thirteen and a half games behind the Brooklyn Dodgers in August 1951. Charlie Dressen, manager of the Bums, pronounced the immortal line: "The Giants is dead." The New York papers debated his grammar, but did not doubt his conclusions. Yet Durocher's Giants persisted, and miraculously tied the Dodgers on the last day of the season. The two teams split the first two games of the playoff. In the last inning of the third and final game, with the Giants trailing by two runs and all apparently lost, Bobby Thomson came to bat with two men on and hit the most famous homer in baseball history. I was nine years old, home alone after school and glued to the tiny TV screen that we had just pur-

The Shot Heard 'Round the World: The New York Giants swarm Bobby Thomson after his three-run, ninth-inning home run beats the Brooklyn Dodgers—and wins the Giants the National League title—at the Polo Grounds on October 3, 1951. *Credit: Bettmann/Corbis*

chased—a family first. I was never so purely and deliriously happy in all my life. Thomson, it seems, was pretty pleased as well:

> To this day, I can never adequately describe the feeling that went through me as I circled the bases. . . . I can remember feeling as if time was just frozen. It was a delirious, delicious moment and when my feet finally touched home plate and I saw my teammates' faces, that's when I realized I had won the pennant with one swing of the bat. And I'd be a liar if I didn't admit that I'll cherish that moment till the day I die.

Janus has two faces because we need to look both ways toward transcendence and reality—somehow titrating both to forge a reasonable approach to life. As Bucky (Fuller, not Dent of the glorious 1978 home run) said: "Unity is plural and, at minimum, is two." And as Amos (the prophet, not Rusie the Hall of Fame pitcher) proclaimed (Amos 3:3): "Can two walk together, except they be agreed?"

The H and Q of Baseball

Books reviewed:

A Whole Different Ball Game: The Sport and Business of Baseball by Marvin Miller

Ted Williams: A Portrait in Words and Pictures, edited by Dick Johnson, text by Glenn Stout

My Favorite Summer, 1956 by Mickey Mantle and Phil Pepe

The Home Run Heard 'Round the World: The Dramatic Story of the 1951 Giants-Dodgers Pennant Race by Ray Robinson

I f you wish to divide Americans into two unambiguous groups, what would you choose as the best criterion? Males and females, east and west of the Mississippi? May I suggest, instead, the following question: "What was Justice Blackmun's worst decision?" Anti-abortionists, and conservatives in general, will reply without a moment's hesitation: *Roe* v. *Wade.* Liberals might need to think for a moment, but if they like baseball as well, they will surely answer: *Flood* v. *Kuhn.* For, in 1972, the same Harry Blackmun who gave us *Roe* v. *Wade* also wrote the 5–3 decision (with the usual trio of Douglas, Marshall, and Brennan in opposition) denying outfielder Curt Flood the right to negotiate freely with other teams following the expiration of his contract with the St. Louis Cardinals, and upholding the admittedly illogical exemption of major league baseball from all antitrust legislation (on the preposterous argument that this game alone—for none other enjoys such a waiver—is a sport and not a business).

Curt Flood was one of the best ballplayers of the 1960s, a fine outfielder with a nearly .300 lifetime batting average. Following the 1969 season, after twelve good years with the Cards, he was traded to the Philadelphia Phillies—and he didn't want to go (or at least he wanted the option, available to any free man, of placing his services on the market and negotiating with other teams). But major league baseball, by explicit judicial sanction, had always enforced a system of peonage based upon the reserve clause. This statement, present in all contracts, "reserved" the player's services to his club for the following season, even if terms had not been reached on a new contract. (That is, the player could be "reappointed"—without his approval, take it or leave it—for a following year at the same terms as the last season.) In effect, the reserve clause provided a perpetual contract because owners granted themselves the power of indefinite extension, year after year. Thus, teams owned players and could pay and trade them almost at will. A player had but one "recourse," really a death warrant, rather than a weapon: he could refuse to sign, but to what avail? No other team would hire him.

Owners insisted that they needed such a provision to prevent baseball's wreckage by bidding wars—an odd argument that management must be protected from itself by oppressing workers. In two previous rulings, in 1922 and 1953, the Supreme Court had upheld baseball's exemption from antitrust legislation, thereby depriving players of any judicial remedy for abuses of the reserve clause. (The Court did not present a constitutional defense of management, but rather passed the buck, stating that any regulation of baseball's traditional ways must be instituted by Congress.) Blackmun's regrettable decision of 1972 includes a mixture of platitudes about the sanctity of our national pastime, combined with a third passing of the buck.

All Americans not living in a hole know that circumstances have since reversed dramatically: the reserve clause is history and players now have adequate power and fair representation in negotiating contracts. Consequently, players are coequal with management, and their gargantuan salaries hog more news than their accomplishments on the field. (I don't want to bore you with figures so endlessly repeated in the press that they have become a litany.)

Two other points are equally obvious to all fair-minded observers, but not so frequently stressed. First, contrary to the doomsday predictions made by owners for more than a century, baseball remains in good health. Owners insisted that free agency would lead to an unfair concentration of talent, but free bidding has increased interest and competition on the field by reducing the differences among teams and giving most a chance for a championship. Between 1949 and 1964 a New York team played in the World Series in all years but 1959. The Yankees alone won nine World Series during this period. These were blissful years for a Yankee fan like me, but not good for baseball and the rest of the country. No such dynasties exist today; talent is too mobile and this year's last can become next season's first.

Second, effective unionizing of players had produced this more equable distribution of baseball's immense revenues. (The vast increase arises from TV and radio contracts, and remarkably effective merchandizing—but owners wouldn't have shared the bounty voluntarily.) I doubt that a better success story for trade unionism can be told in our times. Dave Winfield, a great veteran player and one of the most thoughtful men in the game today, said it all: "I have been a part of the best union for workers in this country. I don't think that baseball players have been greedy, or that the union has been greedy or nasty. The owners used to make all the money. Now they share it."

As much as traditional trade unionists may take heart from this success, special circumstances prohibit a translation into more conventional workplaces. We are, after all, speaking of a few hundred "workers" (major league players) in a market that brings in billions of dollars a year for the exercise of their talents. The average person in an office or on an assembly line simply cannot generate such resources for potential sharing. As Gene Orza, general counsel of the Players Association, once said to me: "Workers vs. bosses just can't be the rhetoric any more. I would rather talk of playing capitalists vs. entrepreneurial capitalists."

I do not generally believe in "great man" theories of history, but I cannot think of a better case for the importance of a single person. The Players Association owes its success to good sense and good fortune in not hiring a management shill to lead a nascent association that would have become a company club (the previous history of players' "unions"), but in bucking baseball's "in-house" tradition and appointing Marvin Miller, lifelong trade union professional, chief economist for the United Steelworkers of America, and a brilliant, persistent, patient, and principled man (also an old Dodger fan from a Brooklyn boyhood).

Miller, who created an effective union out of the Players Association and served as its executive director from the mid-sixties to the early eighties, has finally written his long-awaited account: *A Whole Different Ball Game: The Sport and Business of Baseball*. The jacket copy by the great announcer Red Barber (voice of the hated Bums and later the beloved Yanks in my youth) states with all the one-sided strength of the genre, but with undeniable justice and accuracy:

When you speak of Babe Ruth, he is one of the two men, in my opinion, who changed baseball the most. He changed the construction of the game, the construction of bats as well as the ball. And the second most influential man in the history of baseball is Marvin Miller. . . . Miller formed the players' union. And from the union we have free agency, we have arbitration. We have the entire structure of baseball changed—the entire relationship between the players and the owners.

If we ask how such a radical change could occur so quickly, two factors stand out. (Though we should, following recent events in the former Soviet Union, recognize that complex systems, when they change at all, tend to transform by rupture rather than imperceptible evolution.) First, the new revenues of our TV culture provided a gargantuan pie to divide; no matter how much power players gained, they could not have achieved their current economic might from gate receipts. Second, players had to start very far down in order to rise so far—and we must ask why they were so oppressed (or, rather, "underempowered," if oppressed seems too strong a word for stars in the entertainment industry, whatever their exploitation).

Why, then, did players have so little power in the pre-Miller era? Why were they so underpaid, so devoid of influence over their own lives and futures? Why could the owner's pawn, first commissioner of baseball Kenesaw Mountain Landis, ban Shoeless Joe Jackson and the seven other Black Sox for life—without trial and without any hope of redress—after a court had dismissed charges against them of throwing the World Series? Why did the stigma stick so strongly, and permanently, to yield this, the most poignant of all baseball stories: Jackson ended up behind the counter of a liquor store in his native South Carolina. One day,

Shoeless Joe Jackson, circa 1919. *Credit: Corbis*

more than thirty-five years after the Black Sox scandal, Ty Cobb stopped by. Cobb brought some bottles to the register, but Jackson just looked down, said nothing, and began to ring up the transaction. The puzzled Cobb exclaimed: "Joe, don't you recognize me?" "Of course I do, Ty," Jackson replied, "but I wasn't sure you wanted to know me." (Only Cobb and Rogers Hornsby had lifetime batting averages higher than Jackson's. Cobb himself was widely suspected, probably correctly, of consorting with gamblers and occasionally throwing games.)

The reasons for this underempowerment are complex, but consider two intertwined aspects. Owners played an effective game of "divide and conquer" against a group of mostly young and uneducated players (Rube, the nickname of so many early players, reflected a common background). Hardly any of the early players went to college and few finished high school. Baseball, for all the mythological hyping, really took root as a people's sport in America, while football remained a minor pastime for a collegiate elite. Owners nipped any fledgling attempts at organization among players by providing a few paternalistic scraps and then invoking the same bogeymen that stalled unionization in more fertile fields of factories and mines—"not real baseball people," "trying to undermine the game," "radicals," "outside agitators." A grizzled miner with twenty years in the pits, a huge debt at the company store, and thousands of compatriots might see through the bluff; an eighteen-year-old farmboy, with no one to represent him and only a few hundred colleagues, might never think of mounting a challenge. Moreover, owners had great success in invoking the hoary and elaborate mythology of baseball as a "game" and a "national pastime"—the same line that the Supreme Court has bought three times. "How can you even raise a question about salaries?" owners would intone: "Where else could a person actually get paid for playing a game? Thank your lucky stars, shut up, play, and don't complain." The ruse worked for nearly one hundred years.

This interplay of baseball's sporting mythology and its commercial reality fascinates me more than anything else about the game as a social phenomenon in America. Each year's flood of baseball books can be neatly partitioned into these two basic categories. I shall call them H-mode and Q-mode, for hagiographical and quotidian reality. Such a division seems especially well marked in this season of anniversaries. Miller tells us that he chose this year to publish (in Q-mode) because he wished to launch his book on the twenty-fifth anniversary of the founding of the Players Association in 1966. As for the H-mode, you would have to live in the same hole previously mentioned not to know that 1991 is the fiftieth anniversary for the greatest achievements of two baseball saints—Joe DiMaggio's fifty-six-game hitting streak and Ted Williams's .406 batting average (no one has exceeded .390 since then). The *New York Times* has run a box in every issue this season detailing Joe and Ted's daily accomplishments in 1941. President Bush invited DiMaggio and Williams to the White House on July 9, and then flew them, with baseball commissioner Fay Vincent, up to Toronto aboard Air Force 1 to take in the sixty-second All-Star Game. Bush, who had entertained Elizabeth II in Washington just a few days before, stated: "I didn't think I'd get to meet royalty so soon after the queen's visit."

I will therefore devote this year's World Series–time review of baseball books to a contrast of the H- and Q-modes, in particular to a comparison of Miller's anniversary with books devoted to three milestones in the hagiographical tradition—the story of a career (Ted Williams on the fiftieth anniversary of his greatest achievement), a season (Mickey Mantle's favorite 1956 campaign on its thirty-fifth anniversary), and even of an incident (Bobby Thomson's most famous of all home runs, on the fortieth anniversary of its few-second trajectory from bat to the left-field seats). (The mills of the gods may grind exceedingly fine but the microscope of hagiography probes even more minutely.) I may also cite another, and more immediate, reason for choosing to contrast Miller's book with three different representatives of the hagiographical tradition. The existence of the myth—particularly its unfair, but clever exploitation by owners—made Marvin Miller necessary.

Miller's fascinating story testifies to the power of patience, giving a productive twist to the old Roman maxim for a life of pleasure: *festina lente*, or make haste slowly. Miller held all the cards; after all, how can feudalism be justified or maintained in a democratic age with at least some legislated safeguards? Baseball's owners had prevailed by bluff and force, but they had also become complacent in the absence of any effective challenge for so long. They may even have believed their own rhetoric.

But, as Moses learned, seeing the promised land is one thing, and getting there another. Miller knew that he could win if only he could forge solidarity and union consciousness among players. But how could an intellectual, Jewish, professional union man from Brooklyn prevail on a terrain inhabited by so few of the above? How could techniques for organizing workers succeed in a world where most people viewed "union" as a dirty word? The answer can only be: quietly but forcefully, a step at a time, and, above all, with respect for the intelligence and background of players (something the owners had never learned). Miller's triumph is a credit both to his own skills and to the virtues of professionalism.

Miller's two greatest successes, won sequentially and with help from the arsenal of labor legislation, included the establishment of impartial arbitration for settling contract and other disputes, and the invalidation of the reserve clause, which, as the owners correctly noted, had been the bulwark of their unjust system. None of this could have been accomplished without Miller's success, powerfully abetted by dependable stupidity among owners, in bringing about solidarity among players. Miller can pay no finer compliment than his statement, coming from a man who helped to lead some of the most important industrial actions of the twentieth century, that the players' strike of 1981 was the most principled he had ever seen—for older players, fighting for nothing personal but only for benefits to younger colleagues, held firm, and management eventually collapsed after more than fifty days (following their original prediction that the players would crumble within five).

The story of the reserve clause, and the winning of free agency, best illustrates Miller's method: speak softly and gain little by little. Step 1: by raising consciousness, you can win through losing—the Curt Flood case, previously discussed. Step 2: win a case even if it doesn't establish the general principle. Irascible A's owner Charlie Finley had reneged on a provision of Catfish Hunter's 1974 contract. Miller filed a grievance, went to arbitration (previously established as a first great victory), won his watertight case, and had Hunter's contract voided. The case established no principle, since the outcome only punished Finley for a contract violation, but Yankee owner George Steinbrenner then paid millions to sign Hunter, and the dam broke. Steinbrenner surely made a good move, and Hunter's classy pitching was indispensable in Yankee championships of 1977 and 1978, their first since 1962.

Step 3: take all the marbles. Miller had always insisted—and plain reading seemed to support his view—that the standard language of the reserve clause, as always written, only bound a player to his team *for one additional year* if no contract agreement could be reached. Owners insisted that they could pile on "additional years" in perpetuity. In the famous Messersmith-McNally case (also an arbitration) of 1975, Miller won the principle, and the war. Players, if unable to reach agreement with their owners, could play out their one additional year and then become free agents, able to negotiate with any team.

Miller's book is one of the most important ever published about baseball, but I wish he had done even better. Ironically, *A Whole Different Ball Game* suffers from two features that, above all else, Miller never introduced into his successful negotiations as executive director of the Players Association: some bad organization and a little mean-spiritedness. Miller can't seem to decide whether to write his book as a chronological story or a series of portraits—and you can't have both. For example, an early chapter on Bowie Kuhn (Miller's nemesis as commissioner of baseball) describes in detail the entire history of their relationship, but later chronological chapters go through the same material again.

As for the second problem, a less than optimal generosity of spirit, books just don't work well as devices for settling scores. There is a time to kill, and a time to heal; a time to break down, and a time to build up. Besides, who but you really cares about all the details of potential ingratitude? I didn't mind the harshness about Bowie Kuhn, for he and Miller were serious sparring partners for years, and Kuhn had already gotten his licks in with a previous book. But why go after so many players, including Carlton Fisk, Catfish Hunter, and Dennis Eckersley, for later downplaying the work of the association that had won their benefits? Miller is probably right in his unhappiness with them, but people do lapse into the H-mode as they get older and further from the battles actually fought. They can be reminded gently, and with humor.

Marvin Miller remains one of my heroes, but he is anathema—and quite unfairly—to many baseball fans because they vent upon him their anger and puzzlement about the assault of Q-mode reality upon their H-mode image of the game. How can I uphold the Field of Dreams when salaries and agents get more press coverage than sandlots and extra innings, and if stars, paid in millions, add insult to injury by charging my kid fifteen bucks for an autograph at a card show?

While I can understand and even defend the current salary levels, I do acknowledge some real problems. First, anyone who has a piece of graph paper and knows the meaning of "extrapolate" will easily realize that something has to give. Current trends cannot continue, lest Roger Clemens's salary exceed the GNP. But what can stop a runaway machine fueled by positive feedback? (Remember that "positive feedback" is a technical term for more leading to still more, not a statement about ethics or fairness.) Evolutionary biologists, more than most people, understand that legitimate advantages sought by individuals (tail feathers of a peacock leading to greater mating success) can foster the extermination of collectivities (the entire species becomes vulnerable because such extreme specialization makes adaptation so difficult when environments change). Advantages to individuals and benefits to species need not coincide, and may directly conflict.

Secondly, baseball will be in difficulty if arrogance bred by financial success seriously erodes public sympathy and affection for players. I do not think that this will happen, but sometimes I wonder, especially when I sense that an issue, resolved in financial terms, really isn't about money, but about something so juvenile as "who is king of the mountain." Two years ago, within a week, baseball's three premier pitchers, Dwight Gooden, Orel Hershiser, and Roger Clemens, played leapfrog over one another to become, in sequence (like "king for a day" or "famous for fifteen minutes") the highest-paid player in baseball. (They signed three-year contracts worth between six and eight million dollars; this year, to continue the spiral, Clemens signed a new four-year contract worth 21.5 million!) Can six vs. seven million possibly matter, since either figure should comfortably set up an extended family for life? Is this not a public debate over status, using money as a token? Cash is an awfully expensive token for such an issue. Won't medals do? Or how about pieces of paper proclaiming degrees and written in Latin?

But how can we blame the players, and Marvin Miller, for something entirely of our creation? We have made the world of these gargantuan salaries, and they that have sown the wind . . . shall reap the whirlwind. We want our television programs; we watch the advertisements and buy the products. We turn the people we admire into objects called "celebrities"; we think we own pieces of them, and can deny them the most elementary right of privacy. Sure it's nasty to charge a kid fifteen dollars for an autograph; but when you know that every proprietor in town is hiring kids to get free signatures on large numbers of cards for later resale at enormous profit, do you not feel used and exploited? We are paying out the money that goes to these salaries. What are the players supposed to do? Dig a hole and bury the cash? Give it to the owners? Marvin Miller did a limited and entirely admirable thing: he forced an equable distribution of funds available.

Bruce Bochte, former first baseman of the Oakland A's, helped me to understand this when he said to me:

> Don't think for a moment that any player is under the slightest illusion that, in any absolute sense, his perform-ance is worth the money he receives. The point is that we are members of the entertainment industry, a particularly crazy enterprise. What we do generates this money, pri-marily through TV and radio contracts. Either we get it or the owners get it; and since we are doing the playing, we might as well get our fair share.

You can't blame Marvin Miller for the nature of the system he was hired to work within. Miller did his job consummately, with principled honesty and superlative effectiveness. Don't castigate him because our nutty economy (in a world of poverty) provides so much money in such places.

In this special year of so many H-mode anniversaries, I must ask whether the solution to a fan's distress at Q-mode antics lies in willful abandonment of an admitted partial reality for a home in the bosom of warmth and hope. No real fan can do such a thing for two reasons. First, you cannot even construct an adequately comforting H-mode without an unacceptable degree of fictional-ization—for honorable Q- and H-modes are not fact vs. fiction, but two styles of *truth* à la *Rashomon*. Indeed, we must even fic-tionalize fiction to get the "pure" H-mode of *Field of Dreams*. In Thomas Kinsella's fine novel, J. D. Salinger is the cynic taken to the ball game. In the film version, James Earl Jones plays the part and, in a moving scene, makes a speech about the beauty of base-ball and then disappears with the old players into the Field of

Dreams. They had to use a black man to perfect the H-mode; in no other way could baseball's greatest sin be expiated. In life, most of those older players were racists, and none ever played in the majors with a black teammate. Don't get me wrong; I loved the film. But *Field of Dreams* doesn't tell the whole story; we need *Eight Men Out* (the story of the Black Sox) for symmetry.

Second, a restricted dose of H-mode books soon becomes both dull and limiting. I like all three of the books I have chosen for my H-mode counterpart to Marvin Miller—Teddy Ballgame's career on the fiftieth anniversary of his greatest year (*Ted Williams: A Portrait in Words and Pictures*, by Dick Johnson and Glenn Stout); Mickey's finest season thirty-five years ago (*My Favorite Summer 1956*, by Mickey Mantle and Phil Pepe); and Bobby's transcendent moment of 1951 (*The Home Run Heard 'Round the World*, by Ray Robinson)—all well written, accurate, and fun to read.

But the sameness of the genre begins to wear thin after a while. The two books that treat a specific time (Mickey in 1956 and Bobby in 1951) both begin with a scene-setting chapter in standard form: "It was the best of times, it was the worst of times." The books are eerily similar. We learn what was on TV, who topped the charts of pop music, the content of newspaper headlines, the price of a hamburger. All three books then proceed in chronological fashion, for hagiography is a form of narrative, while criticism is analytical and tends to focus on issues rather than sequences.

But the books also differ in some ways. *Ted Williams* is full of well-chosen (and well-reproduced) photos and other pictorial memorabilia, and the biographical chapters include short essays written by some of baseball's literary groupies, including David Halberstam, Donald Hall, George V. Higgins, and, as I must admit, yours truly (on the statistics of Williams's .406 season). *My Favorite Summer* is particularly well constructed. The 1956 season was Mantle's triumph, climaxed by Don Larsen's perfect game (including Mantle's saving catch) in the World Series. But the chronology of old seasons cannot be as interesting as the usual stuff of drama, and I would have thought such a format difficult to sustain. Phil Pepe, Mantle's "as told to" writer, solves this problem by deftly following a chronological sequence, but using each major incident for a well-paced digression. Mantle's batting in the All-Star Game with Williams prompts a little essay on his reverence for the greatest of all hitters; the introduction of Don Larsen, one of most committed of old-time drinkers, provides an occasion for a discourse on Mantle's own legendary, late-night escapades.

For those benighted enough not to know the context of *The Home Run Heard 'Round the World* (though I don't know why I bother, for such folks can't be fans and probably abandoned this essay long ago), the New York Giants and the Brooklyn Dodgers maintained the greatest of all rivalries (I loved the Giants and hated the Bums; their joint departure for California in 1958 began the serious decline of New York City). In 1951, the haughty Bums were thirteen and a half games ahead in mid-August and the race seemed over. But the Giants fought back and tied the Dodgers at the end of the season, prompting a three-game playoff. They split the first two games, and the entire year hinged on the finale. The Giants entered the ninth inning behind 4–1, and all seemed lost. But they scored a run and had two men on when Bobby Thomson came up, unfurled his bat to October's breeze, and hit the pill heard 'round the world. Russ Hodges, the Giants' announcer, broke into joyous babbling. Red Barber, the Dodgers' man, simply broadcast: "It's in there for the pennant." Red Smith wrote in his next morning's column: "The art of fiction is dead. Reality has strangled invention."

If a season seemed implausible, you wouldn't think that a moment could fill out a whole book. But Ray Robinson prevails, particularly for New Yorkers like me who lived through the event with maximal passion. Predictably, most of the book fills out the entire season, the personalities, and the finer points of baseball's deepest rivalry. But several final chapters treat the moment itself, and Robinson does not run out of things to say. I particularly enjoyed the "where were you when?" final chapter, where many celebrities and ordinary folks recall their spot—for my generation knows this as well as the next remembers where they were on November 22, 1963. I, at age ten, was glued to our newly purchased first TV, home alone after school. I have never known a greater moment of pure joy in my life.

How, then, shall we deal with relationships between the H- and Q-modes, the two deep valleys that house nearly every baseball book (with very few able to maintain a position on the sharp ridge between)? I have thought about this for years, have played with many solutions, and have finally come to the decision that we must leave the two modes alone in their different realities. We need both, but they cannot be combined. They exist like oil and water in a jar—immiscible—and all lovers of the game must own a jar with both components in their separate layers.

Please do not misunderstand me. Hagiographical and quotidian are not true vs. false, exaggerated vs. accurate. Both are equally true, but partial. Hagiography is myth in the honorable, not the felonious, sense. There are no lies in *My Favorite Summer*, only a partial account in the H-mode. But to understand Mantle fully, you need both modes. In the current, H-mode book, Mantle presents the mythological line on salary: I loved the game so much, I couldn't even think of such issues. He writes:

> After the 1955 season, the Yankees sent me a contract for $32,500. To me, that was all the money in the world. My dad probably didn't make that much combined all the years he worked in the mines. I didn't even try to get the

> Yankees to give me more. I just signed the contract and
> sent it right back. I couldn't wait to go to spring training
> to get ready for the 1956 season.

But Mantle also wrote a Q-mode book in 1985, *The Mick*. Here he writes with bitterness about yearly run-ins with George Weiss, his paternalistic, mean-spirited boss. After the 1957 season, which (on paper) was even greater than his 1956 year, Weiss had the audacity to propose a $5,000 pay cut. (The denigration continued. Mantle took a $10,000 pay cut before the 1961 season; he responded by hitting fifty-four home runs, his highest total, and inspiring teammate Roger Maris to break Babe Ruth's record with sixty-one.) Most revealing are Mantle's long descriptions of his financial worries at the height of his career. He was especially concerned about a failing bowling alley that he had started to secure his long-term financial future. His fears reached their peak in 1957:

> I was also getting migraines worrying about my once-
> flourishing bowling alley. Competition had sprouted faster
> than a field of wild daisies. . . . My alley was not luxurious.
> . . . And here I am holding a five-year lease. At $2,300 a
> month there were those nights after closing time where
> I'd stare at the ceiling and imagine myself drilling a hole
> through the floor of the banks above to let some of their
> money trickle down.

Can you imagine anyone of Mantle's status worrying about, or even thinking of establishing, a bowling alley today? A modern Mantle could make three times $2,300 for each at-bat, and could secure his financial future in a single season.

May I venture an analogy to the hoary issue of science vs. religion? This is a supposed conflict, more accurately a pseudoconflict, shouldn't exist at all, but flares up only when one side invades the domain of the other. As inquiries into empirical and moral truth, these subjects form necessary components of a complete life. But they integrate no better than H and Q, or oil and water. Each of us needs to carry a jar with the two layers. Yet some of the world's greatest troubles, intellectual and otherwise, arise from movements by one realm into alien territory—the oxymoronic "scientific creationism," or religion improperly masquerading as science, to choose a prominent contemporary example.

Similarly, in baseball, great and unnecessary troubles arise when one mode invades the legitimate domain of the other. We often label the H-mode passion for events of the pre-Miller era as false and phony because Q-mode oppression was then so real. But Babe Ruth became the greatest icon of America; Lou Gehrig lived and died with nobility; and Bobby Thomson hit that home run, bringing joy or despondency to millions. These splendid men, and their marvelous achievements, are degraded if we deny their legitimacy because the quotidian reality of baseball as a business stressed a different theme. In fact, one might argue that their achievements and their passion became even more admirable because they played with all their heart while patronized and cheated by management.

Even more perniciously, hagiography has always slipped into the Q-world of contracts to gain a great ideological leg up for management: "Hey guys, we are actually paying you to play a game. Just take what we offer and shut up." This is the very incursion that Marvin Miller fought so long, and with complete success. Thanks to his victory, we can now properly separate the modes and, for the first time, treasure both—for Q is no longer oppression, and H can therefore give us unalloyed pleasure.

In other words, we want a détente for this two-sided *Rashomon*. We need a sporting equivalent of the Status Quo, the proper noun, not the common phrase. The Status Quo is the agreement signed in 1852 to regulate the unseemly turf wars among various

Christian factions within the Church of the Holy Sepulchre, site of Christ's crucifixion, in Jerusalem. Under this agreement, times for lighting lamps, opening windows, and saying masses are strictly regulated; and territory is subdivided to the inch. The factions do not love one another, but they survive in imposed and separate harmony mingled with tension—and they do supposedly share a common purpose. Let the H- and Q-modes of baseball commentary execute a similar, if unwritten, pact. They share the common goal of bringing the best in baseball to a nation of fans.

Last year, I participated in a baseball seminar in Philadelphia. I sat on the dais, surrounded by the great pitching heroes of Philadelphia's only World Series in my lifetime—Robin Roberts (of the 1950 team) and Tug McGraw, who got the last outs in 1980, when the Phillies won their first World Series ever. I felt moved to note this passage of H-mode history in my remarks— from the Phils' noble failure in my nine-year-old youth, to their success in my maturity. I said that, although the Phils lost all four games to my Yanks in 1950, people forget that all were close (the first three decided by a single run), and that the Series was far more exciting and closely matched than most people remember. I added that although Roberts lost the second game, he had pitched magnificently, losing 2–1 on a homer by my hero Joe DiMaggio in the tenth inning. Roberts stopped me in the middle of my speech and went to the podium. He said: "I want to thank you for remembering that; so few people do. We were good, and it meant so much to us."

I looked at Roberts, a former hero now aging, and felt suffused by H-mode warmth. But then I remembered: the same Robin Roberts was the primary agitator, the thorn in the side of management, the campaigner for players' rights and better contracts, the man who, above all other players, bears responsibility (and honor) for hiring Marvin Miller. Is there a "real" Robin Roberts to stand up? Is the H-mode man who spoke so movingly to me any less genuine than the Q-mode player who brought Marvin Miller into baseball? Let us instead be thankful that personalities and institutions display such interesting variety.

Sultan of Sentimentality

Film reviewed:

The Babe, directed by Arthur Hiller and starring John Goodman as Babe Ruth

No one, from the most revered statesman to the most feared outlaw, has surpassed Babe Ruth as an American folk hero. Japanese soldiers shouted "To hell with Babe Ruth" as they engaged our men on various Pacific Islands. And an Englishman, forced to respond to an American's taunt of "Go f—— the King" during a barroom argument, could only retaliate, with majestic equality, "Go f—— Babe Ruth." The Babe, to cite a cliché of stunning accuracy in this case, was "larger than life" in all ways—from his physical size, to his appetites (food and women), to his accomplishments (his fifty-four home runs in 1920 exceeded the total of every other *team* in the league but one).

This irreconcilable combination of myth and humanity makes the life of a legend particularly hard to capture in film or biography. Babe Ruth, once served so badly by William Bendix in a 1948

First published as "Say It Ain't So, 'Babe': Myth Confronts Reality" in the *New York Times*, April 26, 1992. Reprinted with permission of the *New York Times*.

film that appeared just before his death, has been sorely cheated again, this time by a fine actor who looks the part (John Goodman), but who could not overcome an irredeemable script and concept. (The task is not impossible; Gary Cooper triumphed as Lou Gehrig, in a moving, if somewhat maudlin, performance in *The Pride of the Yankees*—with Babe Ruth, playing himself in a supporting role, as a fine addition to the cast!)

The Babe is an unqualified failure because the film chooses to follow the most vulgar, cardboard, clichéd version of myth, and ignores both the richness of humanity and the beauty of legend in its subtler and laudable meaning. I do not complain with the prissy fastidiousness of an academic touting a highfalutin theory about veracity, or of a baseball aficionado taking pious and egotistical delight in uncovering every trivial departure from fact. I accept without question the right, even the necessity, for fictionalization in historical films. (In my own domain, I love *Inherit the Wind* as drama, even though the script is grossly inaccurate, in a studied and purposeful way, as an account of the Scopes trial.) For example, I don't mind that *The Babe* epitomizes Ruth's relations with his fellow players by pretending that one central friendship, with third-baseman Jumping Joe Dugan, pervaded his entire career, for such focusing makes good drama. (Dugan was not with Ruth during his early days in Boston. They became close when Dugan joined the Yankees in 1922, but Dugan left New York after the 1928 season, and therefore missed the last six years of Ruth's Yankee career.)

Rather, *The Babe* fails because its fabric of inaccuracy exploits a common theme and purpose—one that patronizes us and cheapens its fascinating subject. This man of so many facets becomes a sheet of cardboard, with no richness of texture and therefore no capacity to win our hearts (however much the dripping sentimentality of contrived events might temporarily exercise our tear ducts). His accomplishments became so bizarre that no one with a modicum of knowledge about the game—a category including most Americans—could possibly credit absurdity. Ruth did not hit, for instance, an infield pop so high that he had circled the bases before it landed—a ludicrous claim that must make any fan laugh in derision. He did, however, twice reach third base on towering pops that landed in front of outfielders, just behind the basepaths. What is wrong with the reality in this case?

Even the accurate bits of this film are usually transposed in time to produce a web of maddening anachronism that fatally dilutes a temporal setting otherwise meticulously constructed. I ended up feeling wrenched from history. Nicknames and identifying features of maturity are attributed to entire careers, and we lose the flow of a lifetime. Ruth is depicted as a home run machine from the start. If we were not shown one quick shot of Ruth on the mound, we would never know that he was exclusively a pitcher during his first four seasons in Boston, with a maximum of four homers in 1915. (Why throw the most truly amazing point about Ruth's career—that he was the best left-handed pitcher in baseball and would almost surely have made the Hall of Fame as a hurler, even if he had never learned to hit?) Ruth is portrayed as bloated and gargantuan from boyhood, but he was firm and trim during his first two seasons. And his nickname at his Baltimore reform school was not Fatso, but Niggerlips (recording another painful reality of American life, totally bypassed in this film). He did not make his famous comment about earning more than the president—"Why not? I had a better year than he did"—while receiving peanuts during his early Boston career, but rather (if he said it at all) as a well-paid Yankee contrasting himself with an inept Herbert Hoover. Lou Gehrig was not called Iron Horse in his first season, before setting a record for consecutive games that earned him that epithet.

If the accurate bits have been so falsely arrayed, the film's fabrications became even more disturbing in their common theme of reducing such a multifaceted life to a single dimension of saccharine sentimentality. *The Babe* wheels out every Washington's

cherry tree of canonical Ruthian lore, and even manages to embel-
lish the old clichés. Here are just two examples. George Ruth Sr.
brings his young son to St. Mary's Industrial School and abandons
him forever. We are told that he never saw his parents again. We
are even given the impression that he never left the school-
grounds until his "parole" at age twenty to join the Baltimore Orioles (the locked gate swings open and the Babe stares in
amazement at the outside world). In fact, Babe was in and out of
the school, spending the intervening time with his parents. His
mother died young, but he remained on decent, if strained, terms
with his father, a saloonkeeper. George Sr. gave his underage son
permission to marry, and then threw a party for the newlyweds in
the apartment above the saloon. Ruth used his share of the 1915
World Series money to set up his dad in a new saloon—and he
worked behind the bar with his father that winter.

The Babe's treatment of legend *numero uno* is even more shameful and manipulative. In the usual version, he visits a seriously ill
(or dying) boy named Johnny Sylvester in the hospital and promises to hit a homer for him the next day (in some versions, he
makes Johnny promise to get well in return). In *The Babe*, poor
Johnny is so ill that he cannot talk at all. When Ruth makes his
promise, Johnny holds up *two* fingers—and the Babe delivers with
a second homer in his last at-bat. In the standard biography of
Ruth's life, Robert Creamer states that the real Johnny was badly
hurt in a fall from a horse. A family friend got Ruth to autograph
a ball and delivered it to Johnny along with Ruth's promise to hit
a home run in the 1926 World Series. Ruth hit four homers in the
series and did pay Johnny a visit afterward. The following spring,
Johnny's uncle approached Ruth to thank him. Ruth, whose
inability to remember names was truly legendary, replied "Glad to
do it. How is Johnny?" When the uncle left, Ruth turned to his
cronies and said, "Now who the fuck is Johnny Sylvester?"

It gets worse in *The Babe*'s version. In 1935, fat, forty, and
washed up, Ruth spent a pathetic partial season with the Boston

Babe Ruth, unvarnished, in 1926. *Credit: Underwood & Underwood/Corbis*

Braves. But he did have one great day when he hit three homers in a single game. To construct a cardboard story of the Babe leaving with dignity, the film then shows him striding over to the Braves owner (who had hoodwinked him into playing with a phony promise that he could manage the team in the following season), throwing his hat on the ground in contempt, and then walking into the dugout for that final stroll into the dark corridor of his future. And now, who should follow him into the dugout but—you guessed it—Johnny Sylvester, grown up! He gives Babe the autographed ball back, saying that it had once brought him luck, a quantity Ruth now needs himself. Babe looks at Johnny and says with simple dignity: "Johnny, I'm gone." (Chalk up yet another transposition. In a true and poignant tale, Joe Dugan visited Babe in the hospital when he was dying of cancer. They drank a beer, and Ruth then said, "Joe, I'm gone," as the two men cried together.)

I know we live in an age of fifteen-second sound bites, and that movies are a medium of mass entertainment. So perhaps this is what the public wants; perhaps we the people deserve no more. I do not believe this pessimistic and cynical judgment. I acknowledge the obvious fact that mass markets will accept and embrace pap when offered nothing else. But complex films of genuine merit can also be great commercial successes. Doesn't so rich and contradictory a man as Babe Ruth, a figure so central in American history, finally deserve a decent, nonexploitive film? Don't America's serious baseball fans, who number in the tens of millions and who pay good money to see movies, merit an honorable version of their chief icon and hero?

I offer one incident as proof that veracity holds both virtue and mass appeal. When I saw *The Babe* in Boston, two young men sat behind me, whispering intelligent baseball commentary throughout. As we left, one said to the other: "Gee, I didn't know that Ruth hit a homer in his last at-bat. Everyone knows that Ted Williams hit one his last time up. If the Babe did the same, especially as the last of three in one game, why don't we ever hear about it?" They, in their naiveté, had never considered the hypothesis that a film might distort. I turned and told them that Ruth had played for another week or two after the three-homer game, and had not left with such power or dignity. They thanked me for relieving their confusion. Do we not deserve the truth in this case, especially when drama does not suffer (and may gain in reclaiming humanity from cardboard), and when a man even greater than Babe Ruth or the king of England once told us that truth might make us free?

Baseball:
Joys and Lamentations

Books reviewed:

My Life As A Fan by Wilfrid Sheed

Fridays with Red: A Radio Friendship by Bob Edwards

The Era, 1947–1957: When the Yankees, the Giants, and the Dodgers Ruled the World by Roger Kahn

The Gospel According to Casey: Casey Stengel's Inimitable, Instructional, Historical Baseball Book by Ira Berkow and Jim Kaplan

O Holy Cow! The Selected Verse of Phil Rizzuto, edited by Tom Peyer and Hart Seely

1.

Change is neutral as a general phenomenon, and can only be assessed case by case. We sit in our unsatisfactory present, surrounded by two mythologies that exalt their respective and conflicting ends—better futures by the fancy of progress, and rosier pasts by the fable of golden good old days. Sports fans are particularly subject to the dangers of nostalgia and a falsely glorified past. Young children deify Babe Ruth, Joe DiMaggio, Mickey Mantle, or even Reggie Jackson (who flourished at the dawn of my middle age)—none of whom they have ever seen in play. But nostalgia is surely silliest in older fans who should be able to grant some strength to the former contestant in a battle between eyewitness testimony and clouds of later memory. (I should mention that "older" has a definite meaning in this particular ballpark. Rooting is generational, and you enter the category of older when you first take your child to a game.) We simply have to be tough in the face of such temptation to moon about better pasts. I confess that I am about to submit to this enticement in choosing to focus this year's review of baseball literature on five books exalting the prime joy of my own youth—New York baseball in the late 1940s and 1950s. I must therefore begin with an apologia.

Consider the twin dangers of arguments about the good old days. First of all, we need only listen to *Kindertotenlieder*, Mahler's searing songs on the death of children, or place a call to Japan by pushing a few buttons, to remind ourselves about unambiguous improvements in the quality of our present lives. Second, I see no sense in fighting to retain old pleasures that have become truly inconsistent with modern life. We may (and should) lament the deaths of friends and lovers, but we cannot hope to retain perpetual youthfulness and must accept inevitability with grace—a time to be born and a time to die; a time to plant and a time to pluck up.

To choose an example involving both dangers, I see no point in decrying baseball's current structure of high salaries, though it has spawned a host of dire consequences endlessly rehearsed in the copious literature of baseball lamentation—including the complacency and self-indulgence of some stars, and the rupture of any loyalty between player and town, as teams become holding operations for the passage of mobile and monied players who spend a year or two and then move on. (Yes, the old days were marvelous, when DiMaggio defined the Yankees for life, Williams belonged to Boston and the Red Sox, and Musial was forever a

Cardinal. But remember that only a few stars used this system to their advantage, and that most players were peons performing for peanuts, prevented by the infamous reserve clause from negotiating their own contracts, and therefore held as vassals to their owners. And I need hardly remind anyone that black men couldn't play in the big leagues at all until 1947.)

Besides, how can we deny players the benefits that modern life has produced? Broadcasting fees have vastly increased the "take" of major league teams. Either the owners keep the windfall, or it goes to the players who actually generate the money. Ballplayers are members of the entertainment industry and are only receiving the going rate (maybe even a bit less, if you consider rock stars) for their services. Do not, therefore, lament things that cannot be anymore, and never were so good anyway.

Let us, instead, save our complaints for preservable goods lost through stupidity, complacency, and avarice. Baseball presents a fascinating duality to students of change and tradition. Nothing substantial has altered on the playing field. We can understand Babe Ruth in 1927, or even Nap Lajoie in 1901, because they played exactly the same game, always changing its style of course (as any dynamic institution must) but operating for more than a century without any major alteration in rules or physical dimensions. (By contrast, I can make no meaningful contact with football and basketball players of my grandfather's generation, for I do not grasp their different games, while the numbers attached to their performances permit no comparison with modern assessments.) Yet, at the same time, the commercial structure of baseball as a business, and the social status of baseball as an institution (including such basics as times and places of play), have altered almost beyond recognition.

I do not like many of these changes (while welcoming others), but I generally resist the strategy so rightly ridiculed in Ko-Ko's proposed beheading of "the idiot who praises, with enthusiastic tone, all centuries but this, and every country but his own." I have, instead, accepted what I didn't like because I could see no alternative that would keep baseball consonant with changed realities in modern American life. "Museums of practice" cannot survive as mass institutions (opera, an elite institution, just barely manages). The miracle of baseball, after all, lies in the fact that on-field play still works so splendidly in its unaltered mode; how did the rulemakers of the 1890s know that they had constructed a game for the ages?

But baseball is now about to institute a change of a different order—erosive (if not destructive), unnecessary, and preventable; and therefore to be lamented. This change is not overtly bigger than others of recent years, but it cuts at the heart of baseball's central joy. As I write this essay, we are witnessing baseball's last pennant races. Next year, teams will no longer play the regular season in pursuit of a meaningful pennant—the banner of victory for first place in a daily struggle lasting from April to the end of September. They will, instead, compete for a slot in an ever-widening, ever-extending, multitiered series of playoff steps to the World Series. Why does this change matter so much?

The National League began in 1876; the American League (still called the "junior circuit"), a quarter century later in 1901. In 1903, the champions of the two leagues met for the first World Series (won by the Boston Red Sox). Each league contained eight teams, concentrated in the east and geographically confined by the practical limits of train travel to a region defined by Chicago, St. Louis, and Washington at the corners. In 1952, the same teams still played in the same places, under a slightly increased and stabilized schedule of 154 games (up from 135–140 in the 1903 season).

In 1953, the hapless Boston Braves moved to Milwaukee (and later to Atlanta). The even more hapless St. Louis Browns moved to Baltimore in 1954, where they have become, as the Orioles, one of baseball's most successful teams. This trickle then expanded to a flood as old teams migrated and new clubs joined. Major league baseball moved into California, Canada, Texas, and most recently, Denver and Miami. Each league now maintains fourteen teams. (You really have to know your history to make any sense of current names. Why should seaside Los Angeles be host to a basketball team called the Lakers? They are the transplanted Minneapolis Lakers of yore. Why should the same city, where no one walks, host a baseball team called the Dodgers to honor wary Brooklyn pedestrians?)

I do not see how any fair person can object to these expansions. After all, by what right could the northeastern segment of the United States continue to wield territorial hegemony over baseball after team travel by airplane made the entire nation accessible? Similarly, how can one lament the first alteration, initiated in 1969, of the balance between regular and postseason play—the splitting of each league into two divisions, with an added round of championship play between division leaders in each league before the World Series? Postseason play for a single club made sense in an eight-team league, but one chance in fourteen (the present number of clubs in each justifiably expanded league) seems too rarefied, while one in seven (the amended probability of victory with two divisions per league) preserves the old balance while implying a round of playoffs before the World Series. Thus very few fans deplored the added intraleague playoffs, which have become a welcome and exciting part of the baseball season. Why, then, do so many of us object so strongly to the second tier of playoffs that will start next season—not as a consequence of fur-

ther expansion (and this observation holds the key to our complaints), but as an end in itself?

To epitomize the new system, each league will be further fractured into three geographical divisions (five teams in the East,
five in the Central, and four in the West). Four teams (the divisional leaders plus a "wild card" second-place team with the best
record across the entire league) will then meet in the added round
of playoffs. The winners of this elimination will then play a second round to determine participants in the World Series. Since
the regular season schedule of 162 games will be maintained, and
since nondomed stadiums in places like Boston and Chicago really
don't permit a beginning much before the traditional April date,
the World Series will now take us nearly to November (if not literally so, given postponements for rain—or snow!).

To understand why this change is qualitative and destructive
rather than merely incremental and inconsequential, we should
consider the packaging of laundry detergent. In this commercial
world, ordinary and regular do not exist; the smallest available
package is marked "large"—and sizes then augment to super,
gigantic, and colossal. Such "promotions" without substance are
merely risible, but more consequential inflations in sport alter the
product itself in fundamental ways, not just the packaging. The
root cause of sporting inflation is entirely obvious: the financial
control and consequent dictation of policy by national TV and its
advertisers, by far the dominant source of modern revenue. Regular season games are regional and for small markets; postseason
championship series can be advertised and promoted nationally
for big bucks.

Basketball, football, and hockey, our other major professional
team sports, have been inflated in this way for years. The so-
called regular season has become something of a farce, with
scarcely more meaning than a set of exhibition games. Few teams

are eliminated from postseason championship play. The rounds of postseason competition have become so numerous that fans now speak of these endless eliminations as a "second season."

We may grasp the structural absurdity of such a situation, but I don't think that lamentations are in order—for football, basketball, and hockey were created (at least as professional activities with truly mass appeal) by television and constructed in its image. Their regular seasons never had a central place in American culture (much as they meant to relatively small coteries of devoted fans)—so demoting regular season play, while silly in a logical sense, has not robbed us of anything precious and formerly possessed.

But baseball's regular season has been, for a century, a joy, and a definition of life's patterns for millions of fans—a rhythm and a drama that buds in spring, becomes our constant companion in summer, burns most brightly for a short time when maple leaves turn red in October, and then ends when the trees become bare. Baseball is not just an occasional three hours at the ballpark. Baseball, through its many months and 162 games, is going to the corner store every morning, buying the paper and a cup of coffee, exchanging a few words with Tom the proprietor about last night's game, and then spending ten minutes at home with the box scores. Baseball is the solace of long summer drives, when a game on the radio beats a Beethoven symphony. These are not romantic images but daily summer realities for millions of Americans.

The World Series was a bonus—a short national blast capping a long regional drama. No one disputed the priorities and balances: a separate and postclimactic World Series, following the primacy of a long regular season, filled (as all drama must be) with moments of adventure and despair, and longer stretches of boredom—and at its climax, a race for a key reward, the league pennant. This popular format, maintained until now as levels of attendance and income continued to rise, has been slain for no reason of complaint or failure—but only because the game's moguls sniffed a source of expanded revenue in destroying baseball's unique emphasis on a regular season. National TV has triumphed over regional loyalty and baseball has adopted the depressing model of other big-business team sports. Our regional, daily pleasures have been sacrificed to a series of staged national productions that can sell advertising for a million bucks a minute.

My complaint is not idiosyncratic or unusually intense. Many players, fans, and writers share my belief that this change differs from all others in marking a fundamental sacrifice and degradation, not a mild inevitability requiring our acquiescence or accommodation. Bobby Brown, now president of the American League, but the Yankee's stylish third baseman in my youth (and later a distinguished cardiologist), expressed his anger and sadness in much the same terms. Michael Madden, the *Boston Globe's* excellent sports columnist, wrote with feeling when baseball's owners, meeting in Boston (of all places) on September 10, made their fateful decision—and also introduced another change symbolic of their servitude to national television:

> Baseball will now have Pete Rozelle's [football's] wild card, and John Ziegler's [hockey's] expanded playoffs, and David Stern's [backetball's] playoff double-headers to be marketed on TV. . . . The circle was rounded when baseball also announced yesterday that it had moved its opener next April from the traditional Monday to Sunday and had sold off that one opener to ESPN. . . . Did they have to do this in Boston? It should have been done in the Great Mall of America outside Minneapolis, in some big TV store, with the owners all standing in front of 100 flickering TV screens behind them, not mere steps from Boston Common.

There is another reason for singling out this change as especially significant—one that transcends the parochialism of baseball and speaks to a fundamental issue at the heart of any general discussion about the quality of life in modern America: regional differentiation vs. commercially driven standardization.

Regionalism is a wonderful thing, provided that each person has a region and that no one is thereby excluded or downgraded. I relish the fact that we New Yorkers talk funny, and that art deco skyscrapers symbolize our city. I am glad that one shot of different buildings, and one sentence from the local cop, conclusively identifies Chicago as the locale of Harrison Ford's *The Fugitive*. But we must set boundaries to this love of variety. I accept the need, even the blessings, of standardization in practical matters: we require a worldwide telephone dialing system and a network of national highways; we cannot move entirely on picturesque one-lane roads passing through every village and hamlet.

We should try to conceive a set of Deuteronomy-like rules about separation: where we will allow standardization, and where we must preserve the key notions of distinctive locality, and of neighborhood. We need domains of standardization, and realms of regionalism, each in its appropriate place, and linked in mutual respect and recognition. I accept and even want McDonalds at the highway interchange—drive-thru and all—but not in my little neighborhood of ethnic restaurants, and not next to the Corn Palace in Mitchell, South Dakota.

The voluminous commentary on baseball's last pennant races has not generally linked our loss to this key issue of regionalism and its virtues; yet, surely, the wider significance lies squarely in this vital debate. I cannot think of a more important or more pervasive example of precious and legitimate regionalism than the traditional structure of baseball's regular season. No one is excluded; everyone has a regional team, now that baseball has expanded throughout the nation and into Canada. The traditional system works; nothing is broken. The local rivalries animate schoolyards, living rooms, and bars; teams—especially the older ones—define a major part of the soul and substance of cities and regions. Why would we surrender something so valuable?

The regular season represents regionalism; postseason play is national. The traditional balance has been just right—a long time of local sharing, followed by a short and intense national contest. Why are we about to downgrade the regional part (while perversely retaining its admirable length after eviscerating the meaning)? I want to travel on the subway to Fenway Park, argue and kibitz with my seatmates Jay, Jenny, and Jeff, follow games in the morning paper; I don't want to spend a month in front of my TV screen watching round after round of eliminations in an ascending series labeled like laundry soap. The elimination of a meaningful pennant after a 162-game struggle, and the addition of a new round of playoffs, is like installing a Pizza Hut in my corner grocery store—and I resent it.

2.

Arguments about historical loss suffer a grave difficulty in any attempt to persuade. How can anyone know what they haven't experienced? Why should younger fans feel an attraction for something they cannot know, especially when most social trends threaten regionalism and boost commercial standardization? Our hope can only lie in testimony from people who have experienced the pleasures of regionalism as fans and players. We can identify a key time and place for the best of a better way (though I will admit to a certain unfairness for the rest of the nation)—New York baseball during the late forties and fifties, when my native city boasted three of the greatest teams that ever played our game, a unique confluence that continues to produce a substantial literature of remarkable quality and variety. I dedicate this year's review to the best years of New York baseball—a symbol for a preservationist battle no less important than any fight ever made to save a building. New York lost its soul when the Dodgers and Giants moved, and when Pennsylvania Station died in wreckers' rubble.

Wilfrid Sheed, in his introduction to *My Life as a Fan*, recounts an intellectual's lament about time spent on sports:

> So there they sat for years, the hours spent mulling and brooding, living and dying over various sports, adding up to a monument the size of a small city to wasted time and attention. Other writers might have gold deposits stashed all around their backyards, but I just had this heap of slag. . . . Yet from time to time I would gaze wistfully at my slag heap twinkling in the sun and ask myself whether it might not be worth at least *something*?

I am delighted that Sheed, a marvelous writer well known to readers of this publication, has decided to join passion with profession—for I regard his book as the best testimony to baseball's hold upon us, and to its frequent (if threatened) internal beauty, since Roger Angell started writing his incomparable prose.

Sheed entered the world of baseball as a double outsider in childhood—first as a foreigner with Australian and British roots, and second as a proto-intellectual who discovered (as I did) that sports knowledge gives you a niche (marginal perhaps, but still a niche) in boy culture:

> He has a place in the gang, though a humble one like a court jester's. "Ask Sheed—he knows everything." You have to be a little weird to know all that stuff, and weird can never be the best thing to be, but you're all right, you've turned your powers to benign, good-guy purposes.

"What do you do, sit up all night and study that stuff?" There is no right answer to this, but you're probably better off with "Yes." It's better to be a crank than a genius. Otherwise you can try "It's just a knack," and try to make up for it with dreadful schoolwork.

Sheed came to Philadelphia in 1940, as a nine-year-old refugee from the Blitz of London. His memories are therefore ten years older than mine, and begin with the bittersweet experience of rooting for a truly terrible local team (the old Philadelphia Athletics). But Sheed soon traded up: "Thank God I had balanced my portfolio with the Brooklyn Dodgers." He therefore knew, as a young man, the joys of New York baseball at its best, including the transcendent moment for his guys (not for mine), when the Bums beat the Yanks for their only World Series victory in 1955, and he (but not I) experienced "the unholy glee that exploded in a million bars and living rooms and offices and came pouring into the streets of Brooklyn on a wave of pure happiness."

Personal testimony provides us with the best way to convey the appeal and value of regional, regular season sport; and Sheed's memories are more telling than most because of his good writing and gentle humor. Consider this description of his first major league game, at the old bandbox of Shibe Park, Philadelphia:

> The first game still sits there shining. . . . Aging commuters will remember how the sight of that park brightened the approach to North Philadelphia station. You had only to hop off the train and be in Wonderland (I hopped off myself one day and landed on my nose—you did have to wait until the train stopped). Anyway, it was love at first sight, a love embracing even the light towers and the back of the grandstand. This was going to be a good place. Yes indeed.

Or this anecdote, about Father Felix, one of Sheed's teachers at his Catholic school, and an avid racing fan:

> Clerical sports nuts were as common as daisies in the old American church. So Father Felix was probably not the only priest to start pawing the ground come spring and flaring his nostrils. . . . He would repair [to the track at Monmouth Park, New Jersey] in black pants and a green school windbreaker and bet such dribs and drabs of money as the vow of poverty allowed him. But one day, before he could slide into the men's room to change into his threadbare disguise, an attendant accosted him in a scary voice with the words "Don't you go in there, Father!" "Why not? What's going on in there?" piped Felix, as a good straight man should, and the attendant wound up and unloaded his high hard one on him. "I seen a lot of priests go in there, Father, and I never seen one come out."

Newspapers and radio supplied the continuity for daily play during the great years of New York baseball. Today, most announcers are interchangeable—little personality and less opinion (though with copious facts dredged from computers about such meaningless arcana as the number of doubles Mr. X hit to the opposite field off Mr. Y in night games at Field Z during 1992). But announcers, particularly on radio where more color and information must be supplied, were once as distinctive and as regionally differentiated as the teams they represented.

New York was fortunate to have two of the greatest announcers, both southerners with deeply distinctive accents, during the glory years—Mel Allen (from Alabama) with my Yankees, and Red Barber (from Mississippi) with the enemy Dodgers. They differed so sharply, and came to define their teams so intently, that when the Bums fired Barber and the Yankees promptly grabbed him, I just couldn't adjust. Barber announcing for the Yanks sounded like Tokyo Rose singing "God Bless America."

Think of any great rivalry between wonderful talents who basically appreciate and admire each other—Pavarotti and Domingo, DiMaggio and Williams. Allen's style was pure corn. He rooted with gusto. (Who can forget his home run mantra of "going . . . going . . . gone"?) He touted his advertisers at any opportunity— home runs were "Ballantine blasts," and near misses were "foul by a bottle of Ballantine beer."

Barber, by contrast, was as cool and even as could be: when Bobby Thomson hit his immortal home run to wrest the flag from the Dodgers in 1951, Barber just stated the fact and then let crowd noises fill the air for a full minute—while Giants announcer Russ Hodges babbled with incoherent joy and, in Barber's opinion, totally unprofessional favoritism. He had more useful information in his head than any modern computer and he made the right connections. He may have spoken without overt passion, but he was a master of words and their uses (including impeccable grammar), and his down-home sayings and phrases illuminated the airways. A wet ball that eluded an infielder was "slicker than oiled okra." As the Dodger starting pitcher began to falter one day, Barber announced: "There's no action in the Dodger bullpen yet, but they're beginning to wiggle their toes a little." I loved both men.

The very best professionals have such love for their work, and such dedication to their calling, that they cannot stop while life and opportunity remain. Much as I admired Mel Allen and Red Barber in their spring and summer, I think that I appreciate them all the more for their work during their eighties, the winter of their lives. Mel Allen now announces for the major league's official television journal *This Week in Baseball*—and how I still look forward to hearing his animated voice. Red Barber died in October 1992, after twelve years as the star of the most popular program ever to run on National Public Radio—his four-minute weekly chat on Friday morning with Bob Edwards ("Colonel Bob" to Red after Barber learned that Edwards, who comes from Kentucky, had officially received this title, one readily conferred upon natives of the state).

Red treated Bob like a son. They talked about flowers, cats, and the weather in Tallahassee, where Red had retired. They usually (but not always) got around to sports. Red charmed millions of listeners with his courtliness, his civility, his urbanity, his professionalism, his stubbornness in conducting each conversation on his own terms, and his immense knowledge. I admired all these traits, but I listened because I so loved to hear that wonderful voice from my youth. I will also confess to an experience worthy of the old cartoon series, "The Thrill That Comes Once in a Lifetime." Red spent one of his broadcasts correcting me for misidentifying the last pitch of Don Larsen's perfect game in the 1956 World Series (I had called it low and outside, but the pitch was high). What a pinnacle: to be corrected by the Old Redhead!—like learning that God himself, or at least the chief rabbi of all history, deems your work worthy of improvement!

Of course *Fridays with Red* is a good book; nothing filled with long excerpts from Red Barber could possibly be bad. But Colonel Bob could have done so much better. He has composed the equivalent of a testimonial or long promotional pamphlet, when be could have written a book about that most elusive, precious kind of relationship, a genuine friendship between men. On the air, Edwards was unassuming, letting Red talk and gently nudging him from topic to topic, and this book contains long and enjoyable extracts from their programs. But I guess the Colonel has been saving his own words for years, and his book contains many editorial statements at too great a length. Moreover, Edwards disrupts his book with long lists of quotations from others, including page after page of eulogistic letters received after Red's death, with testimonials to Red's excellence and his own. Red Barber, a

man of consummate form and timing, would surely have cut
these lines.

Roger Kahn calls the great era of New York baseball "the
most important and the most exciting years in the history of
sport." As a sportswriter for the *Herald Tribune*, Kahn covered all
three teams during these years; he described more than 750 daily
and postseason games, and knew all the players. Kahn has also
written many fine baseball books, including *The Boys of Summer*,
his affectionate and incisive portrait of the men who played for
the Brooklyn Dodgers, considered by many as the finest baseball
book ever written.

Kahn's new book—*The Era: 1947–1957: When the Yankees, the
Giants, and the Dodgers Ruled the World*—wisely violates the conventions of sports writing: the accounts of one game after another
interspersed with anecdotes about extracurricular adventures in
bars and hotel rooms. Instead, drawing on the technique of the
best of TV soaps (and I do not say this at all disparagingly, but in
praise), Kahn ties together the three basic stories for the three
teams, while also including several interesting subplots and tales
about particular players and managers.

Some features of the book seem overly idiosyncratic. Kahn
spends a bit too much time on relatively trivial events that happened to involve him. He has also given the book a most curious
(and regrettable) imbalance by writing at length about the admittedly thrilling beginning of "The Era" and then hurrying through
the equally exciting end. He devotes, for example, a full thirty
pages to the marvelous 1947 World Series, describing every game
in detail, and for once in the conventional narrative mode (so dis-
cordant from the rest of the book that I wonder if this account
was left over from an earlier work).

But he then compresses into the same number of pages all the
dramatic events of 1954 through 1957: the Giants' sweep of the

1954 World Series from the Cleveland Indians, the best team in the history of modern baseball (including Willie Mays's legendary catch off Vic Wertz, and alcoholic utility outfielder Dusty Rhodes's great moment of batting glory); the one and only victory of the Dodgers in the 1955 World Series (how could Kahn, of all people, downplay this singular triumph over the hated Yankees?); Don Larsen's perfect game in the 1956 World Series; and the beginning of the California diaspora.

Kahn argues that the earlier years were more dramatic and important, but I suspect that he just ran out of gas. I, for one, would have read one hundred more pages with delight (and the book would only then have reached the length of *The Boys of Summer*)—for Kahn is the best baseball writer in the business, and shouldn't scrimp.

New York baseball was a marvel during the days of The Era. Ten of eleven seasons featured at least one New York team in the World Series. Seven World Series were "subway" contests between two New York teams ('47, '49, '52, '53, '55, and '56 with Yanks vs. Dodgers, and '51 with Yanks vs. Giants), while one of ours beat an infidel in two others (Yanks over Phils in '50, and Giants over Indians in '54). But the wider appeal of New York baseball lay in the incidents and stories involving the remarkable men who illuminated our athletic stage during The Era.

I didn't know, for example, that Babe Pinelli umpired at second base in the fourth game of the 1947 World Series. With Yankee Bill Bevens pitching a no-hitter with two outs in the ninth, Pinelli called Dodger Al Gionfriddo safe at second in an attempted steal. Had Pinelli called Gionfriddo out—and Rizzuto, who made the tag, swears to this day that Pinelli was wrong—Bevens would have won his no-hitter. Instead, Cookie Lavagetto doubled to ruin Bevens's achievement and, almost cruelly, to win the game as well, as two runners, whom Bevens had walked, scored on the hit. Why concentrate upon this incident? Because the same Babe

Pinelli, umpiring his last game before his retirement, stood behind the plate when Don Larsen pitched his perfect game in the 1956 World Series—and Pinelli made a controversial final call by declaring Dale Mitchell out on strikes on a pitch that was clearly high and outside (the one that prompted Red Barber's correction of my error). Was he atoning for a previous miscall?

Kahn writes best about the ruthless, colorful, crude, imperious, and sometimes principled men who played and ruled New York ball during The Era. What crazy confluence could have brought such people as Walter O'Malley, Casey Stengel, and Leo Durocher together, even in so vast a city? The Dodger boss O'Malley never let a fact stand in the way of a tale and moved the Dodgers to California despite continuing enormous profits in Brooklyn. Kahn tells the story of two prominent sportswriters who challenged each other (one night in a bar, of course) to write down the names of the three worst human beings. Each wrote in secret and produced the same list: Hitler, Stalin, and O'Malley. (Just about right, in my opinion.) Dodger fan Wilfrid Sheed agrees as well, for he brands O'Malley as "this monstrous figure, this walking cartoon. He is the villainous Walter O'Malley, against whom this book is dedicated."

Casey Stengel, who managed the Yanks to a record five World Series victories in a row ('49–'53), sometimes acted like a clown and spoke in syntax so fractured that his style gave the language a new term—Stengelese.[1] But Stengel only used these manner-

---

[1] This year's New York baseball books also include two collections from two singular personalities—a Bible of all key statements in and about Stengelese in *The Gospel According to Casey* by Ira Berkow and Jim Kaplan, and an amusing selection, presented as blank verse but unaltered in text, of the meandering stream-of-consciousness musing developed as a broadcasting style by former Yankee shortstop Phil Rizzuto, in *O Holy Cow! The Selected Verse of Phil Rizzuto*, edited by Tom Peyer and Hart Seely.

isms as a conscious device to lower an enemy's guard, for he was brilliant and ruthless, a complex man capable of both real tenderness and cutting cruelty. When the Yanks beat the Phils 2–1 in the tenth inning of game two in the 1950 World Series, he remarked: "Yes sir, them Philadelphias is a very fine team, make no mistake. It is difficult to beat them, which is why it took us an extra inning today." When the Yanks won 3–2 with two out in the ninth inning of game three, he said: "The Philadelphias are very difficult to beat, as I have told you. Why today, as you gentlemen saw, my fine team was unable to beat them again until the very last inning we were permitted to play." When he took out rookie Whitey Ford for veteran Allie Reynolds to sew up the last game in the final inning, Stengel said: "I'm sorry I had to take the young man out, but as I have been telling you, the Philadelphias is hard to defeat, and I am paid by my employers to defeat them, which is why I went for the feller with the big fastball. Have a nice winter." Sounds aimless, but edit the relative clauses, introduce some agreement, and you have ordinary English. And look what Casey accomplished: he had swept the opposition in four games, but praised them generously, placated a wounded young pitcher, and tempered a rout with comic relief.

Stengel always knew what he was doing. After losing the 1957 World Series to Milwaukee, and wishing to frustrate a young TV reporter who had asked the uncharitable question "Did your team choke up out there?" Stengel just said "Do you choke up on your fucking microphone?" and then clawed at his rear end. He later said to Roger Kahn: "You see, you gotta stop them terrible questions. When I said 'fuck' I ruined his audio. When I scratched my ass, I ruined his video, if you get my drift." He could also be cruel. When Jackie Robinson criticized the Yanks for not hiring black players, and then struck out three times in a Series game against Allie Reynolds, a Native American Yankee pitcher, Stengel remarked: "Before he tells us we gotta hire a jig, he oughta learn how to hit an Indian."

Leo Durocher, who started the era as the suspended manager of the Dodgers (ostensibly for gambling and associating with undesirables, but truly for his sexual behavior and general unwillingness to conform), and then led the Giants in the triumphs of '51 and '54, was cruel and swaggering on one side, brave and antiracist on the other. When Commissioner Happy Chandler announced Durocher's suspension in April 1947, Durocher spoke only one sentence to the reporters at his hotel: "Now is the time a man needs a woman." He then led his new wife, the beautiful actress Laraine Day, into his suite—and didn't emerge for forty-eight hours. During spring training, before his suspension, several Dodgers planned a petition to protest the hiring of Jackie Robinson as major league baseball's first black player. Durocher called a team meeting at one in the morning and told the instigators to "wipe your ass" with the petition. He ended by saying: "I don't want to see your petition. I don't want to hear anything about it. Fuck your petition. The meeting is over. Go back to bed." Robinson had begun his career.

Kahn ends his book by writing: "The Era ended when it was time for the Era to end and that, I believe, is everlastingly part of its beauty and its glory." This I do not dispute. New York could not dominate a national game forever, while clean and dramatic endings beat extended fizzles. But, earlier in the book, Kahn writes of the 1951 regular season that ended with Thomson's home run: "The National League Pennant Race of 1951 belongs to the ages. There has been nothing like it before or since. Nor will it come again." Sadly, this is true—and for a deeper reason than Kahn realized at the time: there will not be another pennant race at all.

On the Wordsworthian theme—"We will grieve not, rather find Strength in what remains behind"—I take solace in what will prevail through any crass and commercially driven sacrifice of seasonal rhythm and schedule: the beauty of a single game well played, and the common denominator of baseball's best performers—obsessive striving for excellence, the mark of all true professionalism. In observing an awesome skill that we do not possess, we tend to misread ease of performance as natural inclination. Even Red Barber so erred in asking Fred Astaire whether dancing came easily to him.

> I was interested in interviewing Astaire to find out the correlation between his dancing and athletic ability. And to my surprise he said, "Well, I wouldn't say that dancing comes so easily to me. I work at it. I practice hour after hour," and suddenly you see a man who does something so effortlessly—seemingly effortlessly—and you find out that each of us who are genuine professionals pays a price.

Intellectuals often make the same mistake in assuming that we struggle to become scholars, while athletes perform by inherited brawn. But Roger Kahn movingly documented the obsessive drive and the incessant practice common to all the Boys of Summer at the Dodgers' apogee. When Billy Cox or Bobby Brown at third, Phil Rizzuto or Peewee Reese at short, dove to field a grounder with such fluidity; when DiMaggio or Mays ran across a whole field to meet a fly ball with precision; when Furillo threw a bullet from right field to home and Campy tagged the runner out by fifteen feet, we watched the equivalent of a poet's couplet, stated with perfect grace, but produced by hours of struggle after a lifetime of discipline. As Yeats wrote:

> *I said, "A line will take us hours maybe;*
> *Yet if it does not seem a moment's thought,*
> *Our stitching and unstitching has been naught."*

Good Sports & Bad

Books reviewed:

Ball Four by Jim Bouton, edited by Leonard Schecter

My Life in Baseball: The True Record by Ty Cobb and Al Stump

Cobb: A Biography by Al Stump, foreword by Jimmie Reese

Cobb, a film written and directed by Ron Shelton

Matty: An American Hero: Christy Mathewson and the New York Giants by Ray Robinson

Hitter: The Life and Turmoils of Ted Williams by Ed Linn

"I Ain't An Athlete, Lady . . .": My Well-Rounded Life and Times by John Kruk and Paul Hagen

Don't Look Back: Satchel Paige in the Shadows of Baseball by Mark Ribowsky

The Catcher Was a Spy: The Mysterious Life of Moe Berg by Nicholas Dawidoff

The Meaning of Nolan Ryan by Nick Trujillo

1.

In "Ode to the West Wind," Shelley wrote one of our culture's happiest lines: "If Winter comes, can Spring be far behind?" Baseball fans have always lived by this maxim, as winter's talk (still called the "hot stove league" to honor older places of public conversation) yielded to spring training and the start of another season. But not this year. While owners and players, tycoons all, continue their pointless and destructive strike, fans are reduced to writing and remembering. In choosing baseball's most ancient and distinctive genre—the sports biography—as my subject for this review, I can at least honor the continuity and change that fans once viewed as inviolable for the game itself, the guarantee of our fealty.

In formulating his optimistic maxim, Shelley called the west wind of autumn "the trumpet of a prophecy." Several of the biographies under review issue their own jeremiads without any overt intent. Their statements about the continuity of baseball, particularly the annual ritual of the World Series (which neither distant war nor immediate earthquake could ever interrupt), ring especially hollow after the rupture of 1994, when baseball's owners canceled both the season's end and the subsequent World Series. In his biography of Christy Mathewson, baseball's first public hero, Ray Robinson discussed the refusal of the 1904 Giants to meet the Red Sox in a World Series (only one had been played before, in 1903, so the Giants were scarcely violating an established tradition). The Giants' owner, John Brush, and manager, John McGraw, hated the "upstart" American League—just formed in 1901, while their own National League dated to 1876—and didn't wish to dignify the new league's existence with such a contest.

> Thus, the World Series of 1904 was never played. It was the last time in the game's modern history that an

owner of a pennant-winning club could unilaterally kill off
the World Series. It wouldn't happen again. Thereafter, the
Series was played every year on schedule, becoming the
ultimate theatrical moment of every baseball season. No
autocrat like Brush, no despot like McGraw would be able
to do a thing about it.

Even the clichés of conventional biographical puffery, the pas-
sages either read in derision or skipped in boredom, have
poignancy in this altered context, as in this bromide from John
Kruk of the Philadelphia Phillies, a key player in the last World
Series of 1993:

> Baseball is a game. Win or lose, you play again the next
> day. If you lose the last game of the World Series [as the
> Phillies did] you can play again next year. It's not the end
> of the world.

I am a paleontologist by trade, a student of life's uninterrupted
3.5-billion-year history on earth. All species die, and new forms
emerge; but continuity has and must be maintained, or else we
would not be here today—for if all life had ever been extermi-
nated, what odds could be placed on reconstitution, especially of
anything as complex as Ted Williams's swing, or Nolan Ryan's
heater? Paleontologists therefore have a special feeling about the
ultimate value of continuity.

If deprived of the thing itself, we must seek a surrogate with
the cardinal properties of persistence and its own interesting history of change. Aside from schedules, scorecards, rule books, and
guides on how to play, the literature of baseball best provides
such continuity (with alteration through time) in its distinctive
genre of biography for star performers.

Such works are as old as professionalization of the sport itself (mid to late nineteenth century). Putative autobiography has always relied upon the services of ghostwriters (the preferred form of yesteryear) or "as-told-to" mouthpieces who craft the conventional sequence of chapters from taped interviews (the modern style). Sportswriters have not been overpaid, and supply often exceeds demand—so a job as trumpet for the stars has always been regarded as potentially lucrative and sufficiently honorable. Moreover, with few exceptions, ballplayers have not been blessed with literary skills to match their physical prowess, so we should not begrudge them their surrogates. Even the pitcher Christy Mathewson, regarded as *the* intellectual among early-twentieth-century players because he had spent some time in college (at Bucknell, though he did not graduate), hired a ghostwriter to compose the many books that appeared under his name.

The history of baseball biography has followed the trend of general culture. Before 1970, almost all published books strictly obeyed the conventions of the hagiographical mode—limitation of treatment to the heroic aspects of on-field play, told as an epic, so that the tragedies of defeat (borne with stoic honor) received equal space with the joys of victory. Statements about personal life, if any, echoed Horatio Alger and told us how diligence and dedication might overcome an early life of poverty and illness. Even the titles of these books conveyed the gratitude of men who might never have emerged from the coal mine, or debarked from the fishing boat, if God had not granted, and the public appreciated, their fortunate skills of body—as in Joe DiMaggio's *Lucky to Be a Yankee* from the 1940s.

Former arbiters of taste must have felt (as so many apostles of "traditional values" and other high-minded tags for restriction and conformity do today) that maintaining the social order required a concept of unalloyed heroism. Human beings so designated as role models had to embody all virtues of the paragon—which meant, of course, that they could not be described in their truly human and ineluctably faulted form.

I confess to some ambivalence about our modern veering to the other extreme of "kiss and tell." We need heroes, and Zeus and Achilles will no longer do (they weren't very nice folks anyway). I don't mind discreet silence about certain categories of private behavior (and I am glad that the press kept out of FDR's bedroom). But I do reject a one-dimensional presentation of public life (and I regret the lost opportunity for private understanding of the man and public knowledge of disability when Roosevelt and the press so cunningly hid his paralysis; think what might have been gained if he had been able to announce, in calm dignity, that he did not govern with his legs).

Ballplayers, as young males living on the road for so many months a year, are notoriously less likely to act as paragons in any case, so the old style seems more inaccurate about these men than about any other putative heroes (except, perhaps, actors and politicians). There is, of course, no final "truth" to be captured by the art of biography, but we can pronounce this postmodern dictum and still allow that some genres depart further than others from salient facts of a person's life. The old hagiographical biographies certainly left a lot out. Had the authors of these books explicitly restricted their narratives to performance on the field, we might criticize them for limited compass, but could not charge gross inaccuracy. Yet these older books do make a claim for providing full and accurate representation of players' lives.

Can we understand Babe Ruth without his drinking and whoring; or Ty Cobb without his paranoia, racism, and general nastiness; or Grover Cleveland Alexander and Jimmie Foxx (and so many others) without the perils of dipsomania? In *The Meaning of Nolan Ryan*, Nick Trujillo tells a story about Babe Ruth and the press that can stand as a symbol of transformation, with all its meanings and ambiguities. An eyewitness provided the perfect example of this change in sports when he told the story about a group of beat writers traveling by train with the New York Yankees in 1928. The group watched in awe as an attractive young woman wielding a knife chased after Babe Ruth yelling, "I'll kill you, you son of a bitch." One of the writers said, "That'd make a helluva story," as his colleagues laughed and continued to play poker, knowing that the story would never be written. . . .

The change to kiss-and-tell biography would have occurred in any case because a cultural alteration of this magnitude cannot be resisted by one segment so firmly tied to the mainstream. But particular items fuel or catalyze any particular transition, and we need to honor these efforts whatever the general inevitability. Jim Bouton was a mediocre pitcher for the New York Yankees at the end of their glory years in the early 1960s. He then played for the hapless Seattle Pilots in 1969, a short-lived team. Bouton wasn't much of a pitcher (sixty-two wins, sixty-three losses, lifetime), but he had one skill vouchsafed to very few ballplayers: he could write. In 1970, he changed the face of sports biography forever by composing a book with the unsurprising title *Ball Four*. His description of life in baseball broke all taboos by trying to describe the tedium, the pettiness, the raucousness, even the raunchiness of this particular male society on the road.

Yet *Ball Four* already seems dated. Bouton has much to say about drinking and pill popping. Some of his scenes are memorable for their humor—particularly the clubhouse election to choose a new catcher for the "all-ugly nine" in 1965 after Yogi Berra retired. But Bouton maintains a discreet silence about a variety of unmentionable subjects, notably dishonesty and race relations, and also about sex, where he lets humor and silliness substitute for action. (In Bouton's most celebrated "exposé," he recounts how Mickey Mantle and Billy Martin would crawl out upon ledges and roofs of hotels for a game of "beaver shooting," or spotting naked women through the windows.)

Now everything hangs out (often to the near exclusion of play on the field as a subject—what an absurd inversion!). Even the most saccharine book for granny and the kids must now include the expletives deleted from Nixon's tapes and a "manly" account of sexual prowess (often with a disingenuous admission of guilt as an attempted nod to the feminists). Jim Bouton himself, on reissuing *Ball Four* in 1981, wrote: "The books that have come after mine make *Ball Four*, as an exposé, read like *The Bobbsey Twins Go to the Seashore*."

2.

A classical device in literature traces the passage of time by permitting the anomalous survival of an oldster into the wonder of a new age—Rip Van Winkle as America's prototype, though paleontologists have their own version in the concept of "living fossils," or creatures like cockroaches and horseshoe crabs that persist almost unchanged for "too many" millennia. This season offers a marvelous opportunity to write about the history of baseball biography because we have just been presented with the finest example of this device in all the days of our sports.

Ty Cobb, who played from 1905 to 1928 (mostly with Detroit and later with Philadelphia), was probably the finest player in the history of baseball. (Ruth, Aaron, and a few others have their defenders, but why quibble among the paragons?) He hit over .400 in three seasons, stole 892 bases, and won twelve batting championships. His lifetime batting average of .367 will, we may state with confidence, never be equaled (although Pete Rose eclipsed his mark for most career hits, while three players surpassed him in stolen bases).

But Cobb was also, and even more undoubtedly, the meanest

Ty Cobb in 1915. *Credit: Bettmann/Corbis*

star in the history of American sport. He delighted in the fact that he had pistol-whipped a man to death. A violent racist, he would beat up any black person who touched him (his teammates once had to pull him off a black laundrywoman). He once dived into the stands to thrash a man who had taunted him (and he continued the beating even when told that the man had no arms, for his tormentor had called him a "half nigger"). Psychobiographers have no trouble attributing this behavior to the great trauma of his teenage years, when his mother shot his adored father to death after mistaking him for an intruder (and why blame her, since Mr. Cobb Sr. had climbed in through a second-story window, apparently on suspicion that his wife was in bed with a lover? And perhaps she was). Whatever the complex causes, Cobb was vicious and probably psychotic. He played brilliantly, made millions in the stock market thereafter, and lived and died absolutely friendless.

In 1960, mired in drunken rages and sensing the approach of death, Cobb hired sportswriter Al Stump to compose a standard hagiographical biography in the defensive mode, as the title indicated—*My Life in Baseball: The True Record*. This book could not be more traditional in style (and therefore becomes a prototype by having the greatest of the great as its subject).

The Cobb-Stump apologia begins with the greatest possible panache, a foreword by none other than General Douglas MacArthur, whose personality and politics made him more likely than anyone else in America to admire Cobb. MacArthur wrote predictably:

> This great athlete seems to have understood early in his professional career that in the competition of baseball, just as in war, defensive strategy never has produced ultimate victory and, as a consequence, he maintained an offensive posture to the end of his baseball days. . . .
>
> Ty Cobb injected much of his own fighting spirit into that aspect of the American character which has put inspiration and direction behind our progress as a free nation.

There follows an even more remarkable preface from E. A. Batchelor, then the oldest active member of the Baseball Writers' Association of America, and a longtime Cobb watcher and apologist. He called Cobb "the greatest ballplayer that ever lived" and praised "the greatest combination of qualities of body, heart, and mind ever given to a professional ballplayer." But what qualities? Batchelor does take up all those nasty rumors about Cobb's demented persona, but he presents a literally incredible explanation for them:

> Early in his baseball life, a canard developed that Ty was a brawler who constantly sought trouble. This misconception seems to have started when he first joined the Tigers, as a slender youth of eighteen, a well-brought-up boy inclined to be friendly with everybody and anxious only to

make good on his own merits. Unfortunately for him, there then were among an otherwise fine group of men on the Detroit roster, a few who were contemptible bullies. These rowdies immediately started to pick on the stripling from Georgia and did everything their disordered minds could think of to make life miserable for him.

Mr. Stump's chronicle then continues for another three hundred pages in the same mode.

Since then, Bouton's revolution came and conquered—and Al Stump watched and waited. Few people get a second chance after the revolution (though Jacques-Louis David, as a Jacobin, voted for the death of Louis XVI and then lived to become Napoleon's court painter). But Al Stump, at age seventy-eight, has just produced a new biography, more simply titled *Cobb*, and largely to expiate the inadequacies of his earlier treatment. The new volume still leans toward the respectful (for the mind cannot be easily cleared of earlier commitments, even so many years later), but Cobb's persona now gets prominent billing, no aspects excluded. Stump himself, substituting for MacArthur in the prologue, writes of his earlier work: "That 1961 autobiography was very self-serving. Cobb had the final say in its contents, accorded him by the publisher. And when we did not agree, which was often, it was his word that was accepted by Doubleday."

In striking symmetry of form with the 1961 volume, but with utter contrast in content, Stump's new book then features a foreword by Jimmy Reese (then ninety-three, the oldest living major leaguer in the Association of Professional Ballplayers—just as the senior professional sportswriter had performed this task for the 1961 book). But Reese, who played against Cobb for many years, remembers the viciousness along with the skill and dedication:

Not many are left who saw Ty Cobb on the rampage in the years 1905–28. . . . What a wildcat he was. . . . We called

him "Jack Dempsey in spikes." The story is quite true that
Cobb filed his spikes to razor sharpness to first intimidate
opponents and then gore them.

Reese then quotes Lou Gehrig, perhaps the most genial of the
star players: "Cobb is about as welcome in American League parks
as a rattlesnake."

Stump's expiation has gained immeasurably greater force by
the conversion of his books into a movie, just released—*Cobb*,
starring Tommy Lee Jones as Ty, and Robert Wuhl as Stump. The
film hardly deals with Cobb's life as a ballplayer, but concentrates
on his dying year and on his relationship with Stump when the
sportswriter ghosted the 1961 version. Director and screenwriter
Ron Shelton (of *Bull Durham* fame) has cast his account of Cobb
in the classic (and rather tired) genre of on-the-road "buddy"
movies, in this case the adventures of an old codger and his
strained but loyal sidekick. Cobb and Stump go to Reno for a bit
of partying, on to Cooperstown (where colleagues honor him at
the Hall of Fame dinner, but will not let him into their private parties thereafter), and finally to Cobb's native Georgia, where he
dies, surrounded by bitter memories of his father's murder.

Among the film's many inaccuracies (mostly exaggerations, for
dramatic effect, of Cobb's lousy driving, impotent loving, and
tempestuous drinking), one item of artistic license stands out as
a symbol of change in the history of baseball biography. Today, we
simply cannot believe that a sympathetic character like Stump
could have acted as such a toady to Cobb's lies and rages. So the
film relies upon a device to remake the 1960 Stump as a post-
Bouton modernist. Stump writes the biography that Cobb requires
on his portable typewriter, but he also stuffs a briefcase full of
handwritten notes with all the true and nasty stuff, hastily scrib-
bled while Cobb was drunk or asleep. These he intends to fashion

into a separate book after Cobb's impending death. (Cobb, of course, finds the notes in one of the film's most dramatic scenes.)

I understand the need for this anachronistic ruse to make Al Stump a sympathetic character in modern terms—a man committed to the "true" record, even while he must humor his bully (in both senses) subject. Yet we distort and dishonor history in such an approach, no matter how good our intentions, just as we falsify a past we need to understand when we "update" racial relations (as in the current Broadway revival of *Show Boat*, first staged in 1927), or change the text of Bach's *St. John Passion* to read "the people" every time the original, and truly biblical, text says "the Jews." Al Stump planned no second "truthful" book when he worked with Cobb in 1960. Why would he have so proceeded against all the accepted standards of his day? In acting as a mouthpiece for Cobb, Stump was doing an honorable job, in a mode that had long been canonical for the genre. Richard Sandomir, interviewing Al Stump in the *New York Times*, wrote: "Stump was not haunted by or ambivalent about not writing a truer version of Cobb's life the first time around." Stump himself then told the interviewer: "I didn't have any secret plan to go around Cobb to write a second book."

3.

As Darwin recognized in devising his own theories for the broad sweep of life's history, evolutionary change encompasses two distinct subjects: (1) trends, or general modification of lineages through time; and (2) diversification, or alterations in the number of entities (loss of species by extinction and gain by branching of genealogical lines). The Boutonian revolution in baseball biography may be judged by both criteria in considering the most interesting books of the last two years.

On the first subject of trending, or general change, the old hagiographies about on-field play are out, replaced, probably forever, by mixtures of psychobiography and social commentary with old-fashioned baseball chronicle. Consider, for example, two recent biographies of heroes (if the term retains meaning in its original sense) from early and later generations: Christy Mathewson (played 1900–1916) and Ted Williams (played 1939–1960).

Who, even in fantasy, could have constructed a better American idol than Christy Mathewson: tall, handsome, God-fearing (he opposed Sunday ball at first), nondrinking, gentle and polite, college-educated (at a time when few people in general, and ballplayers especially, got much formal schooling), and by far the greatest right-handed pitcher of the early game? He also died young, both tragically and heroically—of tuberculosis, just a few years after an accidental gassing in army exercises during World War I (probably unrelated to his early demise, but always so associated in the public mind). Ray Robinson's fine biography sticks mostly to his sports career, but bears the pervasive signature of post-Boutonian writing in its constant linkage of baseball narrative with the main events of history, both domestic and foreign, and in its emphasis upon Matty's relationships with others in the game, particularly with his feisty manager, John McGraw.

In 1991, I participated in a learned symposium to discuss the fiftieth anniversary of Ted Williams's banner season of 1941, when he hit .406 (a pinnacle reached by no one since). After all the panelists had spoken, Jean Yawkey, owner of the Boston Red Sox, rose from the audience and, obviously annoyed by the scholarly and statistical slant of the panelists, addressed a more emotional question to the audience: "How many of you never saw Ted Williams bat?" About half the people present raised their hand. Mrs. Yawkey simply said, "What a pity!" and sat down. I often saw Ted Williams at bat, and he was my mortal enemy (for I am a Yankee fan): he was the greatest.

Unlike Mathewson, Williams was no paragon of personal character. He played with enormous intensity and inward concentration (some called him selfish), and he maintained a constant feud with sportswriters and, to some extent, the public as well (Boston fans have still not entirely forgiven Williams for refusing to reenter the field and tip his hat to acknowledge their thunderous applause after he had homered in his last major league at-bat in 1960). But Williams was at least an adequate hero for our times: he didn't brawl or drink (at least as a public spectacle), and he did sacrifice four prime seasons of his career to fight in two wars. Ed Linn's marvelous biography, *Hitter*, is, again, refreshingly old-fashioned in its focus on his life at bat (Linn, a veteran sportswriter, followed Williams's career from his rookie season in 1939), but also ineluctably post-Boutonian in its exploration of his troubled childhood with a difficult mother and his feuds with the press and, symbolically, in its Sturm und Drang subtitle: *The Life and Turmoils of Ted Williams*.

But the effects of general change are most tellingly recorded not in alteration of the best products, but in transformation of the most ordinary, workaday books; for when potboilers adopt the new style, then the revolution is complete. Consider the usual process of composition for a baseball potboiler: decent player has banner year; sportswriter for the local paper has followed him all season; writer records on tape some tens of hours of interviews with player; writer produces a 250-page book in time for release at the beginning of the next season; book is heavily marketed in the player's hometown and almost nowhere else; enough copies are sold to justify expenses and return some profit.

John Kruk is a perfectly competent ballplayer; he is also a distinctive character par excellence on the current baseball scene—fat and proud of it, and leader of the scruffy-imaged Philadelphia Phillies, toast of a nation, but losers to Toronto in the last World Series.

If you wish to find a good example of literary revolution completed, just read Kruk's book "as told to" Paul Hagen: *"I Ain't an Athlete, Lady . . .": My Well-Rounded Life and Times*. We do hear a bit about baseball, but ever so much more about Kruk's weight, Mitch Williams's unhappiness, and various petty grousings about this and that. The hagiography of play on the diamond has turned into gossip about life off the field. Hardly an improvement.

As for diversification, post-Boutonian baseball biography has also added a variety of styles and subjects that would have been unthinkable in the hagiographical era. All may be viewed as consequences of the transformation of baseball biography into social commentary.

Social commentary thrives on the lives of people who have become marginal within their communities or professions. The post-Boutonian expansion of baseball writing has provided a bonanza of opportunity for biographers of the formerly neglected, most notably the shameful history of those once excluded from major league play by the irrelevancy of skin color. Many of these great players, palpable heroes among blacks, became legendary figures for fair-minded whites (I think of my father and grandfather), who knew that the excluded stars equaled or exceeded their own Ruths and Gehrigs but could never see them compete face to face.

The most famous, and perhaps the greatest, of all black players, pitcher Satchel Paige, finally got to perform in the major leagues—in his late forties, and with sustained excellence, long after most other players had retired. (I well remember the thrill of seeing him when I was a boy.) Although Paige may have been the greatest pitcher of all time, his biography must be written largely as social commentary—and Mark Ribowsky has done a fine job in *Don't Look Back: Satchel Paige in the Shadows of Baseball*. What can one say, except that his story could make any grown man cry, as we learn about Paige's dignity and his good humor as he walked the necessary but impossible tightrope between "acting black" (by white racist expectations) as the situation demanded (and when dignity did not greatly suffer, or could be redeemed by humor or subtle table-turning) and the explicit courage of directly making demands and taking action. Paige was also the Yogi Berra of his generation, "America's greatest existentialist philosopher," Ribowsky tells us with permissible hype. Just consider the poignancy and good spirit of this Paigeian dictum (though incontestably true as well) from a man unfairly deprived of so much: "Bases on balls is the curse of the nation."

Among marginalized players once deemed beyond consideration by conventional hagiography, the lousy performers stand out. Moe Berg, who played sporadically from 1923 to 1939, was a truly poor catcher but perhaps the most fascinating character in the history of baseball. He is therefore candidate *numero uno* for post-Boutonian biography of the marginalized—and Nicholas Dawidoff has responded splendidly in his best-selling *The Catcher Was a Spy*.

Berg was marginal on all fronts within baseball—a crummy player, a Jew, and an intellectual. Berg finished both college and law school, and was a linguist by avocation and partial hype. (In Japan, for example, he did what generations of bluffers, including myself, I must admit, have done to convince people of nonexistent competence based upon marginal effort: he learned the fifty or so symbols of the *katakana*, the syllabary used as a supplementary system to traditional *kanji* characters; with *katakana*, any series of sounds can be written out, at least approximately.)

I had not expected to like Moe Berg much, for I thought that all the standard stories of his life had been egregiously embellished, and that his other exploits might turn out to be as mundane as his baseball. Not so, and I thank Dawidoff for the corrections. Though he thrived on exaggeration, in part concocted by the press to give him a persona that could transcend his play, Berg was a genuinely cultured and accomplished man. (I love John McGraw's comment about Berg's trip to Europe: "Who ever heard of a ballplayer spending his vacation studying Latin—and in Paris?")

Moreover, the well-rehearsed legend of his career in espionage turns out to be true. Chosen for his rare combination of charm, good looks, intelligence, genuine bravery, and linguistic ability, Berg worked at high levels of espionage for the U.S government during World War II. He had a major role in a plot, bizarre and futile in retrospect but not absurd in conception, to kidnap (even perhaps to kill) Werner Heisenberg, if the great German physicist had been making substantial progress toward the manufacture of nuclear weapons. (He wasn't—but no one knew for sure, and Berg could have emerged as a great hero if the German bomb had been a near reality.)

Berg's life ended in sadness, for he could never move beyond his past, or overcome the maddening secretiveness and idiosyncrasy that ultimately drove nearly everyone away. Rejected by the CIA for work in espionage after 1945 (for they found unsupportable in peacetime the same bravado that Wild Bill Donovan had valued for the wartime effort), Berg spent the last quarter-century of his life (he died in 1972) unemployed, moving and mooching from acquaintance to acquaintance, telling the same old baseball and war stories. During all this time, he tried to write his autobiography, but never could—perhaps because hagiography was then dominant, and Berg had too much self-respect to compose in such a mode. Dawidoff writes of Berg's inability to complete the book of his life:

> Alone at his desk, Berg could gloss over and manipulate things no longer. . . . He saw [himself] as a mediocre ballplayer, a scholar only within the unlearned community of baseball, and an intelligence agent whose work had come to nothing. There was no bomb, and the CIA didn't want him.

If lives of the marginalized have added one genre of social commentary to the literature of baseball biography, another may be found in retaining the traditional focus on star players, but in writing about their cultural impact rather than their skill on the field. I trust that this genre will be exploited only so far (for genuine sports talk must not end), but I must confess to great interest in Nick Trujillo's *The Meaning of Nolan Ryan*, the first postmodern biography of a star ballplayer.

Nolan Ryan broke in with the hapless New York Mets in 1966 and pitched until the end of the 1993 season. Very few major league pitchers play into their forties, and those who do usually rely on soft stuff (knuckleballers stay the longest). Nolan Ryan continued to throw the best fastball in the game right to the end. Moreover, he improved through time. He began as a mediocre hurler with no control and no diversity of pitches (the Mets only used him once, in relief for a couple of innings, during the magnificent World Series of 1969). He ended with great control, immense cunning, and a host of additional pitches to augment the heater. In addition, Ryan is a traditional hero in an age that has almost deprived the term of meaning: he is tall, handsome, patriotic, married only once, and living on a ranch, down-home in manner (despite his immense acquired wealth), and gracious and modest. Enter, therefore, the exploiters and the commercializers, for this is America. And enter Nick Trujillo, associate professor of communication studies at California State University, Sacramento.

When Ryan was signed by the Texas Rangers in 1989, Trujillo spent three seasons studying his utility to the team's owners and fans. Once upon a time, we might have defined utility by performance on the field, and Ryan continued to do some marvelous pitching. But now, with ballplayers marketed in every conceivable outlet from autograph shows to pictures on pencils, the financial

value of a genuine hero can be measured only by taking account
of all his salable symbols, with on-field performance as a starting
point of ever-receding import.

We therefore meet the postmodern Ryan of commercial America, fragmented into his salable symbolic roles, none more genuine or truer than the other. Trujillo lists them as follows: "Ryan
the Hall of Fame power pitcher, Ryan the cowboy rancher, Ryan
the family man, Ryan the workaholic, Ryan the profit-seeking
endorser, Ryan the conservative Republican, Ryan the hunter and
fisherman, and even Ryan the sex symbol."

I was most struck by Trujillo's analysis of the power of the
press and television to orchestrate artificial frenzies over trivial
events—particularly the immense publicity (and sale of memorabilia) ignited on the occasion of Ryan's 5,000th strikeout. (No
other pitcher had ever reached this number, but once you get to
4,999, number 5,000 just has to come along the next time—no
big deal when you are averaging more than nine strikeouts per
game. The total accomplishment is, of course, magnificent; the
event of number 5,000 itself is meaningless.) Yet the press and
the publicists told us we should care, and most Ranger fans swear
they can remember their location at the sublime moment, just as
all folks of my generation know where they were when John F.
Kennedy was shot.

The public may be cheapened by this devaluation of play, but
has Ryan (as he became greatly enriched) also been diminished in
turn? In 1975, in vigorous midcareer, Ryan told a reporter: "I try
to spend all my free time with my family. I could make more
appearances and get more attention other ways, I guess, but this
is the life I want." In 1992 he wrote in his autobiography, *Miracle
Man*, about his greater willingness to make endorsements: "I have
a better idea of what they want, and I'm learning to deliver with
every take. . . . Since the extra income allows me to do things for
my family I wouldn't have been able to do otherwise, I carefully
select the right ones and accept them."

I honor and value post-Boutonism, but may this fresh wind not blow us too far from the founding subject. The old hagiographies, at worst, relied on invention and hypocrisy, but at least they talked about baseball and told us how their heroes hit a curve and slid into third base. The new books, when they are good, fill in dimensions previously excluded and give voices to a variety of players ignored by the hagiographers. But, when bad, the post-Boutonian books get so tied up in their sociological analyses (the highfalutin ones) or smarmy kiss-and-tell exposés (the vernacular versions) that baseball recedes into a barely relevant background.

Al Stump's second book is a fine post-Boutonian biography, but the movie version, *Cobb*, has been a crushing failure (and may not even be released nationally) despite some wonderful acting by Tommy Lee Jones. I think that director Ron Shelton lost his bearings and forgot his subject. He became so intrigued with Cobb the aged psychotic that he forgot Cobb the greatest ballplayer who ever lived. Shelton begins with a "newsreel" epitomizing Cobb's playing career, but the rest of the movie is a chronicle of Cobb's dying year, his relationship with Stump, and Stump's anachronistic struggle about integrity. We never again see Cobb on the ballfield.

Hal Crowther, reviewing Stump's second book in the *North Carolina Independent*, wrote:

> [Cobb's] sickness was a distorted reflection of our own. You can make a case that he influenced the outcome of more major league baseball games than any player who ever lived. The question is whether that achievement means anything at all, considering the pathology of the athlete and the human cost he incurred.
>
> At ten, I would have waffled on that one. Now it's clear to me that the answer is "No."

Well, it is not clear to me; and I think the answer is "yes." What price glory, to be sure. Cobb was a vicious bastard, and he brought misery to many around him. But baseball is a beautiful game, an important part of our history as a nation, and a joy and comfort in the lives of millions (if ever the pouting players and owners end their ridiculous pissing contest and return the institution, which they have only borrowed for a while and for their profit, to its true custodians, the fans). And excellence in any honorable form—that rarest and most precious of human accomplishments—must be praised, despite the toll often exacted on the achievers and the victims of their obsessions. Cobb was the greatest ballplayer in American history—and baseball doesn't kill or maim.

Assessing importance is so much a matter of scale. Cobb sowed misery during his living moment to a small circle of people in his direct orbit. But moments and orbits recede as the generations roll, while unparalleled excellence emerges and holds fast. The asteroid that killed the dinosaurs looked terrible to any particular *Tyrannosaurus* witnessing the impact, but worked out wonderfully well for surviving mammals millions of years later. Who knows or cares any more about the foibles of Aeschylus or Sophocles, but I trust that we shall watch *Agamemnon* and *Oedipus Rex* as long as humanity persists.

No one can say of Tyrus Raymond Cobb, as Antony did of Brutus, that "his life was gentle," or that "the elements / So mix'd in him, that Nature might stand up / And say to all the world, 'This was a man!' " Cobb was monomaniacal, and he paid the personal price. But we might say of him, "This was a ballplayer!" Such a judgment should be enough to give life value. Render to Ty Cobb what he couldn't give to others. His viciousness cannot injure anyone anymore; the excellence of his play endures.